Unlocking Agile's Missed Potential

About IEEE Computer Society

IEEE Computer Society is the world's leading computing membership organization and the trusted information and career-development source for a global workforce of technology leaders including: professors, researchers, software engineers, IT professionals, employers, and students. The unmatched source for technology information, inspiration, and collaboration, the IEEE Computer Society is the source that computing professionals trust to provide high-quality, state-of-the-art information on an on-demand basis. The Computer Society provides a wide range of forums for top minds to come together, including technical conferences, publications, and a comprehensive digital library, unique training webinars, professional training, and the Tech Leader Training Partner Program to help organizations increase their staff's technical knowledge and expertise, as well as the personalized information tool my Computer. To find out more about the community for technology leaders, visit http://www.computer.org.

IEEE/Wiley Partnership

The IEEE Computer Society and Wiley partnership allows the CS Press authored book program to produce a number of exciting new titles in areas of computer science, computing, and networking with a special focus on software engineering. IEEE Computer Society members receive a 35% discount on Wiley titles by using their member discount code. Please contact IEEE Press for details.

To submit questions about the program or send proposals, please contact Mary Hatcher, Editor, Wiley-IEEE Press: Email: mhatcher@wiley.com, John Wiley & Sons, Inc., 111 River Street, Hoboken, NJ 07030-5774.

Unlocking Agile's Missed Potential

Robert Webber

Published by John Wiley & Sons, Inc., Hoboken, New Jersey.
Published simultaneously in Canada.

For general information on our other products and services or for technical support, please contact our Customer Care Department within the United States at (800) 762-2974, outside the United States at (317) 572-3993 or fax (317) 572-4002.

Wiley also publishes its books in a variety of electronic formats. Some content that appears in print may not be available in electronic formats. For more information about Wiley products, visit our web site at www.wiley.com.

Library of Congress Cataloging-in-Publication Data Applied for:

Hardback ISBN: 9781119849087

Cover Design: Wiley
Cover Image: © Studio Romantic/Shutterstock.com

Set in 9.5/12.5pt STIXTwoText by Straive, Chennai, India

Contents

Author Biography   *xi*
Foreword   *xiii*
Preface   *xv*
Introduction   *xix*

1   **The Persistence of Waterfall Planning**   *1*
1.1   Introduction to AccuWiz   *1*
1.1.1   The New COO   *2*
1.1.2   Product Management   *3*
1.1.3   PMO   *3*
1.1.4   Engineering   *4*
1.1.5   Customer Perspective   *5*
1.1.6   Synopsis   *5*
1.2   Summary   *6*

2   **Why Agile Has Struggled**   *9*
2.1   Agile Development Fundamentals   *10*
2.1.1   The Agile Revolution   *10*
2.1.2   Scrum   *12*
2.1.3   Kanban   *14*
2.2   Barriers to Real Agile   *15*
2.2.1   Schedule Pressure   *16*
2.2.2   The "Motivation" Factor   *18*
2.2.3   The Mythical Product Owner   *20*
2.2.4   Feature Planning   *22*
2.3   Agile Scaling Frameworks   *22*
2.4   Summary   *23*
            References   *24*

3 **Embracing Software Development Variance** *25*
3.1 The Cone of Uncertainty *25*
3.2 Software Development Estimation Variance Explained *27*
3.3 Making and Meeting Feature Commitments *28*
3.4 How Other Departments Meet Commitments *30*
3.5 Agile Development Implications *31*
3.6 Summary *31*
References *32*

4 **Cost of Delay** *33*
4.1 Weighted Shortest Job First (WSJF) *34*
4.1.1 Cost of Delay Basics *35*
4.1.2 Example *36*
4.1.3 WSJF Proof *38*
4.1.4 CoD and Net Present Value (NPV) Prioritization Methods *40*
4.2 Nonlinear Income Profiles *42*
4.3 CoD for Nonlinear Cumulative Income Profiles *42*
4.3.1 Payback Period CoD Method *42*
4.3.2 Third-Year Income Slope CoD Method *42*
4.3.3 CoD Computation Method *45*
4.4 WSJF and Traditional Finance *47*
4.4.1 ROI *47*
4.4.2 Investment Rate of Return (IRR) *48*
4.4.3 WSJF Versus ROI Prioritization *48*
4.5 Summary *50*
Reference *50*

5 **Investment Fundamentals** *51*
5.1 Investments, Initiatives, and Programs *52*
5.1.1 Investment Hierarchy *52*
5.2 AccuWiz Investment Examples *55*
5.3 Portfolio Allocation *56*
5.4 Investment Forecasts *57*
5.4.1 Development Effort and Cost *57*
5.4.2 Investment Income Forecasts *59*
5.5 Investment Backlogs *62*
5.5.1 Investment WIP *63*
5.5.2 Investment Planning WIP Limits *64*
5.5.3 Minimizing Investment WIP *65*
5.6 Technical Debt Investments *66*
5.7 Summary *68*
Reference *68*

6   Maximizing Investment Value   *69*
6.1   Great Products   *69*
6.2   Business Model Value Considerations   *71*
6.3   Stakeholder Value Analysis   *73*
6.3.1   Gilb Stakeholder Definition   *73*
6.3.2   Ford's Big Mistake   *75*
6.3.3   Trucking Fleet Management Example   *77*
6.3.4   Five Whys   *79*
6.4   User Scenarios   *82*
6.5   Summary   *84*
         References   *84*

7   Planning High-Value Investment Features   *85*
7.1   Avoiding the Feature Pit   *86*
7.2   Feature ROI   *87*
7.3   Summary   *91*
         Reference   *91*

8   Releasing Investments   *93*
8.1   Release Opportunity Cost   *94*
8.2   Investment Release Bundling   *96*
8.2.1   Investment Pricing   *97*
8.2.2   Lack of Customer Acceptance   *98*
8.2.3   Release Overhead Costs   *99*
8.3   Overcoming Modular Release Challenges   *102*
8.3.1   Architecture for Modular Deployment   *102*
8.3.2   Configuration Management   *102*
8.4   Release Investment Prioritization   *103*
8.5   Reducing Software Inventory Costs   *104*
8.6   Summary   *107*
         Reference   *108*

9   Meeting Investment Targets   *109*
9.1   Meeting Commitments   *109*
9.2   Investment Teams   *110*
9.3   Managing Investment Scope   *113*
9.4   Managing Sales Requests   *115*
9.5   Summary   *118*

10   Investment Planning Template   *119*
10.1   Investment Description   *120*
10.2   Proxy Business Case   *120*

10.3   Product Stakeholder Analysis   *122*
10.3.1   Customer Product Stakeholders   *122*
10.3.2   Internal Product Stakeholders   *122*
10.3.3   Constraints   *122*
10.3.4   Competition   *123*
10.4   Acceptance Criteria   *123*
10.5   Go-to-Market Plan   *124*
10.5.1   Pricing Model   *124*
10.5.2   Deployment Model   *124*
10.5.3   Sales Channels   *124*
10.6   Investment Targets   *124*
10.6.1   Development Cost   *125*
10.6.2   Cycle Time   *125*
10.6.3   Income Projections   *125*
10.6.4   WSJF   *127*
10.7   Assumption Validation   *127*
10.8   Summary   *129*
             References   *129*

11   **Managing the Agile Roadmap**   *131*
11.1   The Agile Roadmap Management Database   *132*
11.2   The Agile Technology Roadmap   *135*
11.2.1   Stages of Technology Acquisition   *136*
11.2.2   Investment Technology Roadmaps   *137*
11.3   Summary   *137*

12   **Maximizing Investment Development Productivity**   *139*
12.1   Measuring Software Productivity   *140*
12.1.1   Cost of Quality (CoQ)   *141*
12.1.2   Cost of Quality and Software Productivity   *142*
12.1.3   Sources of Software Rework   *144*
12.2   Agile Cost of Quality   *145*
12.2.1   Reducing Agile User Story Rework   *147*
12.2.2   Reducing Agile Defect Rework   *148*
12.2.3   Agile Cost of Quality Example   *149*
12.3   Summary   *150*
             References   *151*

13   **Motivating Agile Teams**   *153*
13.1   Background   *153*
13.2   Why You're the Only Smart One in Your Organization   *154*

13.3   Consequences and Behavior   *156*
13.3.1   Performance and Organizational Culture   *157*
13.3.2   Behavior and Software Quality   *162*
13.3.3   Intrinsic Motivation   *164*
13.4   Agile and Motivation   *165*
13.5   Measuring Motivation   *167*
13.6   Motivation Advice?   *169*
13.7   Summary   *172*
          References   *173*

14   **Innovating with Investments**   *175*
14.1   Innovation – A Working Definition   *176*
14.2   Investments as an Innovation Vehicle   *178*
14.3   Why Your Organization Can't Innovate   *180*
14.4   An Organizational Behavior Model of Innovation   *181*
14.4.1   An Innovation Tale of Two Companies   *185*
14.4.2   Creating a Culture of Innovation   *188*
14.5   Summary   *193*
          References   *194*

15   **AccuWiz Gets It Together**   *195*
15.1   The Founder Meeting   *196*
15.2   The Announcement   *196*
15.3   Product Stakeholder Analysis   *198*
15.4   Creating the Investment Backlog   *198*
15.5   Customer Management   *202*
15.6   Investment Development   *203*
15.6.1   Project Management   *203*
15.6.2   Managers   *205*
15.6.3   Executive Team   *206*
15.7   Innovation is Revived   *207*
15.8   Synopsis   *207*
          Reference   *208*

16   **Getting It Together in Your Company: A Practical Guide**   *209*
16.1   Step 1: Organizational Support   *209*
16.1.1   Influence Strategy   *210*
16.2   Step 2: Stakeholder Value Analysis   *212*
16.3   Step 3: Stakeholder Research   *214*
16.4   Step 4: Stakeholder Interviews   *215*
16.5   Step 5: Investments   *216*

16.5.1   User Scenarios   *216*
16.5.2   Feature Definition   *218*
16.5.3   WSJF Screening   *218*
16.6   Step 6: Initial Roadmap   *220*
16.6.1   Resource Allocation   *220*
16.7   Step 7: Investment Planning   *221*
16.7.1   Agile Roadmap Alignment Meeting   *221*
16.7.2   Program Review   *223*
16.8   Step 8: Consequence Alignment   *224*
16.9   Summary   *226*

Appendix A   General Cost of Delay Formula   *229*
A.1   Reinertsen WSJF   *231*
A.2   Income Curve Approximation   *231*
A.3   Summary   *234*

Appendix B   Investment Income Profile Forecasts   *235*

Appendix C   Release Cycle Productivity Formula   *237*

Appendix D   Rework and Productivity   *241*

Appendix E   Innovation Behavior Survey   *243*

Glossary   *247*
Index   *255*

Author Biography

Robert Webber introduces a novel approach for Agile portfolio management and planning based on his extensive experience in leading software development organizations at GTE, AT&T, and three successful startups. His roles as VPs of engineering and product management, CEO, and consultant for Fortune 500 companies provided the technical and business perspectives to facilitate Agile planning while improving schedule and financial predictability.

Robert has an Electrical Engineering degree (honors) from the University of British Columbia. He holds five patents and received an Academy of Motion Pictures Arts and Sciences Technical Achievement Award for his innovative work on cable-mounted cameras.

Foreword

As the author of *Code Complete* I have been asked to write forewords for other people's books more times than I can count. I say "no" nearly every time. If readers see a foreword by the author of *Code Complete*, I believe they will expect the book to be as good as *Code Complete*. I rarely have enough confidence in other books to make that promise.

This book is a rare exception.

I have known Bob Webber for more than 20 years, and during that time we have had hundreds of discussions about the topics in this book. We've noted the unique ways that software executives see the world – often correctly, and some-times flawed. We have shared observations about the relationship between the typical software development organization and product management, sales, and top executives. We've analyzed the strengths and weaknesses of Agile implemen-tations – based to some degree on book knowledge, but based more on what we have seen with the numerous teams and companies we have helped first hand. We've puzzled about the reasons that Agile so often fails to live up to expectations. We have had many lengthy conversations about managing portfolios of software projects, releases, value streams, and features – and how all that relates to Agile development.

This book begins with Bob's identification of a major problem: The typical organization's commitment to Waterfall planning undermines its ability to be truly agile, and that in turn prevents it from realizing the benefits of Agile development. Don't mistake this for the common doctrinaire argument, "You can't realize the benefits of Agile unless every remote corner of your organization becomes Agile." Bob's analysis is more focused and far more nuanced – it has to do with the specific interactions between top executives, product management, and software development that give rise to a destructive mismatch between Waterfall planning at the business level that eviscerates the use of Agile practices in the software organization.

After his clear explanations of this fatal weakness in Agile implementations, Bob presents an innovative solution, which is to treat software initiatives as a portfolio of investments, both small and large, and to prioritize them in a specific way that maximizes economic return. The key is in how investments are sequenced – some sequences produce far higher return than others, even when the work in total is all the same. Common sense turns out to be a weak method for sequencing investments, and this book presents a sophisticated approach that works markedly better. There is some math in that section, but it's worth it. When this approach is used, prioritization of "features" and initiatives becomes more objective and easier. Historical friction between engineering and product management dissipates. The organization becomes more successful.

The investment prioritization algorithm in this book – the sequencing – is a core that supports improved organizational performance in other areas. The core provides guidance for roadmap planning, increased productivity, and increased innovation. These are not small benefits. Roadmap planning is perhaps the most common Achilles heel I have seen in Agile implementations. Many organizations treat increased productivity and increased innovation as primary goals. Bob's software investment portfolio approach supports them all.

Despite containing a significant amount of math and some economic discussion, this is not an academic book. It is based on real-world experience, and it provides a step-by-step guide that you can use to implement this software investment portfolio approach in your organization. Bob provides practical resources such as an investment planning template and an extended case study that illustrates how all the concepts and techniques work together in practice.

Most books can't measure up to the promise of *Code Complete*, but the approach in this book can. Most organizations perform their software work in inefficient ways. Simply by doing the same work in a different order – changing the sequence – organizations can increase the returns on their software investments dramatically.

From my conversations with Bob over more than two decades, I can say with certainty that there is no one in the world who has spent more time understanding how to construct a portfolio of software initiatives and how to optimize the returns on such portfolios. This book describes Bob's best thinking on the subject, and I recommend it whole heartedly.

Steve McConnell, author of *Code Complete*

Preface

This is a journey that began in 2011 when I started a second career as a product development consultant. I wanted to leave behind the pressure of delivering software products and transition to a role that would allow me more time flexibility to pursue my interests. I wouldn't change anything in my first career. It provided me with a perspective from the engineering and business side to solve a software industry problem – the missed expectations of Agile development.

I would never have become a consultant if it wasn't for Steve McConnell, an icon of software engineering. I had read his books and admired how he updated proven software engineering practices for the current generation of software developers. I became a client of Steve's training and consulting company, Construx Software.

When I decided to leave the corporate treadmill, Construx was the only company for which I wanted to consult. Steve let me determine how I could best contribute and gave me the flexibility to focus on my interests. It gave me the opportunity to apply my knowledge and experience to help software companies build higher value software and release it faster. It also provided me with insight into what was really going on in Agile, and it wasn't the Agile I was reading about in books.

This was a period when everyone was "going Agile." I saw larger companies stumble when they tried to apply a simplistic Scrum model designed for small organizations. Product development organizations had the biggest challenges. Where is the product owner who knows everything about everything in an international organization with a complex domain and diverse customers? And how can engineering do real Agile development when product management plans large releases with fixed schedules stuffed with features?

My consulting assessments always pointed out that organizations were not really doing Agile. A basic tenet of Scrum is that teams have time to incorporate feedback and correct defects during sprint development. Instead, teams were still driven by imposed schedules and barely had time to create basic functionality. Teams were demotivated from continually missing schedules. Sprints were not "potentially shippable." Defects mounted up during sprints which led to major rework in a "hardening sprint." Engineers were feature implementors instead of providing innovative solutions to problems conveyed to them in user stories and epics.

The value of releasing faster seemed obvious. Why did these organizations continue to use traditional Waterfall release planning methods with fixed schedules and content? Waterfall planning hadn't ever achieved the predictability they sought. How did they think that Agile roadmap commitments could be made prior to requirements development given that requirements were allowed to change?

Companies continue to use Waterfall planning because they are forced to make multiyear financial commitments. The sales organization needs to know the products and features they can sell before they will commit to revenue. And projects need financial justification based on delivery schedule and content commitments. Internal operations groups must budget with the expectation of increased productivity dependent on new features. Agile didn't address these issues. The somewhat flippant response of the Agile community was, "The business needs to be more Agile." Even though Waterfall planning leaves a lot to be desired in terms of predictability, it is the only way product managers know how to plan.

Some companies implemented the SAFe Agile framework to integrate business planning and Agile development. However, SAFe just institutionalized feature-based Waterfall planning. Product managers liked it because they didn't have to change the way they planned large releases at the feature-level. SAFe included an option for Lean Canvas planning but is not widely used in larger organizations. It's difficult to get funding approved for market experimentation. The business wants to see the releases and features they are paying for before funding development.

I've experienced a few epiphanies in my career. One occurred at the annual Construx software leadership summit in 2011 that influenced this book. Donald Reinertsen, author of *The Principles of Product Development Flow* [1], was a keynote speaker. His book presents a queue-based model of software development analogous to manufacturing organizations. The book includes a concept that can potentially change the way software is planned. It's called "Cost of Delay."

Cost of Delay is a simple yet elegant perspective of the software development process: "How much more money would you make if you could release your software one month earlier?" Reinertsen went on to show that prioritizing projects based on something called, "Weighted Shortest Job First" (WSJF), would optimize income. WSJF is the Cost of Delay divided by the project cycle time. It essentially says that companies make more money when they limit functionality and release and earn income faster. I recognized that WSJF can facilitate the mythical "Minimum Marketable Feature Set" (MMFS) advocated by Agile. I say mythical because sales organizations refused to compromise on functionality. They wanted anything and everything that could possibly lead to a sale in any country.

Thus began the journey to this book. Cost of Delay and WSJF were great concepts, but they were not widely adopted. Companies found it difficult to calculate Cost of Delay for non-linear post-release income profiles. Reinertsen's formula works for linear income profiles with constant income per month. I recognized that WSJF had to be simplified and product managers need to have methods and tools to simplify the calculations for any income profile.

My conclusion was that most companies have not achieved the potential of Agile because they are not really doing Agile the way it was envisioned. They are still trying to force-fit Agile into a Waterfall planning framework. This book enables these organizations to reap the benefits of their investments in Agile development by incorporating Agile planning and deployment. It also lets larger organizations replicate the powerful dynamics of a startup instead of the divisiveness and friction I observed between product management and engineering. The book describes how larger organization can build collaborative Agile product teams.

There is one other major influence that helped shape my solution. Tom Gilb has a long history of contributing to the software industry in the areas of software metrics, software inspections, and evolutionary development processes. Tom gave a talk on stakeholder value analysis at Construx in 2011. His method provides a way to dig down to what users really want before getting into requirements detail. It was the perfect fit for my proposed approach to Agile planning.

I want to thank Steve McConnell for his patience and support for this journey. Steve is a deep thinker who kept me on track by challenging many of my assertions. His philosophy of hiring smart people and letting them figure out how they can best contribute gave me the freedom to pursue my ideas. I also had the benefit of stimulating collaborations with other Construx consultants. Steve's recent book, *More Effective Agile* [2], is a useful and practical guide for engineering leaders that complements my work.

Don Reinertsen's book and principles provided the foundation for this new approach for Agile planning. He is an inspirational speaker with the analytical mind of an electrical engineer. I had the pleasure of talking to Don about some of my ideas at the Construx leadership summit he attended two years after his first talk. I highly recommend reading, *The Principles of Product Development Flow*. WSJF was a way to illustrate the value of reducing cycle time. The book contains much more. He goes on to show how cycle times can be drastically reduced by managing queues that build up in software development.

I have one other person to thank – my wife, Susan. In addition to being a great partner and mother, her PhD in Psychology and experience in leading change at high-tech companies gave me insight into the "soft" side of software development that needs to be addressed to realize the full potential of Agile. We can put all the procedures and processes in place, but little happens without human motivation.

This book explains how Agile can create high-performance self-directed teams, yet how it has been squandered by the constraints and controls from traditional development, especially those driven by the perpetuation of Waterfall planning.

And, of course, I want to thank Susan for infinite patience and support for the years I've spent developing and refining the Investment approach.

References

1 Reinertsen, D.G. (2009). *The Principles of Product Development Flow: Second Generation Lean Product Development*. Celeritas Publishing.

2 McConnell, S. (2019). *More Effective Agile: A Roadmap for Software Leaders*. Construx Press.

Introduction

The Lost Potential of Agile Development

I wrote this book because I want to see Agile development fulfill its promises. My assertion is that organizations that retain Waterfall planning have not obtained the true benefits of Agile. I found that organizations often referred to their software development frameworks as a "hybrid" approach. After almost a decade of software development consulting, I learned to recognize that the term "hybrid" was a sure sign of a failed Agile implementation. It meant that engineering was still held to fixed schedule and release content commitments. This book will show that Waterfall planning is the antithesis of Agile. However, product managers can now adopt new planning methods that support Agile development while meeting the business need for predictability. Engineering can finally do Agile with content flexibility.

After a successful career in software development, I joined Construx Software as a consultant. I gave seminars on requirements, innovation, and project management. I also conducted software development organizational assessments, which included many Fortune 500 companies. I reviewed their practices and organizational structures to recommend how to improve software development productivity and predictability, and to reduce time-to-market. I had the opportunity to see what was really happening "under the hood" in Agile.

While at Construx, I also had the opportunity to moderate group sessions at the annual Construx Leadership Summit where software executives shared their challenges and solutions. I heard the same concerns over and over. Engineering was still being held accountable for schedule, scope and budget commitments made during the release planning stage. Many reported that they had not been able to deliver on the expectations of Agile because of the continued use of Waterfall planning.

In this book, we will consider "Waterfall planning" to be any development framework where release development cost, schedule, and scope are fixed during an initial planning period. Scope is typically defined in terms of features. Development may be split up into several increments of release functionality, but the overall release schedule and scope have already been determined.

Waterfall planning with fixed schedule, scope, and resources undermines the fundamental Agile principles of evolving requirements to incorporate feedback and additional knowledge during development. Agile teams were supposed to pull work from queues at their own pace to ensure they can incorporate feedback and new requirements during the development cycle. Variable content was supposed to give teams time to correct defects to maintain "potentially shippable" software instead of building up mounds of defects that had to be corrected near the end of Waterfall projects. Agile teams were supposed to deploy software faster, with the ultimate goal of continuous delivery. However, planning begins with the assumption of large releases that are then "filled up" with myriad features of questionable value.

This book mainly addresses issues observed in larger organizations with separate product management departments. I've seen many cases where Agile works great with small teams under the guidance of a knowledgeable product owner who truly understands customers and the market. However, something seems to go wrong when silos go up around formalized product management departments. There is a major disconnect between the Waterfall planning perpetuated by product managers and the variable content necessary for Agile development. Product managers have not been provided alternatives to Waterfall planning that meet the predictability needs of the business and the schedule and/or content flexibility required by engineering.

I've also observed that there are common characteristics of the Agile examples touted by the Agile community. They are mostly in companies with a Business to Consumer (B–C) business model where the engineers have a solid understanding of the domain. Consider Facebook or Apple versus a medical device company serving international patients. The second characteristic of these example companies is the ability to attract the top percentiles of engineering talent. The third is that engineers are not constrained by Waterfall planning mandated to try to meet quarterly and annual financial targets.

Engineers with deep domain knowledge, especially when they are potential consumers of the product, can work effectively with little guidance. They can fill in the blanks of high-level user stories without frequent interaction with product owners. The Business to Business (B–B) companies that I assessed have complex domains and were never able to convey the necessary requirements detail through user stories alone. As an example, I worked with a company where Indian engineers were implementing highly regulated casino management software from user stories when they had never been in a casino in their lives! It wasn't Agile development – just code and fix.

Talent is another critical factor. I've worked with teams of talented engineers that can deliver software with little or no software development framework or methodology. These are the top 15% of self-motivated engineers who will overcome anything in their way. And they can write virtually error-free code. Who gets this demographic? The "cream of the crop" goes to startups or fashionable companies like Google, Microsoft, Facebook, and Spotify. The rest of the industry is left with average engineers who need a solid development framework and detailed requirements.

The third Agile success element is the main subject of this book. The example companies have abandoned Waterfall release planning and embraced Agile planning, often because they are dominant in their markets and can set their own schedules. They are probably not like your company with a demanding sales team committed to quarterly revenue based on what is available for them to sell. I have not seen an effective Agile implementation where Waterfall planning persists.

Putting these three Agile success elements together, one realizes that most of the "ideal Agile" examples and literary advice is based on a small fraction of the software industry comprised of startups and sexy B–C companies that have embraced Agile planning and are loaded with engineering talent. I always felt bad for the Construx summit attendees who listened with envy about amazing Agile implementations and wondered what was wrong with them. It is not them. They could be making the same presentations given the same ideal conditions discussed above.

This book is for the frustrated "silent majority" of software development organizations where Agile has not met expectations. It addresses the typical large company with complex domains and average talent. These companies can now adopt Agile planning and deployment and improve predictability for the business. This book describes how highly motivated Agile product teams can be built around business problems with quantified value. Engineers are provided with the problem to solve instead of trying to convey detailed implementation requirements through user stories with an uninvolved or uninformed product owner.

The word Agile in this book refers to methods other than just Scrum, like Kanban. I use Scrum terminology in this book, but the same investment planning principles and methods apply to any Agile method using iterative development with evolving requirements where self-directed teams pull their work from backlogs.

There is one other term used throughout this book that needs to be clarified for those of you with some knowledge of company financials. When I use the term "income" I am referring to "Net Income," which is the income received with product cost, expenses and taxes removed.

Missed Business Expectations

Agile has not addressed the real-world need for financial predictability in business. We do know that roadmap commitments were usually not met with Waterfall development. We learned there is a limit to the accuracy of software development effort and schedule estimation. With the advent of Agile, engineering was now expected to make commitments even before requirements were developed, exacerbating the predictability problem.

The Agile community response of, "The business needs to be more Agile" did nothing to help product and project managers who were still held accountable for long-term commitments of schedule, scope, and cost. This widened the division between product management and engineering. Engineering is frustrated by not being able to do Agile development the way they were taught, having to resort to "hybrid" methods. Product and project management are frustrated because of the reluctance of engineering to make release commitments.

Certainly, there are organizations that have been able to manage variable content with Waterfall planning by reserving software development contingency. But these organizations are rare because contingency doesn't typically survive the pressure to commit during release planning.

I don't blame product management for the continued use of Waterfall planning. They weren't provided with an alternative. Product managers were left out of Agile because, in the view of the Agile community, they could be replaced with product owners who sit with a team to provide verbal clarification for everything they need to know. And, according to the Agile community, there was no need to get requirements right because they could release small increments and gain the benefit of rapid customer feedback. We went from the Waterfall world where we tried to know everything about everything before development starts to the purist Agile view where we can't know anything about anything.

Agile did not account for the real-world challenges faced by software product managers in established organizations. In the real world, sales departments must commit to future revenue so that projected earnings and growth rates can be met. These commitments become part of multiyear business plans committed to a board of directors. Of course, sales people naturally want to know what they will have to sell and when they can sell it before they can agree to sales quotas. This results in expectations that product managers can predict delivery at the feature-level on a multiyear roadmap.

Agile grew quickly from a methodology for small development teams to major projects and products without defining methods for product managers to meet the predictability demanded by the business.

My experience as a VP of engineering, VP of product management and a CEO in the software industry has enabled me to view Agile development from all sides. It has given me a good perspective on how the needs of all stakeholders need to be addressed for Agile to be truly successful. Agile development is trying to swim upstream in a current of established business processes based on financial reporting requirements. The business will always demand predictability as long as our capitalist system requires CEOs to make earnings projections. Agile needs to meet business predictability expectations to be deemed successful. "The business needs to be more Agile" is a naïve response from the Agile community. I doubt that any business leader would argue with this, but agility can only exist within the predictability constraints of the business.

A New Approach to Agile Planning

Let's examine what predictability actually means to the business world. Multiyear financial forecast commitments must be made to shareholders and other stakeholders. Your company's executives really don't care about software estimation uncertainty. They want financial predictability. Agile can deliver predictability for the business in two ways. The first is to learn to make commitments that have high probability of being met, which is addressed in this book. The second is to plan and focus on delivering predictable financials and R&D Return on Investment (ROI). The Investment method described in this book enable product management and engineering to work together to balance income projections and development costs to meet financial targets.

Today features are still the primary planning element in software development. Features are an increment of value with a common understanding of benefit by sales, product management, and engineering. However, it is generally not possible to estimate financial return on a feature basis at the planning stage. The best we could do was feature prioritization with subjective rating methods. Some of you may be familiar with T-shirt sizing, where both "business value" and development effort are weighted for a feature. Features with the highest "business value" and lowest cost have higher priority. T-shirt sizing has been a useful method for subjective prioritization of features, but it doesn't project income on a feature basis.

The need for financial predictability on the business side, combined with the inherent Agile development need of content delivery flexibility, led to the Investment planning approach introduced in this book. "Investment" in the Agile planning context is defined as the smallest increment of software functionality that has the potential to increase income and/or reduce operational expenses. To generate income a customer must perceive value. Willingness to pay for something affirms business value.

Here are some examples of Investments:

New Sales

- Interactive dashboards to reduce customer operational costs by 10% to increase annual revenue by 5% over the next three years

Defense

- EU competitive features to prevent market loss of 20% over three years

Expense Reductions

- Multi-tenant capability to reduce annual hosting costs by 15%

Refactoring

- Deployment simplification to accelerate $3M in income over the next three years

Investments become the Agile planning element with this new approach. Features can then be justified and prioritized within an Investment based on their relative contribution to the financial target instead of trying to prioritize hundreds of features. This book uses Cost of Delay principles to show that Investments that generate the highest income with the lowest development effort should be prioritized higher.

The condition "potentially deployable" is used to separate the release packaging problem from the prioritization of development work. There are often valid reasons why multiple Investments may be packaged in the same release. Regulatory validation requirements are an example. Or there may be deployment process constraints involving retraining of operations staff. However, even if we are planning to release multiple Investments in a release, they should be developed in the order of highest value.

We want to be "agile" by being able to replace lower value Investments with higher value Investments at any time during the development cycle. With the ability to assign income to increments of software development, we can finally quantify the millions of dollars that are delayed because of the inability to deploy individual Investments. This can be viewed as "the opportunity cost of not being Agile." Investments in software infrastructure and deployment processes to release faster can now be justified.

Product managers may view Investments as conventional "initiatives" they have traditionally used in planning. There is a key difference. Initiatives relate to marketing programs of which R&D costs are only one component. Marketing initiatives include all activities necessary to develop, market and profit from a product. Investments defined in this book are based only on R&D cost so we can prioritize work within constrained software development capacity to maximize ROI. In effect, an R&D "Investment" is one component of an "initiative."

Engineering may view "Investments" as the Minimum Marketable Feature Set (MMFS) long advocated by Agile development. The comparison is valid for the case where an MMFS is associated with a financial forecast. However, the MMFS term is also used to describe an increment of functionality that adds any perceived "value" for the customer. An Investment can be an MMFS, but not every MMFS is an Investment. The book will show, however, how the Investment approach facilitates the MMFS because Investments with lower development cost are prioritized higher. A Minimum Viable Product (MVP) may be created to validate the perceived benefit of an increment of software without revenue expectations just to obtain customer feedback. MVPs are Investments only if they generate income.

You may be questioning at this point how we can assign income forecasts at the Investment level because it requires commitment from sales and/or operations during the planning stage. Obtaining revenue and cost reduction commitments prior to starting development has long been a goal of product managers. However, release price bundling and the inability to forecast income at the feature-level have made this impractical. Product management can now get income commitments on an Investment before it can be prioritized within the Investment backlog. Methods to collaboratively plan income impacts with sales and operations prior to development are provided in this book.

Addressing Traditional Software Development Challenges

Don Reinertsen introduced Cost of Delay and Weighted Shortest Job First (WSJF) in his book *Principles of Product Development Flow* [1], but these calculations have not been widely adopted. Reinertsen introduced "Weighted Shortest Job First" (WSJF) as a project prioritization method. He showed that prioritization by monthly income divided by cycle time always provides the optimal development order of projects. He refers to monthly income as the "Cost of Delay." Although widely acknowledged as the optimal prioritization method, WSJF has posed a challenge for the software industry. It's not possible to prioritize software development within a release because features typically don't have income projections. His WSJF based on Cost of Delay in terms of income can now be used to prioritize Investments.

Inability to reduce technical debt has long been a point of frustration for engineering. It's not realistic to expect product managers to prioritize work with nebulous financial value ahead of the feature demands of their stakeholders. Engineering can now propose Investments for technical work that can be prioritized against business investments. The catch is that engineering needs to justify how these technical Investments improve financial results to offset their development costs and the cost of delaying income from other Investments. This book teaches engineering how to do that.

Investments also facilitate collaboration between product management and engineering. Relationships between product management and engineering departments have often been adversarial because they have conflicting objectives. Product management pressures engineering to incorporate features into releases under pressure from sales and operations. Engineering naturally avoids commitment because they are the ones that end up being held accountable, especially when they know that additional work will come in without schedule relief. Product managers and engineering can now share common goals with Investment planning. Their shared objective is to define Investments with the lowest development costs that maximize income. They also need to ensure that Investment scope does not increase without offsetting income to maintain WSJF priority. Product teams with common goals can now be formed around Investments.

Agile teams can be staffed on the basis of Investments. We want Agile teams to be focused on value rather than functionality. By definition, Investments provide quantifiable value. Consider the higher motivation of an Agile team working together to solve problems directly related to customer value, rather than implementing pre-determined functionality. This achieves the original objective of Agile development of delivering increments of true customer value.

Lastly, Investment planning addresses the role conflict between product managers and product owners. I have observed product managers who still dwell on the details of requirements definition, even down to User Interface (UI) layouts. Investment planning elevates the role of product managers to focus on value rather than functionality. Product managers can concentrate on identifying opportunities for customer value for which customers are willing to pay. Product owners can focus on the functionality necessary to achieve that value. Investment planning provides complementary roles for product management and product owners that facilitate collaboration and innovation.

Motivation and Innovation

I have included a chapter on each of these topics based on some amazing insight and training I received early in my career. I felt that this book would be incomplete without addressing the organizational cultural aspects necessary to fully realize the potential of the Investment approach and Agile development.

Motivation must be established in your organization to adopt and use the practices provided in this book. Most organizational change implementations fail because they don't provide the motivation to follow new practices. And can you really change the divisive and confrontational relationship between product management and engineering in your organization? Can product management ever get sales to accept the MMFS instead of continual pressure for features of little value? You'll see that there are established principles of organizational behavior that show how to align consequences with new practices to facilitate sustained behavior change. These principles have been taken into account for all the practices defined in this book. The practices themselves drive culture change.

Innovation is at the end of the Agile rainbow. However, the potential of Agile to ignite innovation is rarely achieved. The Investment model described in this book facilitates innovation by allowing engineering to contribute at the planning stage. Investments convey the problem to solve instead of constraining engineers with features and prescriptive requirements. However, even with new practices to facilitate collaboration and innovation, it won't happen unless you can create the nebulous "culture of innovation."

Culture is defined in terms of the organizational behavior model of motivation. We will see that innovation is a product of behaviors that must be frequently reinforced in your organization. Presenting ideas or building a proof of concept on one's own time are examples of behaviors observed in companies with a "culture of innovation." Behaviors require motivation, hence the connection with the organizational behavior model. Chapter 14 tells you exactly what your organization needs to do to reach the end of the Agile rainbow where product managers and engineering collaborate to produce innovative products within short cycle times that outdistance your competition.

Your Organization

This book provides everything you need in terms of practices, templates, and tools for you to implement the Investment model in your organization. The final chapter in this book provides a step-by-step guide, from gaining internal support to creating your first Agile Investment roadmap. It also tells you how to align consequences in your organization to make lasting change. This book provides references to downloadable spreadsheets to support Investment planning, including Cost of Delay calculations. They can be accessed at: www.construx.com/product-flow-optimization-calculators.

Reference

1 Reinertsen, D.G. (2009). *The Principles of Product Development Flow: Second Generation Lean Product Development*. Celeritas Publishing.

1

The Persistence of Waterfall Planning

The benefits of increased business agility have been well documented by the Agile community. Who would argue that organizations that can rapidly react to changing market conditions will prevail? Or the potential for increased R&D Return on Investment (ROI) using the "Minimal Marketable Feature Set" (MMFS) approach to provide value at lower R&D cost? Yet, most organizations constrain Agile development with Waterfall planning practices and large releases with fixed content and schedule.

We'll start with a fictional startup accounting company called AccuWiz that used Agile development to become successful. As the business grew, they turned into a company many of you may recognize if you work for a large company. AccuWiz tossed aside the Agile planning and development practices that made them successful and became like companies from which their Agile developers fled. For those of you in smaller companies, this is the fate that awaits you as your company grows from entrepreneurship to a product organization expected to set and meet financial commitments.

Although these changes were mysterious to the developers, we'll see that there are natural business forces that explain the changes. The example demonstrates how Waterfall planning will continue to constrain Agile development unless ways are found to satisfy the business need for predictability.

AccuWiz will be revisited in a later chapter to see how they were able to use the Investment approach to restore them to an innovative organization with highly motivated Agile teams, while meeting the predictability needs of the business. There is hope for your organization.

1.1   Introduction to AccuWiz

AccuWiz was a startup that leveraged Agile development to get traction in the crowded accounting software market. The founders, Ken and Brett, brought in a

Unlocking Agile's Missed Potential, First Edition. Robert Webber.
© 2022 The Institute of Electrical and Electronics Engineers, Inc. Published 2022 by John Wiley & Sons, Inc.

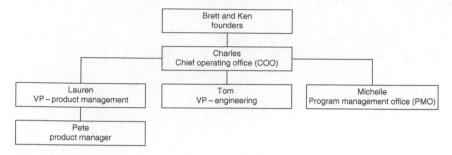

Figure 1.1 AccuWiz organization chart.

new chief operating officer (COO), Charles, to establish financial predictability to support their goal for acquisition or a public offering.

As companies grow, departments evolve that have different, and even conflicting, objectives. AccuWiz adopted the typical product development organization (see Figure 1.1).

1.1.1 The New COO

Charles, the new COO, was the VP of product management of a large established company that has dominated the accounting software market for years. Charles was brought in to establish the financial predictability sought by the founders. There is no way AccuWiz can be acquired or go public without a record of financial predictability.

Charles created a product management organization and hired Lauren from his previous company to lead the department. Lauren is expected to implement roadmap planning to support AccuWiz financial growth objectives. Lauren hired product managers with years of experience in the accounting field. Pete, for example, is a trained accountant who developed a keen interest in software by working with several traditional accounting systems. He can't wait to share his experience with software developers. He has so many great ideas. He especially likes the idea of being the "Voice of the Customer."

Tom was the first technical person hired by the founders and rose to the position of VP. He built his development organization around Agile development. Tom and his team provided many of the technical innovations that differentiated AccuWiz.

A new program management office (PMO) headed by Michelle was formed. Charles brought her in from his prior company because of her reputation for holding people accountable. She is supposed to improve software project schedule and cost predictability.

The founders, Brett and Ken, feel they have established the organizational infrastructure to take them to the next level.

1.1.2 Product Management

The new product management department brought structure into the planning process. They organized the hundreds of feature requests from sales into a prioritized list and allocated them to annual releases on a three-year roadmap. Lauren pushed Tom to commit to as many features as possible in each release.

However, Pete, the product manager, has become frustrated. This isn't the dream job he expected. He is under intense pressure from his boss, Lauren. It seems that all Pete does is pass on feature requests from sales to development. The VP of sales often goes directly to the founders to complain that they will miss their revenue commitments next year without these new features. Sales has a lot of influence with the founders, especially through their weekly golf outings. Pete has had to put all his great ideas on hold and can hardly keep up providing requirements for the myriad feature requests.

Pete must pressure developers to reduce estimates. His boss, Lauren, is very unhappy when he comes back from a meeting with engineering where they refuse to commit to a feature in the next release. She tells Pete to keep pressing. She knows they have slack. Whenever they apply pressure, engineering finally accepts the features.

When Tom balks at including features in a release, Lauren often sets up a meeting with Tom, Charles, and the VP of sales to emphasize the importance and potential impact on revenue. Tom is in the "hot seat" and usually commits with no relief in schedule or feature commitments.

1.1.3 PMO

Agile development was new to Michelle. Tom told her that releases must have feature content flexibility in Agile because requirements are created and changed throughout the release cycle. He also tried to explain the natural uncertainty in software estimation, but Michelle feels this is just a wishy-washy way to avoid commitment. Tom also explained that the teams must incorporate feedback during development to deliver what customers really want. Tom says, "The business needs to be more Agile."

Michelle has no idea how she is supposed to meet her roadmap commitments. There is no schedule or feature content flexibility. The schedules were established without any contingency, and any changes will impact financial commitments. And she and Charles know from their prior company that contingency reduces pressure on development, and they slack off. She has already observed that there are very few developers in the office when she comes in at 8:00 a.m. and has passed the observation on to Charles.

Michelle took an introductory Agile class for management to try to get on the same page as Tom. However, there was nothing about how multiyear business roadmap and financial commitments can be planned and achieved with any predictability. She heard the same expression used by Tom – "The business needs to be more Agile." She can't imagine Charles telling the founders they have to invest millions over the next three years, but he can't commit to financial returns because sales doesn't know what they'll have to sell. "Just be more agile." Charles wouldn't be around long.

1.1.4 Engineering

Tom, the VP of engineering, has been with the founders from the start. It was his idea to use workflow to differentiate their product in the market. Tom chose Agile development to quickly respond to individual customer needs. He soon found that versioning became a major headache. Although his teams could create frequent releases, customers weren't upgrading. Engineering had to support multiple releases. Tom acknowledges that moving to major releases can help, but he still wants to use Agile development because the engineers are highly motivated, and teamwork is great, and direct customer feedback during sprint development has helped them build a great product.

Tom's developers have become disillusioned because he is unable to set schedules they can meet. The Agile teams don't create their own sprint objectives anymore. They must meet sprint commitments to support the feature schedules tracked by project managers. Developers barely have time to get the basic functionality working and don't have time anymore to create robust, high-quality software. Nobody seems to care as long as the features get checked off.

Product managers have been designated as product owners. However, they're never available when developers need to make design decisions. Developers just make assumptions because they must meet feature schedules. Developers don't get any direct feedback from customers anymore. The product managers feel they have enough experience to know what the customers need. They can just tell engineering what the customer needs.

Sprint reviews are tough. This is where developers are told everything that is wrong with what they've built. Many of the assumptions they had to make during development are ridiculed by product managers. They go away from the review with lots of changes, but the feature schedules stay the same. They're just going to have to let the defect backlog grow, hoping they have time before the release date to correct them. Developers don't include software for unlikely use cases and focus more on demonstrating the bare minimum to get them by the next sprint review. They hope to have time to account for these cases later. Unit testing is being bypassed to try to maintain the schedule.

Developers have started to leave the company. Tom's wife wants him to leave the company. He works long hours and comes home complaining about his day.

However, Tom has too much vested in the product and is loyal to the founders. He will hang on a bit longer hoping he can instigate some changes to make it more like the company he loved. He just doesn't know how to do that at this point.

1.1.5 Customer Perspective

AccuWiz was viewed as a breath of fresh air in the world of accounting software. They brought some novel ideas, especially around workflow to simplify the work for accountants. The decision to bring in AccuWiz was made by Adam, the head of his company's accounting department. He was willing to forego some of the bells and whistles of currently available accounting applications because AccuWiz made their routine work so efficient. They also got great support for small changes they wanted.

Their AccuWiz sales rep told them they were moving to annual release cycles. She explained that customers will benefit by getting more features with higher value, and customers will only have to upgrade once a year. Adam was okay with this because recent upgrades have surprised his staff with unexpected changes. They can now plan and do retraining prior to upgrading.

Adam is not happy with the way things have turned out. Only one of the ten features promised by their sales rep made the release. The release was three months late, and there were many quality issues. Adam noticed that the functionality they are seeing in this new release looks a lot like accounting packages they used in the past. He's wondering whether they just should have stuck with their old accounting software. The accounting staff is now angry about having to use AccuWiz, and their IT organization is complaining of the high level of support required.

1.1.6 Synopsis

AccuWiz represents the point in a company's life cycle where it transitions from entrepreneurship to bureaucracy. Scaling introduces organizational structure at the expense of communication and speed. Departmental goals become self-serving and often conflicting. For example, software development wants time to deliver with quality. Product management wants faster feature delivery and long-term roadmap commitments. Project management just wants to keep checking off features to meet the schedule, and sales wants every feature they believe can get them even one sale. The deeper the organization, the higher the organizational walls.

Of course, AccuWiz is a fictional company. It is made up from my early career experience in large companies and over ten years as a Construx consultant working with Fortune 500 companies. The pattern was observed over and over. There is intense pressure on engineering to commit more features than what they can deliver. Engineering questions the value of the endless requests for features, many of which end up not being used by customers. Engineers can't meet schedules and become disillusioned and frustrated.

The pressure is not the fault of product managers. They are under pressure from the sales department. If you are a product manager in a large company, you may remember being told to force feature commitments on engineering under pressure from the sales department, often supported by the CEO – "don't come back without the right answer." It creates an antagonistic relationship between product management and engineering.

Let's also recognize that this situation is not the fault of the salespeople. Imagine that more than half of your income depends on making sales that depend on features being available on time. What would you do? Of course, you would use any leverage you have to push for features that could increase your income.

Another observation. If you switched the players around and ignore skill issues, what happens? Say Pete, the product manager, is moved to the sales department and Tom from development goes to product management. You will likely see them assume the same behaviors as their predecessors. You have likely observed this when people you work with have moved to jobs with different responsibilities. They start to behave differently. That means that there is something about how we define job responsibilities that impacts how people behave in organizations. We'll see that individual consequences drive behavior, and different roles have different consequences. We'll discuss consequences in detail in a later chapter on organizational behavior principles that will allow you to align role consequences with desired behaviors to change your organizational culture.

Does it have to be this way? Is there an approach that realizes the vision of Agile to deliver higher value faster with increased predictability in larger organizations? Can we create a culture of collaboration and teamwork between product management and engineering? We'll revisit AccuWiz after we describe an alternative that puts product management and development on the same side to achieve the Agile vision. The simplicity of the Investment approach will surprise you.

1.2 Summary

1. Financial reporting constraints drive the business need for multiyear predictability in terms of software delivery and development costs.
2. These constraints cause organizations to retain Waterfall planning practices that limit the business agility of Agile.
3. Organizational structures are typically based on the need for business predictability and divide organizations at the highest level with conflicting goals.

4. Engineers should be educated on real-world business constraints to create Agile development frameworks that meet the business need for predictability.
5. Knowledge and acceptance of real-world financial constraints usually explain the mysteries of business decision-making for engineers. "Follow the money." Accept it. It's not going to change.
6. Feature-level planning limits the value that Agile development can add by constraining solutions. It also leads to low-level feature commitments that are impossible to schedule with predictability.
7. The evolutionary requirements approach of Agile increases the likelihood that engineering will miss delivery and cost commitments, reinforcing a perception of poor productivity and lack of motivation.
8. The software industry needs to embrace the variability of software estimation to improve business predictability.
9. Replacement of Waterfall planning in Agile requires an approach that provides business predictability while retaining the tenets of the Agile development vision.

To make Agile successful in the eyes of the business, we need to understand why it is viewed as a failure in many organizations. That is the topic of the next chapter.

2

Why Agile Has Struggled

The principles of Agile development are great. What's not to like about a development framework where engineering teams are guided by knowledgeable product owners helping them build great products. Teams work without schedule pressure or management interference. Developers have time to develop robust software, not just a facade of functionality written for the "happy path." Teams have time to incorporate feedback from sprint reviews to build what stakeholders really want, and to correct defects to retain the software in a "potentially shippable" state. I like to say that with Waterfall, we developed products that customers would finally accept. With Agile, we can create products that delight customers.

Construx has an annual leadership summit where clients hear industry leaders talk about the latest advances in software engineering. There are small group sessions where attendees talk about specific topics of interest. I've had the pleasure of moderating some of these groups at each of the Construx summits for several years. I recently did an impromptu survey with the 15 engineering leaders who attended my group sessions to get their perspectives on the perceived success of their Agile transitions.

The question was "Please indicate how you believe your stakeholders feel about your Agile transition." Possible answers and scores were the following:

1. Met promises and expectations of Agile
2. Has not met expectations
3. Worse than before

They were allowed to provide fractional answers for anything in between. Only 3 of the 15 indicated that Agile had met the expectations of their stakeholders. The average of the scores was 1.8, indicating that expectations have not been met in most cases. This is a small sample, but isn't it alarming that only 3 of 15 software leaders say their Agile implementation has met business expectations? And I'd love to hear the business perspective in their organizations. The informal survey results agree with my observations and support the premise of this book.

Unlocking Agile's Missed Potential, First Edition. Robert Webber.
© 2022 The Institute of Electrical and Electronics Engineers, Inc. Published 2022 by John Wiley & Sons, Inc.

This chapter starts with some Agile fundamentals to get us all on the same page as to what really constitutes Agile development. My years of assessments revealed that most organizations are not really "doing Agile," mainly because of the constraints imposed by Waterfall planning. Many development organizations use Waterfall practices with short development cycles claiming they are using Agile development. Some organizations were surprised to discover that their engineering departments had "gone Agile" without them knowing it. Suddenly, Agile terms like "stand-up meeting" and "sprints" crept into the vocabulary while nothing really changed.

I recall a few good examples. I asked an engineer during an assessment exactly what they had changed to say they are now Agile. His answer was "We're now doing stand-up meetings and writing less documentation." A junior engineer in a maintenance group at a different company went through a detailed explanation of how they were "Agile" because they had established a "backlog" of issues and were releasing fixes for them in quarterly releases. I said it sounded just like a standard maintenance process. Her response was, "Oh, I don't know. I was just told we're now doing Agile." The best was from an engineering director – "We've pretty much got Agile down. We just need to figure out the product owner role."

Feature-level planning has persisted, although Agile provides an approach to focus on value rather than functionality with epics and user stories. We'll explain why feature planning isn't going anywhere and needs to be incorporated within Agile development in a way that lets engineering add value.

Lastly, we'll discuss a major reason why Agile has missed expectations unrelated to Waterfall planning that needs to be addressed for Agile to be viewed as successful. I haven't seen an effective product owner implementation in any of the large companies I assessed over 10 years with Construx. Yes, I've seen it work well in small companies and in isolated "start-up" groups in larger organizations, but these are exceptions. It calls into question the feasibility of the product owner role as currently defined. It's a problem that needs to be addressed.

2.1 Agile Development Fundamentals

You can skip this section if you feel you have a good understanding of the history and principles of Agile development. However, you may find that you're not really doing Agile development based on the description below.

2.1.1 The Agile Revolution

Agile development was a grassroots revolution that began in engineering. Lack of success with Waterfall development frameworks drove engineering to find an alternative. In my view, the biggest attraction of Agile for engineering was the elimination of the fixed schedules of Waterfall to allow them time to build good software without punishments imposed for missed schedules.

We know that few organizations were successful in achieving the commitments of cost, schedule, and scope with Waterfall planning. The path to failure started in the planning stage where engineering was pressured to make long-term development commitments based on vague or no requirements. Engineering had little power. Sales could always play the trump card at the CEO level by claiming impacts to their sales forecasts if they didn't get features they wanted. Product managers were under intense pressure from sales to get commitments from engineering.

As development progressed under Waterfall, new "must-have" features came in with no relief in content delivery or schedule. Feature functionality grew from new requirements. This resulted in late releases, or, often, partially developed or tested features being dropped from the release as the deadline approached. A significant portion of the release development effort was wasted. The net effect was lower R&D Return on Investment (ROI).

There were also negative customer impacts with Waterfall. We really didn't want to get customer feedback during release development because it would put us further behind. We stood behind the 1000-page detailed requirements document to fend off new requests during release development – "You signed off on this." Customers were offered "workarounds" and were promised "enhancements" in a future release, which usually didn't happen. "That's on our roadmap" became the standard answer.

Agile development was the promised solution for these problems. Engineering was going to work more closely with users to build what they really valued, rather than just be implementers of prescribed features.

Agile, as we know it today, had its beginning in the Manifesto of Agile Software Development[1] proposed by a group of 17 influential people in the software industry. It was an engineering perspective of what was necessary to overcome a perceived lack of success caused by the impossible predictability demands of the business. Engineers wanted to have time to build software they could be proud of within a collaborative and motivational environment.

The Manifesto was based on 12 principles:

1. Customer satisfaction by early and continuous delivery of valuable software.
2. Welcome changing requirements, even in late development.
3. Deliver working software frequently (weeks rather than months).
4. Close, daily cooperation between business people and developers.
5. Projects are built around motivated individuals, who should be trusted.
6. Face-to-face conversation is the best form of communication (colocation).

1 Agile Alliance, June 2010.

7. Working software is the primary measure of progress.
8. Sustainable development, able to maintain a constant pace.
9. Continuous attention to technical excellence and good design.
10. Simplicity – the art of maximizing the amount of work not done – is essential.
11. Best architectures, requirements, and designs emerge from self-organizing teams.
12. Regularly, the team reflects on how to become more effective, and adjusts accordingly.

This led to the creation of different Agile frameworks like Extreme Programming, Scrum, and Kanban. There were others, but Scrum has become dominant in the software industry, followed by Kanban. I will use the term "Agile" to represent both Scrum and Kanban, or any other development framework where development teams select small increments of work from a queue and develop them in two- to four-week cycles.

2.1.2 Scrum

Scrum provides agility by allowing requirements to change throughout the development cycle. Requirements documentation was reduced to facilitate rapid change and reduce effort. Verbal communication was preferred. Requirements in Agile could be described in the form of a short "user story" that could be clarified by someone called a product owner during development.

A user story is a short statement of need in the form:

As a <specific role>
I want to <what the user wants to achieve>
In order to <the reason behind the achievement>

For example, "As accounting clerk, I want to identify late invoices so I can follow-up and obtain payment."

The level of decomposition of a user story is determined by the requirement that it can be completed by the team within a sprint, a development cycle of two to four weeks. Agile accounted for definition of "epics" that are higher-level statements of need that can be decomposed into user stories. The emphasis of Agile is on conveying the problem for engineering to solve rather than providing them with prescriptive functionality.

The product owner is responsible for what gets developed by an Agile team. Teams are comprised of five to seven engineering staff. The product owner prioritizes the work of the team and expands on the user stories during development to ensure that the right thing is built. The product owner has final approval and declares a user story "done" at a review at the end of each sprint. Engineers are

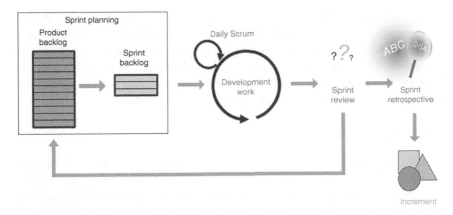

Figure 2.1 Scrum development cycle overview

given time in the next sprint to incorporate feedback, as well as any new requirements identified. Defect correction takes a higher priority than new development.

Engineering teams set their own goals for the sprint user stories. They are encouraged to lower sprint targets if they miss objectives.

Figure 2.1 shows a high-level view of Scrum.

The team selects user stories for each sprint from a prioritized list called the "product backlog" that contains stories targeted for the release "increment." The product backlog content and priorities are controlled by the product owner. Sprint retrospectives are done by the team at the end of each sprint to find ways to increase throughput and improve quality.

There is one more important distinguishing factor of Scrum. Each story is supposed to provide working functionality that can be demonstrated, instead of just a chunk of development. For example, assume the user needs to drill down in a report to get the information they need to satisfy the user story. Before Scrum, a wireframe for the full report would be generated and reviewed, followed by the complete layout of the UI. Drilldown capability for the entire report would then be developed.

In Scrum, a user story would be defined around the need that is driving a specific drilldown case. For example, "As an accountant I want to determine the accounts that contribute to the accounts payable balance in order to follow up with the customer." A page with a single button would be created in a sprint. However, the button is functional. When the product owner clicks on the button, a summary of accounts displays.

We can see that Scrum is incompatible with the long-term feature-level predictability demanded by the business. It is impossible to make feature-level predictions when requirements haven't been developed, and how do we account for the extra time necessary to incorporate feedback during and after the sprint? We also can't account for the indeterminate time it will take to fix defects at a higher priority than new functionality in the next sprint to keep the software "potentially shippable." Contingency can be built in to achieve predictions, but my experience is that contingency doesn't last long under the intense pressure on product management and engineering to deliver more features.

2.1.3 Kanban

It's easier to describe Kanban by comparing and contrasting it with Scrum. In terms of similarities, both involve small development teams pulling small increments of work from queues at their own pace. Both advocate small development increments. However, the product owner title is not used in Kanban. Similar positions are "service request managers" or "service delivery managers."

One difference is that Kanban provides more flexibility in how requirements are defined. There is no requirement for user stories.

Work items are represented by cards on a board (see Figure 2.2). The columns represent the order of work. Work items can be "In Process" or "Done." To add to the confusion, many Scrum teams adopt Kanban boards to focus the team's work, but it doesn't mean they're "doing Kanban." As long as they are using user stories under the guidance of a product owner and conducting Scrum "ceremonies" like stand-up meetings and retrospectives, they are still doing Scrum, which could be called "Scrum with a Kanban board."

There is much available on the web on the history of Kanban. It started in Japanese auto manufacturing to control parts inventories. Big stacks of parts would build up at manufacturing workstations. For example, brake pads may pile up for wheel assembly. This represents money tied up in the manufacturing process that shows up on financial reports. It also leads to delays in the manufacturing line when upstream work must stop while a bubble of inventory is processed. Manufacturing needed some way to prevent the buildup of parts in the manufacturing line.

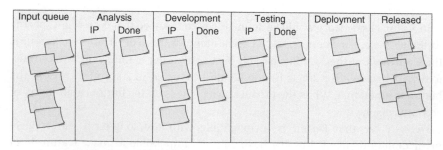

Figure 2.2   Kanban board example

"Kanban" means signboard or billboard in Japanese. The simple solution was to create cards to signal the number of parts to be delivered to a workstation. The preceding workstation knows how many parts to provide to the subsequent workstation to prevent parts from piling up. It reduces the amount of capital tied up in parts sitting on the manufacturing floor and reduces delay by limiting queue sizes.

Kanban used the concept of "Work in Process (WIP)" to account for value of parts waiting in queues. It became an important manufacturing Key Performance Indicator (KPI). WIP limits could be established for the number of queued parts. WIP limits also defined a minimum number of parts to account for variation in the manufacturing process to prevent "work starvation."

Kanban used in software today was heavily influenced by Don Reinertsen, the same person we can thank for Cost of Delay and Weighted Shortest Job First (WSJF) discussed in Chapter 4. He modeled software development as a series of "workstations" taking work delivered by preceding workstations and applying a development process step. For example, flow of Agile development artifacts may include multiple queues.

Epic > User Story > Test Plan > Coding > Testing > Done

Work can build up at each interface and cause the same impediments to efficient flow that occur in manufacturing. One difference is that partially completed elements of the software process are not quantified in terms of inventory cost. It doesn't appear on the financial report.

The same book referenced for Cost of Delay and WSJF, *The Principles of Product Development Flow*, contributed much to optimizing the flow of work through the software development cycle. Reinertsen supports his principles with queuing theory – an interesting and insightful contribution to software development.

2.2 Barriers to Real Agile

Frankly, I've never seen Agile implemented the way it's described in Agile books. I believe there are some smaller organizations, especially startups, that have effectively implemented Agile, and there are likely some good implementations out there in large organizations. One could argue that my perspective is colored because I was only brought in to assess organizations that had problems. However, ten years of moderating Construx summit leadership group sessions have confirmed that very few of the larger organizations are doing Agile the way it was envisioned. I called our leadership group meetings "group therapy" because attendees were relieved to find out they weren't the only ones.

Interestingly, I did have the opportunity to do an assessment for a summit attendee who claimed to have it all together during the group discussions. I found he was out of touch with what was really going on in his organization. The Agile implementation was no better than any other company I worked with. Things can look pretty good, the higher up you go.

Other Construx consultants and I recommended improvements for clients, but within the organizational constraints we observed. The major theme of this book is that Agile development can be a very powerful development framework if engineering is allowed to implement it the way it was envisioned.

There are three significant constraints in most software organizations today that need to be addressed:

1. Schedule pressure
2. Realization of the product owner role
3. Feature-based planning

2.2.1 Schedule Pressure

Agile was predicated on variable content and fixed release cycles determined by a "timebox." Requirements are expected to evolve during development. Feedback is provided throughout the development cycle to prioritize building what users really want over schedule. Agile teams pull work from queues at a pace they determine, and they prioritize correction of defects over new production to keep the software in a "potentially shippable state." However, most large organizations today are still using a traditional Waterfall planning process that forces schedule and content constraints on Agile teams, undercutting the Agile tenet of variable content.

From the engineering perspective, Agile can actually improve predictability for the business. The fixed effort, schedule, and content model of Waterfall planning was an illusion. Companies made huge investments in large releases that rarely met schedules. Any that met effort, schedule, and content commitments usually compromised quality. As ship dates drew near, partially completed features were shed from the release like ballast released from a sinking balloon. Agile broke down software development investment into smaller increments with lower risk and improved predictability. Why would Waterfall planning be retained?

Agile failed to address the business need for multiyear financial predictability that the business sought from Waterfall planning. These needs must be addressed to make the variable content of Agile development a reality. To start, let's examine the drivers behind the business need for predictability that need to be satisfied. Fortunately, we only need to learn how a few line-items in financial reports drive the quest for predictability and the perpetuation of Waterfall planning. You don't need a background in finance or accounting to understand it.

There are three documents that drive the need for business predictability. The first two are the income statement and balance sheet that can be found in the annual report of a public company. These documents also exist in nonpublic companies. Investors and boards of directors rely on them to justify investment in the company. The third document is the business plan, an internal document that describes how the company will attain the objectives of the financial statements.

2.2.1.1 Income Statement

This is the quarterly summary of sales, expenses, income, and earnings per share (EPS). Companies are expected to show EPS that justify continued investment in the company. Investors will decide to move their money elsewhere if they can obtain higher returns. However, they may initially accept a lower return in anticipation of growth. In either case, investors want to see trends that maintain or increase EPS.

EPS is the source of the quarterly predictability that drives business decisions. Engineers are often mystified by such decisions. "Why would they reduce R&D expenses in a quarter when we're making so much money? Why was the travel budget eliminated in the fourth quarter?" Accept the fact that decisions will be based on the short-term impact to quarterly projections and roll with it. It's not going to change unless we throw out our entire capitalist economic model, which isn't likely to happen.

2.2.1.2 Balance Sheet

Investors and owners need to understand the current worth of companies represented by the balance sheet. The balance sheet is a snapshot in time of current assets and liabilities. Companies often capitalize software development costs according to strict accounting rules to turn them into assets on the balance sheet.

R&D costs do not appear as expenses on the income statement when software is capitalized. Although it reduces pressure on quarterly R&D development expenses, capitalization negatively impacts another performance indicator called "Return on Equity (ROE)" where the denominator is the asset value, including capitalized software development costs. ROE is income divided by shareholder's equity, which is the company's assets minus its debt. Companies may or may not capitalize software, based on how they want their financial report to look for investors.

The takeaway for engineering is that software capitalization is not free money for R&D. There will still be pressure to minimize software development costs.

2.2.1.3 The Business Plan

You may be wondering why organizations expect multiyear projections for product development since financial statements are only released each quarter. The answer provides the key to understanding business decisions that impact software development. Company departments are expected to contribute to a multiyear plan that projects profit and loss, and company value. The business plan establishes confidence for the CEO, CFO, owners, and any Boards of Directors that the company can predict and deliver positive financial statements in upcoming years. CEOs who fail to do this don't stay around long. It's the desire for financial statement predictability that drives most business decisions.

Let's look at how the business plan evolves and how it impacts Agile development. The CEO and CFO need to predict quarterly income generated by new software development and related R&D costs. They need revenue projections from sales and operational expense forecasts from any internal operations departments, as both impact net income. The first question from sales is, "What can I sell in these upcoming years?" Operations asks, "What software tools can I count on to reduce my operational expenses?" The mold is set at this point.

Product management is expected to make software roadmap commitments in sufficient detail to convince sales and operations that they can meet these projections. The CFO needs to quantify the quarterly R&D investment required to make these financial commitments to ensure adequate funding exists, and to support R&D ROI predictions. Income, R&D expenses, and software capitalization need to support the goals of the projected Income Statement and Balance Sheet.

Our capitalistic system drives the need for business predictability and Agile must provide a way to achieve predictability while allowing teams the content flexibility fundamental to Agile development.

2.2.2 The "Motivation" Factor

This section exposes an unspoken reason why the fixed schedule and scope of Waterfall planning persist in Agile development. In the eyes of the business, Waterfall schedules create deliverable accountability used to prod engineering to work harder to meet deadlines. The prods are in the form of negative project meetings that "motivate" engineering to avoid showing up with deliverables off-schedule.

How do I know that? In every Agile transition I've been involved with, I've stressed to management that they have agreed to implement self-directed teams that pull work from queues at a pace determined by them. The first reaction is invariably, "How do we know they're working as hard as they can?" My response is, "So, you're saying that the only way this company motivates people is to overload them with work and prod them when they drop behind?" Unfortunately, this is the sad truth. Executives publicly state that they accept self-directed teams in Agile, but they still believe that pressure from fixed schedule and scope commitments are necessary to create motivation.

I've seen attempts to retain individual accountability in Agile. I've attended Scrum stand-up meetings where attendees are asked one by one by managers what they've completed in the last day. I've seen many cases where the backlog for a fixed-length sprint is chosen by product or project management. Missed the sprint objective? "Well, we need to load them up with even more next sprint, so we get closer to what we need to meet the release schedule." I've seen project managers who continue to track at the task level. The problem is that most companies don't know how to motivate Agile teams without negative schedule accountability.

You may be wondering why engineering motivation is always questioned. Engineering leaders often hear comments from other department leaders that question their motivation, especially in front of the CEO – "I was on the engineering floor at 8:00 this morning and I didn't see any of your developers." In most of the organizational assessments I did, product management described their major issue as poor engineering productivity. They had all the right plans if only engineering could develop them.

Engineering productivity is questioned because they miss the impossible commitments based on the fixed schedules and content of Waterfall planning. From the perspective of the outside world, they clearly need more motivation. Additional functionality is piled onto large releases and project management increases pressure to deliver. It's a no-win situation for engineering.

The other major reason for questioning engineering motivation is that under pressure, many engineering leaders end up committing to additional features and functionality without insisting on trade-offs, and they often deliver, at least from the perspective of the outside world. Clearly, engineering had slack that was only taken up under intense pressure.

Engineers know how this really happens. They resort to developing software that works for the "happy path." Demonstrating the "happy path" requires only a fraction of the code required to create robust and reliable software that covers all situations. Under intense schedule pressure, the software to handle unusual cases and exceptions is sacrificed, resulting in error-prone and unreliable software. Testing time is constrained to include only the most visible and rudimentary cases. The outside world can't tell the difference until customer complaints roll in. However, engineering did meet the schedule despite the addition of new features and functionality. They obviously just needed more pressure to increase their motivation.

I've been in the position of an engineering leader under intense pressure at the executive level, so I don't blame these engineering leaders. Careers are at stake. I do have a tip on how engineering leaders can better handle these situations. I realized once I got out of engineering that engineering leaders usually push back immediately when faced with the challenge of adding functionality within the current schedule. The engineering mind immediately starts to verbalize obstacles when presented with a problem. This gives the impression that they will not really try to find ways to get it done.

Try this. When confronted with a challenge, immediately respond that you understand the importance to the business, and you will get your team together to look at every conceivable way to get it done. No thinking out loud of why it may not be possible. Go back with your team and try to find ways to get it done. At the same time consider trade-offs that might be presented as well as *what you could deliver* within the requested time. You will find the audience to be much more receptive to accept trade-offs when clearly presented, and they will believe you and your team have tried your best to meet their needs.

Many organizations still believe they need the fixed schedules and content commitments of Waterfall planning to motivate engineering. A later chapter dedicated to motivation will show that pressure works, but it limits employee engagement. Motivation should not be an excuse for retention of Waterfall planning.

2.2.3 The Mythical Product Owner

The envisioned role of the all-knowing product owner was not effectively implemented in most of the organizations I assessed. There were pockets of success, but larger product companies with established product management organizations struggled. A successful product owner implementation is crucial for successful Agile.

The product owner role defined in Scrum was a great idea. Engineers using Waterfall were tired of being blamed for missed requirements. At the end of the day, if the product didn't meet expectations, it was engineering's fault. "They should have known, or they should have asked." The idea that engineering could have an individual assigned to their team to tell them everything they needed to know was attractive, and to take the blame when they didn't get it right. I have sometimes heard product owners referred to by engineering as "One Neck to Grab (ONTG)," or the "single wringable neck." The expressions reflect the pressure engineers are under. Of course, it's better from the engineering perspective that the product manager gets their neck wrung when the wrong thing is built.

User stories reduced requirements documentation, but under the assumption that a product owner would be engaged with the team to add the detail necessary for engineers to write their code. Construx refers to user stories as "topics of discussion." At a minimum, user story detail should be included in an acceptance test written prior to inclusion in the backlog. Any cases not explicitly described in the acceptance tests were supposed to be clarified by a product owner fully engaged with the team throughout sprint development.

Product managers were no longer required in the Agile vision. After all, they were the perceived source of the pressure on engineering. Engineers also didn't want product managers constraining them by telling them how to build it. Engineers just wanted someone who would work closely with the team to ensure they built the right thing. Tell them the problem to solve. Product managers were written out of the Agile vision. They could be replaced by product owners.

The name "product owner" led to confusion in organizations with established product management departments. Product managers have always been "product owners" in that they have ultimate responsibility for the success of the project, sometimes at the Profit and Loss (P&L) level. Therefore, in their minds, they were the logical "product owners."

However, much of the time of product managers is taken up by the insatiable demands of sales. Failure to respond to a sales request could put a product manager in front of the CEO explaining why they have sabotaged this year's financial commitments. Product managers were also driven by other priorities, like preparing for trade shows or performing customer demonstrations. Near-term priorities gave them little time to interact with Agile teams during a sprint development cycle, and often no time to thoroughly review their implementation at the end of a sprint. Agile teams took their best shots at building functionality based on a one-sentence user story, only to find they're wrong as the release date drew closer, or often after it has been released.

Many organizations realized the futility of using product managers in the product owner role and assigned product owners from within engineering. Product owners had more time with the teams, but they lacked exposure to customers and the market. Now engineering was isolated from the customer through two layers, product owners and product managers, and sales often presented a third layer.

Even with the assignment of a qualified product owner, they rarely sat with the teams to give them the level of verbal communication expected in Agile. Engineering was left to interact through e-mail, chat, or by requesting meetings. This way a product owner could handle multiple teams. Certainly, remote communication would be sufficient. Product owners and teams could be in different buildings, across the country, or even offshore in different time zones.

Let's look at what happens when engineers can't get the answers they need, especially when they're under schedule pressure. They make assumptions based on their peepholes into the domain, and they are often wrong. One of the scariest things in the world is listening to a couple of junior engineers with no domain experience discuss how something should be implemented. I used to tell product managers that if you don't specify what should happen, assume that decision will be made by an engineer fresh out of college. Engineers must make assumptions or miss schedules.

Product organizations struggled to establish the product owner envisioned in Agile because they build software for a diverse set of users who can't be represented by an individual. Product organizations must aggregate needs and constraints from worldwide markets with diverse product stakeholders and regulatory requirements. The product owner role did not include standard requirements elicitation processes to create and prioritize product requirements. Get it wrong? "Oh, just fix it in the next sprint."

I worked with a large energy company that brought in field engineers as product owners. Engineering commented that their last product was always built for the last field engineer, missing many of the requirements for international deployment.

So Agile went forth without clarification of how the new Agile roles would fit within a larger established organization. The role of project management was also written out. They could be replaced by scrum masters who support the team instead of pestering engineers to get their project tasks checked off. Management roles were also excluded. "We don't really care what they do as long as they stay out of our hair."

The net result is a reduction in software development productivity due to massive rework caused by incomplete requirements. Please hear me out. I'm not going to advocate going back to the Waterfall days. As I said, my goal is to make Agile successful in the eyes of the business. Agile has the potential to reduce wasteful rework to levels we could never attain in Waterfall. However, the failure to implement a successful product owner model results in high levels of waste, and what's worse is that this waste is no longer visible to the business because it just gets added to sprint backlogs.

The bottom line is that making Agile successful in larger organizations requires clear role descriptions for the product manager, product owner, project manager, and management that complement each other.

2.2.4 Feature Planning

Agile development was supposed to replace features with epics and stories. Agile teams could add value by understanding the problem to be solved, rather than just implementing features based on detailed requirements. Feature-based planning is still the norm at most organizations. In my experience, the vast majority of Agile teams are adding predefined features to a code base with little opportunity to add value. Many organizations define their product backlog in terms of features.

Product managers need processes that allow them to focus on value prior to any discussions on features, and the value must be conveyed to engineering in terms of a problem for them to solve. We'll see later that there is a place for features, but starting there severely limits the ability to add business value.

2.3 Agile Scaling Frameworks

Agile scaling frameworks were developed to reduce the frustrations of trying to apply simple Agile principles in larger organizations, especially those with existing product and project management infrastructure. Engineers were also challenged with exponential communication paths among multiple teams working on the same large software base. While many scaling frameworks are attractive to the business side, they constrain the potential of Agile development, and many engineers are dissatisfied with what they view as their inherent imposition of Waterfall planning practices.

The Scaled Agile Framework (SAFe) [1] has by far become the most popular Agile development framework in large organizations. However, it got there by institutionalizing Waterfall release planning in Agile. Existing company Waterfall planning processes could now coexist with Agile. The business side didn't have to know what went on "under the hood" in their Agile implementations. They could just continue to pile on features and blame engineering for missing their commitments.

I'm not criticizing SAFe, because they've done their best to introduce Agile planning to the business. They did include the Lean Canvas approach developed by Ash Maurya [2]. However, Lean Canvas does not account for the pressure on product management from sales and operations that perpetuate large releases filled with predefined features. Also, few established companies are willing to "gamble" by directing a significant portion of their R&D investment portfolios toward the exploratory nature of Lean Canvas. Lean Canvas can certainly be effective in an isolated area of a larger organization to refine new product ideas given separate funding, but it has not been widely adopted within most large companies that require a scaling framework.

SAFe now advocates the adoption of "Business Epics" at the beginning of the planning process. Again, a great idea, but from my perspective, the uptake has been low. Planning in most SAFe organizations starts with the "Release Train" of Waterfall planning and then stuffs them with features.

SAFe perpetuates Waterfall planning by even defining a dedicated role as "release train engineer." They're not "deployment engineers" tasked with planning development increments that can be released independently. The "release train" is a foregone conclusion when planning starts.

SAFe provides many great methods and structures to manage Agile development at a large scale, but it has not been able to move the industry toward Agile planning. The business is comfortable with the way they have always done it, blissfully unaware of the opportunity cost of not leveraging the power of Agile development. I see the Investment approach as a complementary solution for SAFe to deliver on the best of both worlds – high quality and effective scaled Agile development with Agile planning. In fact, Investments can be the instantiation of Business Epics with quantified financial targets.

2.4 Summary

- Scrum and Kanban are the two most popular instantiations of Agile development.

- Agile has not met the expectations of the business in many organizations, especially in larger organizations with established product management organizations.
- The requirements process in Waterfall rarely met the expectations of users. Agile can adopt user feedback during development *if engineers are given the variable time needed to implement it.*
- Business expectations for detailed schedules at the feature-level were not met with Waterfall. Agile has exacerbated the problem because detailed requirements are not created before the major development effort starts.
- The product owner role envisioned in Agile has not been successfully implemented by many organizations, especially product organizations with product managers.
- Scaled Agile frameworks like SAFe have institutionalized large releases filled with features by providing a Waterfall planning wrapper around Agile development.
- Agile must provide the business with the multiyear financial predictability they need to be successful.

A lot of promises have been made so far of the ability of the Investment approach to solve the biggest problems perceived by the business while establishing a true Agile development environment for engineers. I don't blame you if you are skeptical that such a simple idea can have such far-reaching industry impact. We have two more chapters to get through before describing the Investment approach. The first key is finally accepting software engineering estimation variance. The second is Reinertsen's Cost of Delay, which was the impetus for the Investment approach.

References

1 Leffingwell, D. (2016). *SAFe 4.5 Reference Guide: Scaled Agile Framework for Lean Enterprises.* Addison-Wesley.
2 Maurya, A. (2012). *Running Lean: How to Iterate from Plan A to a Plan that Works.* O'Reilly Press.

3

Embracing Software Development Variance

Engineers have found it difficult to convey the reality of software unpredictability within their organizations. Organizations must accept the reality of software development schedule and content variability to ultimately increase predictability. The business side needs to recognize that Waterfall planning has not, and will never, achieve the level of predictability they seek.

The chapter begins with industry data that demonstrate the software industry's inability to achieve schedule and effort predictability over decades of trying. For many years, the software industry assumed that predictability was just a case of improving software estimation methods. Software engineering pioneers like Barry Boehm and Steve McConnell made significant contributions that helped improve estimation processes. Yet, there is a natural limit to the degree to which software development effort and schedule can be estimated. Steve McConnell referred to it as still being a "black art." [1] This chapter provides an explanation of how the nature of software development makes it impossible to make accurate predictions for both schedule and content.

The chapter ends with the answer to a puzzling question, "Why can other departments like sales and manufacturing make and meet long-term commitments?" It provides insight into how engineering leaders can better deal with expectations of long-term projections.

3.1 The Cone of Uncertainty

Steve McConnell is well known in the software industry for defining the term "Cone of Uncertainty" to document software estimation error. The cone is based on analysis of hundreds of software projects. We'll review the traditional Waterfall cone and then relate it to Agile development (see Figure 3.1).

Unlocking Agile's Missed Potential, First Edition. Robert Webber.
© 2022 The Institute of Electrical and Electronics Engineers, Inc. Published 2022 by John Wiley & Sons, Inc.

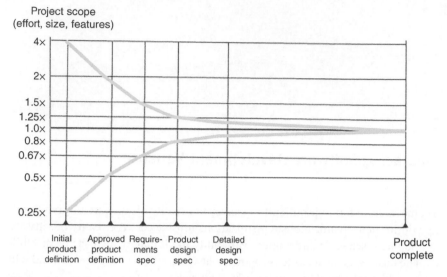

Figure 3.1 McConnell Cone of Uncertainty. Used with permission of Steve McConnell.

The vertical axis shows relative estimation error in software effort. Most projects fall within the error bounds of overestimation and underestimation by factors of 4x and 0.25x, respectively, where x is the actual effort when the project is completed. Estimates tend to grow rather than shrink because they're based on what is known at the time of the estimate. Further analysis usually identifies additional requirements. Therefore, the top half of the chart tends to be denser reflecting that most software projects go over schedule and budget.

A company could narrow the cone through improved estimation techniques and requirements best practices, but it didn't change the characteristic shape. Attempts to fix schedule, content, and resources with Waterfall planning typically ended up with missed schedules and/or dropped content. And, today, Waterfall planning with Agile expects that estimates for schedule, content, and resources can be done prior to requirements development.

Of course, the business rejects the idea of the cone. They don't get Cones of Uncertainty from sales or manufacturing, and we don't see it presented by hardware engineering. Some departments do make longer-term commitments that they usually achieve. I've heard some people in the software industry explain the lack of predictability relative to hardware engineering as "software being harder." Hardware engineering has many uncertainties that software doesn't have to deal with, from device availability to electromagnetic interference, so that's not the reason. Don't try to tell them that software is harder.

3.2   Software Development Estimation Variance Explained

Whether the business likes it or not, software has characteristics that limit the accuracy of effort and schedule estimates. It is because software development requires hierarchical decomposition into smaller components, eventually resulting in "modules" with defined functionality and interfaces. This is the point when the work can be understood by an individual developer and reasonably accurate estimates can be generated. The number of "modules" that can be done in parallel is only known after detailed design, so schedule estimates prior to detailed design have large uncertainty. The problem is that the "detailed design specification" point in the Cone of Uncertainty is well beyond the planning stage. Commitments have already been cast in stone. In Waterfall, software development commitments are expected at the requirements stage and even during the conception stage.

I've used a tax preparation analogy to explain the software estimation challenge for people without software development experience. Suppose you were asked to determine how many accountants could be added to prepare an individual's tax return to minimize schedule. The number of tax forms varies for an individual based on the types of income and deductions. The specific tax forms to be completed, and their inputs, are only determined during the tax preparation process. Therefore, the shortest tax preparation schedule could only be estimated with any reasonable degree of accuracy after a "detailed design" step has been completed to determine the number of forms, their inputs, and the approximate effort for each accountant, which would take a significant part of overall tax preparation schedule.

However, the business simply cannot accept the large opening at the planning stages of the cone. How likely is it that you would get project approval by saying the project will cost somewhere between $250K and $4M, and it will take anywhere from 10 to 16 months? And in today's Agile world, we would want to add that we're not sure which features will actually be delivered. The cone has been viewed by the business as an attempt by engineering to avoid commitment.

So, why is hardware engineering able to make commitments earlier in the development cycle? I've managed hardware development. Hardware typically serves as a foundation for software functionality. The way users interact with the system is mostly determined by the software and must cover an almost infinite combination of cases. This is what drives pages and pages of software requirements. In hardware engineering, the architecture, number of circuit boards, and interfaces can usually be estimated fairly accurately at the system design stage where a hardware block diagram is available. Hardware engineering then estimates with proxies like the number of inputs and outputs and estimated component count. Software estimation uncertainty is analogous to asking hardware engineering to estimate schedule and cost without knowing the number or types of circuit boards to be developed. Would they be predictable?

Estimation uncertainty was supposed to be addressed by Agile. It was supposed to reduce long-term commitments to be able to deliver in shorter cycles with increased predictability. The product owner sets the priorities for the work, and engineering provides them with progress in the form of a burndown chart. Content delivery can be changed based on actual team velocities. A product owner is dedicated to the team to provide implementation guidance throughout sprint development to make sure the team builds the right thing.

As established in Chapter 2, Waterfall planning continues to be imposed on Agile development. The business response was, "You can call how you develop anything you want, but you're still going to have to make delivery and cost commitments like everybody else." This leaves an impossible problem for the poor project manager still accountable for schedule, cost, and content.

What about just adding resources when estimates increase or a new functionality is added? This fallacy was exposed in the classic book *The Mythical Man-Month* [2] by Fred Brooks where he showed that adding staff to a late project makes it later. It's as true now as it was then. Software development requires specific knowledge about the domain, software base, and development practices that take months to acquire. This presents a drain on current staff. Organizations need to assume fixed development capacity and make trade-offs between schedule and/or content.

3.3 Making and Meeting Feature Commitments

Construx provided methods to meet Waterfall schedules using the same variable content concept adopted by Agile. The Cone of Uncertainty could be used to initially commit to a set of features and make additional commitments as estimation accuracy improved during the development cycle. We will show later how this method can be applied at the Investment level.

The Cone of Uncertainty provides guidance on estimation variability. It shows that estimates vary between 0.5x and 2x at product definition and 0.67–1.5x when requirements are complete. Detailed requirements are not available in Agile development when effort forecasts are required. I recommend an expected variance between 1.5x and 2x depending on the level of epic and user story decomposition.

Features are ranked by priority in the chart below. The top bar represents committed features. The bottom bar shows features that will not be included in the release. The bar in the middle marks features that are still targets for the release (see Figure 3.2).

Figure 3.2 Feature content forecast chart

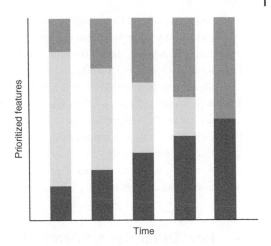

We need to account for the potential variability of remaining features using the minimum Cone of Uncertainty factor of 1.5x or more. At each update, the effort of the remaining features is multiplied by 1.5 to account for worst case. Features likely to be completed within the schedule are those that can be completed based on current capacity. These features are targets. Features with effort that falls outside of the capacity limit are not likely to make the release.

Consider five features expected to be delivered in a release, each with estimated effort of 200 hours shown in the first column in Table 3.1.

Given a capacity of 1200 hours that can be completed within the development interval, it is possible that all can be delivered if the estimates are accurate. Of course, we know that's not likely, so we multiply them by the Cone of Uncertainty factor of 1.5 to estimate worst-case effort. Features A and B have been completed by

Table 3.1 Feature content forecast example.

	Forecast	Worst-case	Actual	Forecast	Cumulative forecast
Feature A	200	300	175	175	175
Feature B	200	300	230	230	405
Feature C	200	300		300	705
Feature D	200	300		300	1005
Feature E	200	300		300	1305
Feature F	200	300		300	1605
Totals	1200	1800			

this reporting week and the actual hours can be entered in the table. The Forecast row includes the actuals from the features completed and the worst-case estimates of remaining features. Cumulative effort is shown in the last column.

Given a capacity limit of 1200 hours, Features C and D can remain as targets because they can be completed within the projected capacity. Features E and F are unlikely to be delivered. Of course, estimated capacity may also vary and be accounted for in the feature forecasts.

In reality, this method was not adopted by many organizations because of the perception that pressure was the only way to motivate engineering to achieve, or get close to, development targets. Contingency was viewed by project managers and executives as an opportunity for engineering to slack off.

3.4 How Other Departments Meet Commitments

The business expects forecasts from sales, operations, and manufacturing that are also based on risky assumptions, so why is engineering any different? Cries of "software is more complex" won't cut it. I've managed hardware development and have also been exposed to the challenges that manufacturing faces. For example, unforeseen component shortages or loss of a vendor may require a quick redesign or a substitute device approved by hardware engineering. Manufacturing is dependent on deliveries from hundreds of suppliers and must react quickly to changes in their production forecasts.

I'll share my experience on how other departments make and meet commitments. Manufacturing is managing an ongoing process where they build the same thing over and over, which is easier than estimating new development effort from a set of requirements for each project. As discussed above, software development estimation involves sequential decomposition where accurate estimates can only be derived later in the project, and we've already established that hardware development can usually do this decomposition earlier in the project. Nevertheless, manufacturing deserves a lot of credit for excellent processes to rapidly respond to change to avoid production losses.

Sales need to meet revenue forecasts for the company to achieve company financial commitments. They also deal with many variables, like new competition and late products. However, they are, by the nature of their roles, great negotiators. They preserve contingency when they make their forecasts. In fact, they want to set forecasts low so they can exploit sales accelerators that increase commissions with higher sales volume. They've learned to play the game.

So, why doesn't engineering play the game? First of all, they're just too darn analytical. If you ask an engineer for an estimate, they will do their best to provide you with an answer with the precision of two decimal points. It's a problem to solve, not a game to play. The second reason is that they are under intense pressure to commit to shorter schedules and lower development costs from project management, ending up with the "prove you can't deliver it sooner" schedule.

3.5 Agile Development Implications

There is no major release milestone for completion of detailed design with Agile development. The design takes place incrementally during each sprint. This means that Agile estimation uncertainty is, at best, at the product definition phase on the Cone of Uncertainty where estimation errors vary by a factor of two. This is certainly outside the bounds of business expectations at the time of project approval and financial forecasts. There are some good Agile estimation methods that may reduce this uncertainty, but it is not likely to be less than the cone variance factor of 1.5.

The demand for corporate financial predictability perpetuates Waterfall release planning despite its inaccuracies. Agile has not provided product and project managers with an alternative. The solution involves embracing software estimation unpredictability to improve business predictability. This seems like an oxymoron, but it can be achieved by balancing long-term commitments and development capacity contingency, and by reducing the fraction of development capacity allocated to committed features. We also need to recognize that the business financial reporting demands financial predictability, not predictability in terms of feature schedules. Product management creates feature schedules, so changing to a more predictable way to achieve financial targets is within their control.

3.6 **Summary**

- Software estimation variance must be accepted by organizations to successfully implement Agile.
- The Cone of Uncertainty shows that estimates and schedules set by Waterfall planning were usually not met.
- Software development estimates lack accuracy prior to the design stage because the number of elements to build is not known.
- Hardware is a platform for software functionality and the number of circuit boards and elements can usually be estimated without detailed functional requirements, providing more accurate development effort and schedule estimates earlier in the development cycle.

- The only way to achieve Waterfall schedules is to leave contingency for features that may not be delivered.
- A different approach for achieving financial predictability is within the control of product and project management.

References

1 McConnell, S. (2006). *Software Estimation: Demystifying the Black Art*. Microsoft Press.
2 Brooks, F.P. (1974). *The Mythical Man-Month and Other Essays on Software Engineering*. Addison Wesley Longman Publishing Co.

4

Cost of Delay

Donald Reinertsen, in his book, *The Principles of Product Development Flow,* introduced the concept of "Cost of Delay (CoD)" in software development. It's a simple yet elegant concept. CoD is the loss in income if a project is delayed one month. He also showed that prioritizing projects by CoD divided by cycle time, which he refers to as "Weighted Shortest Job First" (WSJF), results in the lowest "Net CoD," which is the cumulative cost of delay for a set of projects that must be prioritized because of development resource constraints.

For product managers, Net CoD is the same as opportunity cost. Opportunity cost is the profit or income lost by choosing one alternative over the other. Given two development projects P_1 and P_2, prioritization of P_1 defers income from P_2, which would be referred to as the opportunity cost for doing P_1 first. The role of product management in Agile is to define and prioritize R&D work for the backlog to minimize opportunity cost. This chapter illustrates how Reinertsen's CoD and WSJF principles can accomplish that.

Although CoD, or opportunity cost, has always existed in software development, it has been difficult to quantify. Features with unjustified financial value have traditionally been bundled into large periodic releases. However, the importance of adopting a CoD approach has substantially increased today because of the ability to develop and release value faster with Agile development. Increasing the number of releases within a planning period increases the permutations of project development order. For example, breaking an annual release into four increments results in 24 unique development order permutations. Which one maximizes R&D Return on Investment (ROI)? That will be the case where the Net CoD is lowest.

Unlocking Agile's Missed Potential, First Edition. Robert Webber.
© 2022 The Institute of Electrical and Electronics Engineers, Inc. Published 2022 by John Wiley & Sons, Inc.

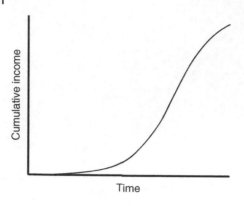

Figure 4.1 S-curve income profile.

Software organizations have found it difficult to implement WSJF prioritization because Reinertsen's formula is based on projects with constant CoD. Total income generated by a software release usually follows an adoption ramp defined by the classic "S-curve" (Figure 4.1). Initial market penetration is low, followed by rapid adoption and then saturation. This is true for new products and software upgrades. It is even true for subscription pricing models where the curve is determined by deployment rates.

This chapter introduces three methods for estimating Net CoD for nonlinear income profiles, each with increasing complexity and varying accuracy. The third method is the most accurate, but it requires significant computing power to calculate the permutations of backlog Investment order. It is included for completeness, but any of the first two methods should be adequate. I stress not getting hung up about WSJF accuracy. The lack of precision in development effort and financial estimates used in the calculation exceeds the variations based on the model chosen. The main goal of WSJF is to provide a clear financial trade-off between development effort and income forecasts. This is a discussion that normally doesn't take place in software development.

The last section compares WSJF prioritization with traditional ROI prioritization.

4.1 Weighted Shortest Job First (WSJF)

WSJF was historically used in computing to prioritize batch jobs. Batch job priorities were weighted in terms of importance and estimated execution time. WSJF was calculated by dividing the weighted importance by estimated execution time.

WSJF for software projects can be calculated using Reinertsen's formula:

$$\text{WSJF} = \frac{\text{CoD}}{\text{Cycle time}}$$

where cycle time is the duration of the project. Projects that have a higher CoD generate higher income per unit time, which means that delays are more expensive. We want to prioritize projects with the highest CoD and the shortest development time, generating the maximum income from constrained R&D resources.

4.1.1 Cost of Delay Basics

Let's start with Reinertsen's description of CoD from *The Principles of Product Development Flow* [1]. The chart assumes three software projects with different CoDs and cycle times. The example assumes that each project generates uniform income per month. Income is used throughout this book in relation to CoD instead of profit. Either could be used, but profit calculations add another layer of complexity beyond what is necessary for software project prioritization.

Reinertsen uses the example of three projects with different CoD and cycle times (Table 4.1).

Reinertsen depicts the projects in Figure 4.2 to show accumulated Net CoD for project order A, B, and C.

Table 4.1 Reinertsen project CoD example.

Project	Cycle time	CoD	CoD/cycle time
A	1	10	10
B	3	3	1
C	10	1	0.1

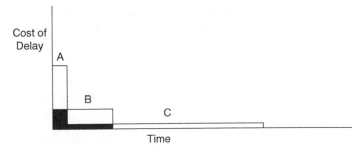

Figure 4.2 Reinertsen project Cost of Delay (CoD) example order A, B, C. Used with permission of Donald Reinertsen.

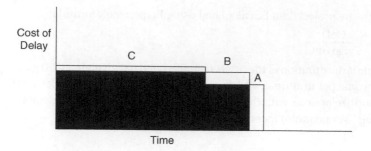

Figure 4.3 Reinertsen project CoD example order C, B, A. Used with permission of Donald Reinertsen.

Table 4.2 Project WSJF productivity example.

Project	Time (mo)	CoD ($K/mo)	WSJF
P_1	3	30	10
P_2	9	45	5

Project A generates cumulative income over a period determined by its CoD multiplied by time. In the first example, Project A is developed first, delaying the start of development of Projects B and C by the development duration of Project A. The Net CoD for developing Project A first is the sum of the Costs of Delay of Projects B and C multiplied by the development duration of Project A, represented by the first dark rectangle on the left of the chart. Project C is delayed while Project B is developed, creating the Net CoD depicted by the second dark rectangle. There are no projects delayed while Project C is being developed.

Figure 4.3 shows the reverse project order. It is the worst case because higher income per month is deferred for longer periods of time.

Reinertsen asserts that Net CoD is minimized by prioritization by WSJF for the case of linear income ramps (constant CoD). Net CoD is incurred in software development any time there is a defined set of projects that cannot start at the same time. Of course, this is the typical case. There is always more work than can be developed in parallel by constrained R&D resources. CoD can also be viewed from the perspective of income generation. Consider an example of two projects of different durations and Costs of Delay as shown in Table 4.2.

4.1.2 Example

The WSJF calculation shows that P_1 should take priority. Figure 4.4 shows the cumulative net income when we develop in the reverse WSJF order with P_2 first.

Figure 4.4 Reverse Weighted Shortest Job First (WSJF) prioritization income generation.

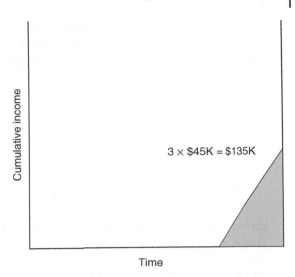

P_1 income of $45K per month starts after completion of P_2 and generates $135K over the last three months of the year. P_2 adds $30K per month starting at the end of the year for a running total of $75K per month beyond one year.

The cumulative income profile for WSJF prioritization is shown below (Figure 4.5). In this case, the income of $30K per month from P_1 starts after three months and contributes $270K for the year. The income beyond one year is the same as in the first example.

Figure 4.5 WSJF prioritization income generation.

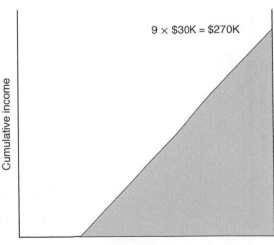

Total productivity is Value Out/Value In. It's simply the income or profit generated by a software release divided by the cost to develop the software. Productivity can be calculated for both cases. R is total productivity, I is the income for the year, and C is the development cost for both projects.

$$R_1 = \frac{I_1}{C}$$

$$R_2 = \frac{I_2}{C}$$

Development cost cancels out when we take the ratio of productivity.

$$\frac{R_2}{R_1} = \frac{I_2}{I_1}$$

For this example, total productivity improves by a factor of $270/135 = 200\%$.

This is a simplistic view that ignores software capitalization, taxes, and NPV. It also assumes that income is the same as profit. The engineering organization would need to double its productivity to attain the same result with the reverse WSJF prioritization.

4.1.3 WSJF Proof

We can prove that WSJF prioritization optimizes income for the case of linear income ramps assumed in Reinertsen's formula. Consider two projects P_1 and P_2, each with CoD and duration T. Figure 4.6 shows the cumulative income for the case where P_2 is done first. The total period is the sum of the durations for both projects.

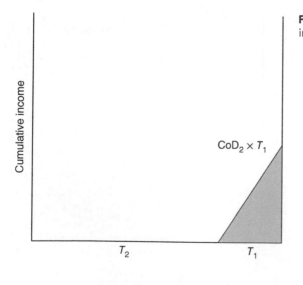

Figure 4.6 Cumulative income with P_2 first.

Figure 4.7 Cumulative income with P_1 first.

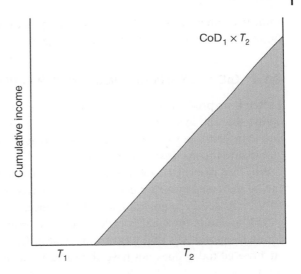

Figure 4.7 shows the case where P_1 is completed first.

P_1 should be prioritized when greater income is generated within the same period. The income generated with P_2 developed first is the CoD of P_2 multiplied by the cycle time of P_1. Income generated when P_1 is developed first is the CoD of P_1 multiplied by the cycle time of P_2. P_1 should be prioritized when

$$CoD_1\, T_2 > CoD_2\, T_1$$

By cross multiplying we get Reinertsen's WSFJ formula.

$$\frac{CoD_1}{T_1} > \frac{CoD_2}{T_2}$$

It's interesting to look at the units of the WSJF calculation. The units are in currency per unit time squared. We can consider currency per unit time to be analogous to velocity of an object. Velocity is in terms of distance per unit time. Acceleration units are distance per unit time squared. For example, acceleration due to gravity is 9.8 m/s², which means that your falling speed, neglecting friction, increases by 9.8 m/s every second. WSFJ represents income acceleration. A WSJF of \$100K/month² means that income is deferred by \$100K per month for every month of delay. Projects with higher WSJF accelerate income.

Before moving on to WSJF calculation methods, I want to stress something.

> The most valuable aspect of WSJF in Agile development is that it establishes incentives for the Minimum Marketable Feature Set (MMFS)

It's not so much about having a precise calculation of CoD and WSJF. Dividing income generation by cycle time prioritizes projects that can generate the greatest value that can be developed in the shortest cycle time, which encourages the least functionality required to meet financial targets.

4.1.4 CoD and Net Present Value (NPV) Prioritization Methods

I often hear product managers say that CoD is just an NPV problem. They recognize that the income in our example above is only different for the first year, and then $900K per year is generated after that at a rate of $75K per month. The cumulative income is shown in Table 4.3.

Why then prioritize by WSJF? It just looks like an issue of income timing which can be addressed by NPV calculations. Before answering the question, I'll explain NPV for those of you not familiar with the term.

NPV accounts for what is called the "time value of money." NPV is used to compare alternatives that return money at different times in the future. A dollar invested today does not have the same value as a dollar earned three years from now.

For example, assume a dollar is invested at an annual return of 10% paid out at the end of each year. It would be worth $1.00 \times (1 + 0.10) = \$1.10$ after the first year. After the second year, it would be worth $1.10 \times (1 + 0.10)$, which is $1.00 \times (1 + 0.10)^2$. After three years the value is $1.00 \times (1 + 0.10) \times (1 + 0.10) \times (1 + 0.10) = \$1.33$ which is $1.00 \times (1 + 0.10)^3$. So, if you could get a return of 10% on your money, $1.00 you expect to receive in three years is only worth $1.00/(1 + 0.1)^3$ today, which is an NPV of $0.75.

The general NPV formula is

$$NPV = \frac{R}{(1 + i)^t}$$

where R is the net cash flow at time t and i is the "discount rate" for the period t.

The discount rate is the same as an interest rate in the example above. However, companies calculate the discount rate based on how they value money. Their ability to raise cash is limited by financial considerations like current debt and investor risk. Your CFO determines the discount rate for your organization. The discount rate is unique to your company and is typically higher than prevailing interest rates. Otherwise, investors may as well secure their money in banks.

Table 4.3 CoD cumulative non-discounted income example ($K).

	Year 1	Year 2	Year 3	Year 4	Year 5
P_2 First	$135	$1035	$1935	$2835	$3735
P_1 First	$270	$1170	$2070	$2970	$3870
Increase	100%	13%	7%	5%	4%

The NPV formula is used to calculate your mortgage rate payments. It determines the monthly payments required to reduce the NPV of your mortgage to zero by the end of the mortgage, based on the mortgage interest rates. Companies don't have access to the low interest rates of safe mortgages backed by property. They get their funding from a wide variety of capital sources like business loans, corporate bonds, and stock sales. Their NPV discount rate is based on the Weighted Average Cost of Capital (WACC) which can be different for each company.

A 2019 KPMG study [2] states that the average WACC for all industries was 6.9%. Companies calculate WACC based on their access to capital and use it as the discount value in NPV calculations. The technology sector average WACC was 8.1%, which is applied to Table 4.4 to calculate NPV for our example cashflow.

The percentages increase slightly in each year. However, it still seems like it's not worth the effort to calculate WSJF and we can just use NPV to prioritize projects as we've always done. It turns out that the importance of WSJF prioritization increases substantially for Agile development.

NPV calculations assume you can forecast income over a long period of time. We know this is a dangerous assumption in today's dynamic world of software development. Agile development enables competitors to rapidly take advantage of new opportunities. Platform as a Service (PaaS) offerings like Microsoft Azure and Amazon Web Services enable startups to quickly build enterprise applications with virtually unlimited scalability that can replace enterprise software. Companies want to minimize exposure with software releases with short payback periods, usually less than three years.

NPV prioritization does not significantly differentiate between projects with different cycle times over a multiyear planning period. However, consider using WSJF prioritization for new projects every year. In this case, the income from new projects in each year is doubled.

In summary, traditional NPV calculations do not sufficiently factor in the cycle times of Agile projects approaching weeks or months. WSJF prioritization should be used. However, we will consider NPV in one or our WSJF calculation methods discussed in Section 4.3.2.

Table 4.4 CoD discounted cumulative income example ($K).

	Year 1	Year 2	Year 3	Year 4	Year 5
P_2 First	$135	$895	$1608	$2267	$2876
P_1 First	$270	$1020	$1732	$2391	$3001
Increase	100%	14%	8%	6%	4%

4.2 Nonlinear Income Profiles

The WSJF formula doesn't work in the case where the rate of income generation is a nonlinear function of time, which is true in most cases for software releases. It's not possible to cross multiply Reinertsen's formula to calculate a value for WSJF independent of the cycle times of other projects. We need a practical way to calculate WSJF for non-linear income profiles, like the S-curve in Figure 4.1.

4.3 CoD for Nonlinear Cumulative Income Profiles

Scaled Agile Framework (SAFe) claims to use WSJF, but they have reverted to a subjective weighting system based on "user-business value," "time criticality," and "risk reduction-opportunity enablement value." There is no mathematical correlation with Reinertsen's WSJF calculation. And the weights are subjective, open to opinion, and political influence.

There are three methods described in this section to prioritize Investments with nonlinear income profiles:

1. Payback Period CoD Method
2. Third-year Income Slope CoD Method
3. CoD Computation Method

4.3.1 Payback Period CoD Method

There is a relationship between CoD and payback period. A project with a CoD of x dollars per month reaches its payback point when CoD multiplied by time equals the development Investment. Therefore, CoD for software development can be approximated by the project labor cost divided by the payback period. For example, a project that costs $360K with a three-year payback would need to return an average of $360K/36 months = $10K per month. CoD can be estimated as $10K per month. This simple calculation provides a linear approximation for non-linear income profiles.

4.3.2 Third-Year Income Slope CoD Method

This is the simplest and recommended approach. It assumes a three-year planning period to support prioritization of projects that can start within the next year. CoD is the rate at which income is shifted beyond three years.

Cycle time and income projections beyond three years are questionable. And with Agile development, it's likely that any projects planned within three years will change. In fact, the value of WSJF prioritization is not planning the optimal development order for a set of Agile projects over the next five years. It is to determine which project to start next. We want to look at the rate at which income will be shifted out of the three-year planning period depending upon which projects we start next. It is a dynamic calculation based on today's view.

Consider the S-curve case shown in Figure 4.8.

The rate at which income is deferred beyond three years can be approximated by the average slope of the curve between Years 2 and 3. This linear approximation applies for delays of up to one year. Figure 4.9 shows that a six-month delay places the linear approximation at the edge of the three-year boundary.

The linear approximation results in a simple way to calculate monthly CoD. It is simply the income generated in the third year divided by 12.

Another reason for using a three-year planning period is that NPV impacts are relatively small compared with the estimation error of income projections and can be ignored. Figure 4.10 shows the effect of excluding NPV from multi-year income projections.

The lines represent discount values ranging from 6% to 10% per year. For example, the NPV of $1000 received in Year 2 at a rate of 10% is $1000/(1 + 0.10) = $909. Neglecting the cost of money creates an error of (1000 − 909)/1000 = 9%. At an average discount of 8% typical of the high-technology sector within the three-year period, the error is less than 15%, well within the accuracy of income projections three years out.

The third-year cumulative income slope method provides sufficient accuracy for project delays of up to one year. The CoD approximation is effective for determining the next software increment to be released in Agile development.

If you need to consider income beyond three years, you can use the NPV of the income beyond three years for all projects. In this case, the CoD is the NPV divided

Figure 4.8 Third-year income CoD calculation.

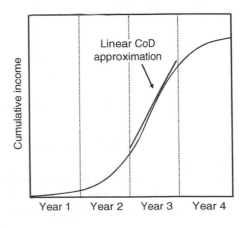

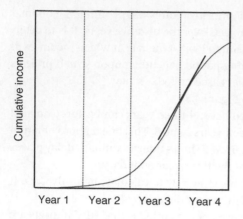

Figure 4.9 Third-year income slope with delay of 2.5 years.

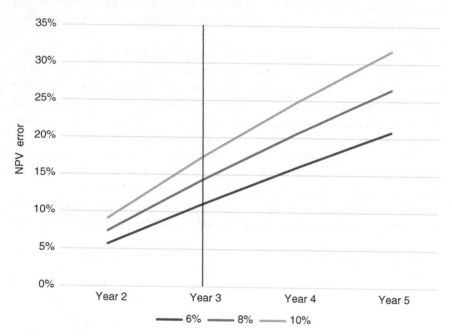

Figure 4.10 Net Present Value (NPV) error based on discount period.

by 12 months. However, a risk factor should be incorporated before calculating NPV that far out.

Consider the following project annual income profile (Table 4.5):

Assume a discount rate of 8%. Years 4 and 5 are discounted for the number of years beyond Year 3 after applying the risk factors.

Table 4.5 Net Present Value (NPV) beyond three years example.

	Year 1	Year 2	Year 3	Year 4	Year 5
Income ($K)	20	60	90	120	200
Risk Discount				20%	50%
Risk-Adjusted Income ($K)	20	60	90	96	100

$$NPV_4 = \frac{96}{(1 + 0.08)} = 89$$

$$NPV_5 = \frac{100}{(1 + 0.08)^2} = 86$$

$$Year\ 3 = 9 + 89 + 86 = 184$$

$$Year\ 3\ CoD = \frac{184}{12} = \$15K\ per\ month$$

NPV should be calculated for the five-year period for all projects to be prioritized. The third-year slope method can result in a CoD of zero, as shown in Figure 4.11.

For example, a modular deployment may be deployed within a period of two years. What is the priority with a CoD and WSJF of zero?

This answer is nonintuitive. If your goal is to optimize income within a three-year planning period, projects that don't generate income in the third year can be prioritized lower, because the income will still be captured within the planning period.

4.3.3 CoD Computation Method

Net CoD can be calculated for any set of projects where the income profile can be modeled as a function of time. Consider two projects P_1, P_2 with the nonlinear

Figure 4.11 S-curve for income returned within two years.

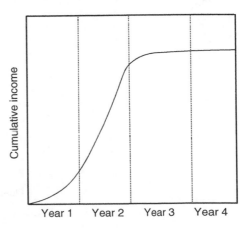

income ramps developed in project order P_1, P_2 with cycle times T_1 and T_2. The Net CoD for delaying P_2 by the cycle time T_1 is the income that would have been generated by P_2 up until the time when P_1 is complete. Figure 4.12 shows the cumulative income for each project, with P2 delayed by three quarters by the development of P1. Each income profile is modeled with a function of the form:

$$f(t) = at^b$$

Now consider three projects. The Net CoD for order P_1, P_2, and P_3 is:

$$N_{123} = f_2(T_1) + f_3(T_1 + T_2)$$

The income generated by f_3 starts after both P_1 and P_2 are complete.

If the order is reversed, the Net CoD is:

$$N_{321} = f_2(T_3) + f_1(T_2 + T_3)$$

The Net CoD for a set of n projects must be calculated $n!$ times because there are $n!$ permutations of project order for n projects. Appendix A provides an example of three projects where the income curves are in the form:

$$f(t) = at^b$$

Any function of time will work, including the logistics curve function (S-curve) described by

$$f(t) = \frac{L}{1 + e^{-k(t-T_0)}}$$

L = maximum value

k = slope of the curve at the inflection point, also called the logistics growth rate

T_0 = the time value at the inflection point

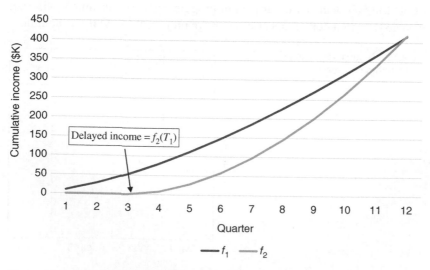

Figure 4.12 Cumulative income based on project order.

We can prove Reinertsen's linear WSJF formula for the case of linear income ramps when income is a constant multiplied by time:

$$f(t) = Ct$$

where C is the CoD. P_1 should be prioritized when the income delayed for order P_1, P_2 is less than the delayed income of order P_2, P_1:

$$C_1 T_2 > C_2 T_1$$

which is the same as the WSJF formula:

$$\frac{C_1}{T_1} > \frac{C_2}{T_2}$$

4.4 WSJF and Traditional Finance

WSJF can be related to traditional finance terms used in project planning. This section looks at ROI, IRR, and payback period.

4.4.1 ROI

ROI is income returned over a planning period minus the investment divided by the investment.

$$\text{ROI} = \frac{\text{Income} - \text{Cost}}{\text{Cost}}$$

Table 4.6 shows the annual income generated over a five-year planning period for the two different development orders of the projects P1 and P2 in Table 4.2. Both projects complete in the first year so R&D investment for Year 1 is the same in both cases. Income in Years 2 and 3 is based on $75K per month after the first year for both cases.

Table 4.6 Three-year income projections for WSJF example.

Project order	Year 1	Year 2	Year 3
P1 First	$270K	$900K	$900K
P2 First	$135K	$900K	$900K

Many companies impose a minimum payback period by which they must recover project investment. Income in later years is more difficult to predict, especially in the dynamic world of software development. Therefore, companies want to reduce risk by recovering their R&D costs within a shorter period. The exact value is established by your CFO. A payback of one year will be assumed in this example. Development cost is equal to the sum of the first-year income which is $405K.

Table 4.7 shows ROI after each year:

Table 4.7   Return on Investment (ROI) impact of WSJF prioritization.

Project order	After Year 1	After Year 2	After Year 3
P1 First	−33%	189%	411%
P2 First	−67%	156%	378%

The table demonstrates that WSJF prioritization provides return on an investment sooner but approaches the same value with increasing planning periods. However, it significantly decreases ROI risk because returns are more predictable in earlier years.

4.4.2   Investment Rate of Return (IRR)

IRR is another financial calculation impacted by WSJF prioritization. IRR is a common method for comparing the financial value of projects. IRR is defined as a "discount rate" that makes NPV zero in a discounted cash flow analysis. The interest on your mortgage is the IRR. For example, the IRR of a 30-year mortgage is the interest rate to pay off the mortgage after 30 years of monthly payments. If you were a mortgage lender, you would want to receive the highest IRR possible.

Excel calculates IRR based on a series of cashflows. Table 4.8 shows the IRR for both orders of P_1 and P_2.

Table 4.8   IRR impact of WSJF prioritization.

Project order	After Year 2	After Year 3
P1 First	567%	655%
P2 First	233%	314%

We see a similar pattern where near-term IRR is improved but converges over time.

4.4.3   WSJF Versus ROI Prioritization

Companies using traditional ROI project prioritization are losing millions of dollars in opportunity cost with Agile development. Consider five Investments with development costs and Costs of Delay as shown in Table 4.9. As in traditional planning, ROI is calculated separately for each Investment to determine priorities. Over the 12-quarter planning period, Investments generate income at the rate determined by CoD. For example, Investment 1 returns income of $25K per quarter × 12 quarters = $300K with a development cost of $100K so ROI is ($300 − $100K)/$100K = 200%.

Table 4.9 ROI prioritization example.

Investment	Development cost ($K)	Income ($K/quarter)	ROI (%)
Investment 1	100	25	200
Investment 2	75	35	460
Investment 3	50	30	620
Investment 4	130	40	269
Investment 5	90	45	500

Table 4.10 WSJF prioritization example.

Investment	Cycle time (quarters)	CoD ($K/quarter)	WSJF
Investment 1	1	25	25
Investment 2	2	35	18
Investment 3	2	30	15
Investment 4	3	40	13
Investment 5	4	45	11

Investment ROI priority order is 3, 5, 2, 4, 1.

We now consider cycle time and apply the quarterly income as CoD to calculate WSJF (Table 4.10).

WSJF prioritization shows the optimal Investment order is 1, 2, 3, 4, 5.

Figure 4.13 plots cumulative income by quarter for the ROI and WSJF priority order cases and adds a line for the worst-case reverse WSJF order:

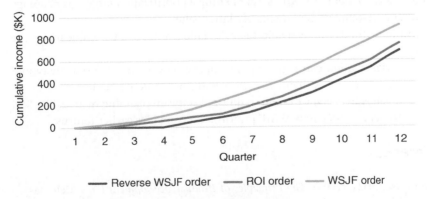

Figure 4.13 Cumulative income by prioritization method.

As expected, WSJF prioritization produces the greatest income of $950K within the planning period. ROI prioritization generates $750K. The worst case of reverse WSJF order results in $685K.

Three-year ROI can be calculated for each case (Table 4.11).

Table 4.11 ROI comparison based on prioritization method.

Prioritization method	Three-Year ROI
WSJF	106%
ROI	69%
Reverse WSJF	54%

This is only one example. But it demonstrates that ROI prioritization is likely to result in an ROI somewhere between what could be attained with WSJF prioritization and the worst case of reverse WSJF prioritization. ROI prioritization is not likely to result in the optimal ROI, especially with the larger number of permutations of Agile projects.

4.5 Summary

- CoD is the profit or income lost by delaying a software project by a unit of time.
- Software projects prioritized by WSJF optimize income over a planning period by minimizing Net CoD.
- WSJF prioritization has become more important with shorter release cycles enabled by Agile development.
- Reinertsen's WSJF prioritization formula is based on linear income ramps. Software release income ramps are more likely to be nonlinear.
- The greatest benefit of WSJF is establishing a prioritization target to encourage smaller development increments of higher value.
- Multiple methods are available for calculation of CoD for nonlinear income profiles.
- WSJF prioritization can significantly improve development productivity and ROI using currently available resources and development practices.
- Relationships between CoD and traditional software planning metrics like ROI and IRR demonstrate how WSJF prioritization provides earlier returns.

References

1 Reinertsen, D.G. (2009). *The Principles of Product Development Flow*. Celeritas Publishing.
2 KPMG, *Cost of Capital Study*, 2019. https://home.kpmg/de/en/home/insights/2020/10/cost-of-capital-study-2020.html.

5

Investment Fundamentals

This chapter expands on the Investment definition introduced earlier and provides a practical method for forecasting income projections to support Cost of Delay (CoD) and Weighted Shortest Job First (WSJF) calculations. Investments are the smallest increment of software functionality that has the potential to increase income and/or reduce operational expenses. This allows CoD to be associated at the Investment level.

We start by differentiating Investments from initiatives and programs commonly used in portfolio management. Portfolio management is the process used to distribute funds across numerous potential projects to maximize the benefits for the company. It is like your stock portfolio where you allocate money to investments that maximize your Return on Investment (ROI) and manage risk.

An Investment relationship hierarchy, or "schema," is introduced in this chapter that plans value independent of release planning. Investments bundled into releases increase Net CoD because each Investment could have generated income earlier if it had been released independently. The schema also introduces profit and loss (P&L) centers that can be used to allocate portfolio ROI responsibilities.

It may be difficult to estimate income to calculate CoD for some Investments. For example, penetration of a new market may be difficult to estimate prior to product introduction. Or income may be expected beyond a planning period used to calculate WSJF. There is a section on how to allocate your R&D portfolio to account for what are called "strategic Investments" with payback periods greater than three years.

In many cases, sales or operations may be reluctant to commit to a revenue or income profile. In the past, they have been able to push for features without financial justification. This chapter provides a method to determine income profiles necessary to satisfy a target payback period based on development cost and projected growth rates. This opens a collaborative discussion among sales

Unlocking Agile's Missed Potential, First Edition. Robert Webber.
© 2022 The Institute of Electrical and Electronics Engineers, Inc. Published 2022 by John Wiley & Sons, Inc.

or operations and product management to determine the optimal balance of expected income and payback period.

Investment backlogs are introduced, including how to prioritize strategic Investments. Investment Work in Process (WIP) is addressed. It includes the effort for Investments that have been started and not completed, and introduces a one-year backlog planning WIP limit.

Lastly, this chapter discusses a topic near and dear to engineering leaders – technical debt. It shows how technical debt reduction can be justified as an Investment.

5.1 Investments, Initiatives, and Programs

Initiatives are defined by product management to implement a strategy to achieve a business goal. The initiative defines the responsibilities of departments to make the initiative successful. For example, a company wants to penetrate a new market by funding an initiative. The initiative may entail new development from R&D, support from field services to deploy the software, and new marketing collateral to sell the product. It may also involve new hardware. The training department might develop training material for sales and customers. The initiative defines the responsibilities of all departments involved and estimates total implementation costs.

Investments, as defined in this book, are limited to the R&D contribution to an initiative or business goal. The Investment model is intended to optimize the order of development of software development work so external costs are not included. Investments may define the R&D work necessary to accomplish an initiative.

For completeness, we should understand the difference between "initiatives" and "programs." Programs specify the deliverables of departments and their inter-dependencies to achieve the initiative or business goal within schedule and cost constraints defined in the business plan. Programs are usually owned by a different organization, often called a "program management office," or PMO.

5.1.1 Investment Hierarchy

Investments facilitate a shift in traditional product management thinking. They change focus from functionality to value. Investment value depends on the willingness of a customer to pay for an Investment. Value is no longer a nebulous concept. It is determined by having a CoD.

With Waterfall release planning, R&D work usually starts at the feature-level. An endless stream of features is bundled into large releases. This is also true in the many Agile implementations where Waterfall planning persists. Financial value is usually determined at the release level, making it impractical to calculate CoD to prioritize smaller elements of work within a release. The conventional planning hierarchy is represented in Figure 5.1.

Planning typically starts with the assumption of a major release that needs to be filled up with features.

The number 1 and the infinity symbol (∞) indicate that multiple child releases can be funded from the R&D portfolio, each with multiple features. This is referred to as a "one-to-many" relationship.

Figure 5.2 shows how Investments establish a planning element between portfolio and feature levels.

Release bundling should be viewed as a problem to solve rather than the first step in Agile planning. Releases increase Net CoD because they delay deployment of Investments that could generate income earlier. Recall that every Investment has associated income. Bundling Investments extends payback periods and

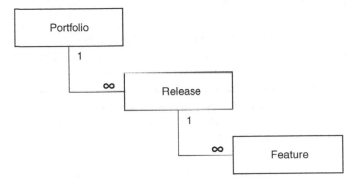

Figure 5.1   Release feature-level planning hierarchy.

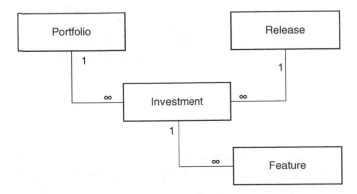

Figure 5.2   Investment planning hierarchy.

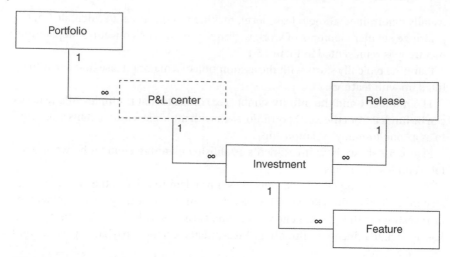

Figure 5.3 Investment planning P&L centers.

reduces near-term R&D ROI. Chapter 8 quantifies the additional Net CoD posed by releases and provides guidance on when Investments should be bundled within a release.

Figure 5.3 introduces P&L centers that can provide another level of financial control and accountability between the portfolio and Investment levels. For example, there may be separate P&L centers for different regions, like North America or Asia. There may be separate P&L centers for market segments, like the North American large, medium, and small markets. This provides flexibility for multiple product managers to share functionality in a common release while separating financial responsibilities and product planning.

P&L centers also provide finer control of resource allocation. Resources may be shifted at any time based on P&L performance. Financial projections of P&L centers can be created based on increased resource allocation for comparison. For example, what would three-year financial projections look like if each P&L could increase staffing by 10%? This would allow money and resources to be shifted from lower- to higher-performing P&L centers.

Figure 5.4 shows how Investments can be driven by strategies and initiatives. The connections with the infinity symbol at both ends indicate that any number of Investments can be associated with any number of strategies in a so-called "many-to-many relationship."

Investments can be derived from strategies or initiatives. The relationships also ensure that strategies and initiatives are adequately supported by R&D investment.

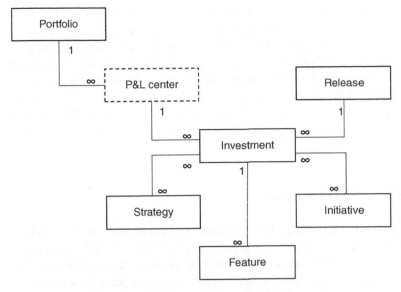

Figure 5.4 Investments related to strategies and initiatives.

5.2 AccuWiz Investment Examples

Below are examples of Investments that AccuWiz came up with after applying the practices described in this book. Each Investment is associated with a clear business objective and has the potential to increase income.

Investment	Objective
Quick Close Capability	Increase quarterly customer financial predictability
Workflow Enhancements	Reduce customer accounting staff costs
European Version	Expand AccuWiz market
User Interface (UI) Enhancements	Reduce AccuWiz customer churn rates
Data Analytics Connectors	Increase customer financial predictability by supporting personalized dashboards
Enterprise Integration	Reduce customer accounting costs and increase accuracy by reducing redundant data entry
Customer Support Enhancements	Reduce AccuWiz customer churn rates and increase customer references
Mobile Application	Retain AccuWiz market share

How was AccuWiz product development able to arrive at software functionality that creates value that customers pay for instead of taking feature orders from sales? How did AccuWiz change their organizational culture from conflict to teamwork and collaboration among the three department heads to agree on priorities? The principles and practices necessary to do this in your organization are the subject of this book. We'll return to AccuWiz in a later chapter to see how it happened. I'll give you a glimpse. Charles, the chief operating officer (COO), doesn't make it. His controlling style is not necessary anymore to achieve financial predictability.

5.3 Portfolio Allocation

It may not be possible to assign financial value to every Investment. For example, changing the product UI to improve branding. We can account for this by separating portfolios into tactical and strategic pools. We define a strategic Investment as one with an uncertain payback, or a payback period greater than three years.

Consider a case where your marketing department wants to change the UI to strengthen branding. Marketing feels strongly that this will result in increased income, but they just can't say by how much. These requests are "bets" rather than Investments. Just as with your personal Investment portfolio, you limit "bets" on high-risk Investments to a fraction of your portfolio. You want to invest most of your portfolio in safe Investments that can provide more predictable returns.

The recommendation is that your company's R&D portfolio be separated into "strategic" and "tactical" Investments. Strategic funding goes to the "bets" where income can't be forecast or payback is beyond three years. Tactical Investments pay back within a three-year planning period. The tactical fund generates the predictable income the business needs to meet financial commitments.

Figure 5.5 shows a recommended R&D portfolio allocation.

It's very difficult to forecast financial returns for Investments in innovation. If you could, the funding would come out of the tactical Investment allocations. Innovation funding is like the small portion of your stock portfolio you might allocate for high-risk, early-stage startup companies. Funding for innovation should not compete with Investment portfolio allocations because it is not possible to calculate a value for WSJF.

Software maintenance has a specific definition in this model. It is limited to fixes and technology changes necessary to maintain the viability of the product. For example, updates for browser compatibility would qualify as maintenance. Maintenance does not include changes to provide additional value to a customer. These would be part of the Investment allocation.

Figure 5.5 Investment portfolio allocation.

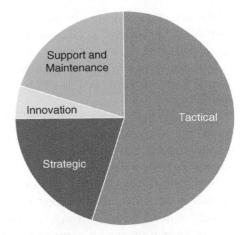

I assert that strategic Investments can be justified financially in more cases than we believe. In the branding case, the question would be, "How many more customers would we add or retain with the UI rebranding?" What tests could marketing set up to show that customers exposed to the new UI are more likely to purchase or retain the product? How much money would we lose if we don't do the rebranding or cut the funding in half? Investments bring up hard questions to justify allocation of precious development resources.

5.4 Investment Forecasts

5.4.1 Development Effort and Cost

The term "forecast" will be used in place of "estimate" to stress that effort estimates should be expected to vary in Agile development. Initial forecasts are done without detailed requirements and may change based on newer information and sprint feedback. Software effort forecasts should be like sales forecasts, where variability is managed through feedback and decision-making at a weekly sales meeting focused on sales targets. Sales expects that specific sales predictions will change, so they carefully manage their pipeline to achieve revenue commitments. The Investment approach embraces estimation variability to increase predictability.

Forecasting Investment effort and schedule should not involve a lot of planning effort. The purpose of these forecasts is to determine backlog priority, not to fix schedules. A later chapter will discuss how Investments can be timeboxed by adjusting feature content and functionality based on the rapid feedback provided by Agile development.

Additional planning and estimation effort should not be wasted on Investments with very low WSJF scores. We want to do an initial screening based on

WSJF as soon as possible with as little effort as possible. There are several good "top-down" estimation techniques, like estimation by analogy and estimation by statistical methods. Top-down estimation does not require software design and decomposition to provide an estimate. These and other estimation methods can be found in Steve McConnell's book, *Software Estimation: Demystifying the Black Art* [1].

A common Agile approach is decomposition into epics and user stories to estimate story points, which is a form of "estimation by analogy." Engineering defines a scale to enable relative effort comparisons. The scale is anchored by assigning a story point value to one user story, for example, 100 points. A user story estimated to be twice the effort would be 200 story points. Story points allow the team to target stories that can be accomplished within a sprint based on the total story points completed in prior sprints, which is the team's velocity.

Even though engineering may estimate effort in terms of story points, they must be related to hours at some point. Project approvals require estimations of development cost before development starts. Companies are not willing to fund the development without prediction of what will be delivered when, and the investment required.

Engineering is often reluctant to provide a conversion from story points to hours because they end up being committed to schedules and content they can't meet. I often hear complaints from product managers about outrageous development estimates. This is usually a sign that engineering has been forced into commitments they can't make. Initial Investment estimates are more likely to be reasonable because they are not used to fixed schedules. They are only used to forecast development costs for initial screening. Section 5.4.2 will show how development cost forecasts are used to determine income that must be generated by an Investment to justify development.

Once an Investment passes initial screening, traditional "bottom-up" estimation techniques may be applied, or epics may be broken down to the user-story level. WSJF can be refined to ensure the Investment should proceed to the backlog. Cycle time can be refined to set Investment timeboxes. A timebox assumes a fixed schedule but allows delivery content to change to account for increased estimates and new requirements.

Consider one more factor that provides flexibility on Investment content. Your CEO and CFO don't really care about which features are delivered. They want financial commitments to be met. Sales wants products and upgrades customers will pay for. The Investment model allows commitments to be made above the feature-level, giving product management and engineering more control over feature content.

5.4.2   Investment Income Forecasts

Investment income forecasts are required to calculate CoD. This can be a challenge. Asking your sales organization for a revenue commitment upfront or asking operations to commit to expense reductions is not likely to result in the answer you want – "We just know that the number is big!" This section provides a way to establish mutually agreed Investment income forecasts to support a CoD calculation.

A relationship can be drawn between CoD and payback period. An Investment or project is expected to generate a specific return within the payback period to recover development costs. For example, an Investment of $180K with a payback period of three years would need to generate an average of $60K per year, which is an average of $5K per month. This is also the cost of a one-month delay if we assume a linear income profile. However, we've already established that income profiles are not linear and often follow a growth curve. We can account for non-linear income profiles with a bit of algebra.

Most organizations have payback targets for software development. The period is typically short because of the high risks in the dynamic software market. Periods of one to three years are typical. If you don't have a target payback period provided by your CFO, as a product manager you should establish a reasonable target that balances the payback period with the risks of your industry.

As an example, the AccuWiz "Quick Close" Investment requires a sales forecast to justify development. However, sales is reluctant to commit to a number. AccuWiz product management has established a target payback period of three years for Investments. AccuWiz product management now avoids investing in new development without a sales commitment to achieve the payback revenue. This is a new game for sales. They could always just apply pressure in the past to try to get what they wanted. What can product management do?

The Investment development cost is estimated at $570K in this example with a target payback period of three years. Product management only needs to ask sales what they think the relative profile of income by year will be. If the income from year 1 is 100%, what would future yearly revenue be relative to year 1? I would argue that the company shouldn't be making large Investments in a case where sales cannot even predict a growth rate.

This example assumes the Investment generates sales revenue, but the same calculation can be done for the case of expense reductions where internal operations should be willing to commit to productivity improvements to justify tactical Investments.

Assume a revenue growth rate as shown in Figure 5.6.

In this case, second-year income is expected to be 5% higher than the first year's income.

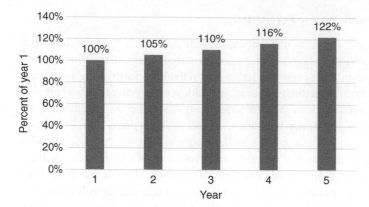

Figure 5.6 Relative annual income forecasts.

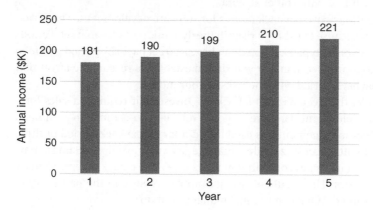

Figure 5.7 Income profile example.

Figure 5.7 shows the income necessary to meet the payback period of three years. Appendix B shows the math behind the calculation and includes a reference to a downloadable Investment Income Profile Calculator spreadsheet you can use to determine income profiles needed to meet payback targets based on development cost estimates.

In this case, the income for the first three years is the same as the development cost of $570K, meeting the payback period objective. Revenue can be estimated by dividing by projected margins. In the case shown in Figure 5.8, margin of 80% in each year is assumed.

The downloadable Investment Income Profile Calculator accounts for fractional years. For example, it will calculate the correct income profile for a payback period of 2.5 years.

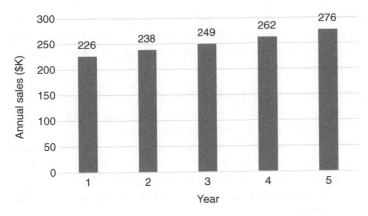

Figure 5.8 Sales revenue calculated from annual income forecast.

The intent of this calculation is to establish a collaborative dialog with sales or operations to balance payback period and income commitment. A director or VP of sales may initially balk at the calculated income profile. "This is much higher than I think we can meet." The next step is to consider what could be done to make it more reasonable. Increasing the payback period will reduce the revenue commitment, but it increases financial risk for the company, and your CFO may have absolute limits on the maximum payback period. The conversation naturally leads to ways to decrease development effort to decrease the required income to an acceptable level.

Consider the following collaborative discussion with a sales director:

Product manager: "We understand that this Investment could significantly increase sales. However, based on payback targets it would require this much revenue over the first three years."

Sales director: "Wow! That's much higher than I expected. How can we reduce the sales commitment?"

Product manager: "We can reduce development effort or justify a lower payback period. However, I know our CFO is firm on software development payback periods."

Sales director: "What's the next step?"

Product manager: "Perhaps the features or functionality you said are essential could be simplified or deferred. There's a possibility of reducing the functionality by focusing initially on a narrower market segment. What if we put out an initial release that can only be sold in North America where most of the sales are generated in the first three years anyway? There are several features we wouldn't need. And I can also ask engineering to propose functionality simplifications to reduce development effort."

Sales director: "I really appreciate you looking at alternatives to make this happen. I certainly will consider reduced functionality to get this done. And I'll go back to see if we could generate additional sales to justify the functionality we want."

Aha! The illusive Minimum Marketable Feature Set (MMFS) appears! An often-antagonistic discussion turns into one that can substantially improve company financial results and relationships. Everybody wins.

We now understand why the MMFS has not, and will not, propagate until there are trade-offs that sales and operations understand. There are no perceived financial consequences for continuing to pile on functionality. The Investment approach provides a practical way to present these trade-offs in early planning stages where options still exist.

You may be thinking that sales will just agree to a higher forecast to justify higher priority in the Investment backlog. There is a catch. The individual Investment income forecasts add up to the sales VP's commitment for new development. The projections are used to establish sales quotas for the VP and directors. You can be sure they will vet the income assumptions to end up with a sales quota they believe they can achieve.

5.5 Investment Backlogs

WSJF is used to prioritize Investments to create an Investment backlog. However, actual order may vary from strict WSJF order based on judgment of risk, strategic value, and the credibility of supporting data.

Strategic Investments can be interspersed within the backlog to obtain development resources. Even though the funding comes from different portfolio allocations, they must still be prioritized relative to tactical Investments that have quantified WSJF. Insertion of a strategic Investment in the backlog increases Net CoD of tactical Investments beneath them. The actual financial impact of a strategic Investment is the cost of development plus the increase in Net CoD of the lower-priority tactical Investments. A strategic Investment to improve UI may have a development cost of $100K, but costs millions of dollars when the additional backlog Net CoD is considered.

One way to compare strategic Investments with delayed income is to use Net Present Value (NPV). Although NPV is not used to compare tactical Investments, the long-term income from strategic Investments may be discounted to the third year of a three-year planning period. However, income beyond three years should also be heavily discounted for risk.

Strategic Investments may be first prioritized among themselves with a weighted point system that considers more than income generation.

For example:

- Support for company vision
- Support for company strategic plan
- NPV forecast
- Risk
- Competitive positioning
- Contribution to company brand
- Leverage of company core competencies
- Ability to expand market

5.5.1 Investment WIP

The importance of minimizing WIP was discussed in the earlier description of Kanban. Even though it is associated with Kanban, minimization of WIP should be an objective of every software development process. Reducing WIP reduces system delays. It also reduces R&D capital tied up in partially completed Investments.

WIP is a Key Performance Indicator (KPI) for manufacturing organizations. The cost of WIP appears as a component of the inventory asset account on the balance sheet. Components of products are assumed to have value. For example, a completed LCD screen to be installed in a television set in the next manufacturing step has financial value that adds to the inventory asset account. The WIP cost for the LCD screen includes material costs and the labor to produce it. Manufacturing organizations strive to keep WIP costs low. It represents capital tied up in the manufacturing process. WIP added to the balance sheet reduces shareholder Return on Equity (ROE).

WIP in software organizations also represents tied up capital. Material costs are negligible, but every document or line of code has an associated labor cost. At any point in time, a large portion of the R&D budget is tied up in partially completed components targeted for the next release. However, software organizations do not focus on WIP costs because they do not directly impact financial reports. Reduction of WIP in software development can increase total productivity and free up capital that can be invested in new development.

The Investment model provides a vehicle to manage and reduce WIP without requiring a detailed accounting system. We will consider two types of WIP that we want to make visible and quantify. The first is Investment planning WIP to minimize wasted planning effort. The other WIP is the labor cost accrued during Investment development prior to completion. In Chapter 8, we will introduce one other form of WIP analogous to manufacturing finished goods WIP.

It should be noted that zero WIP is also not a good situation. There should be some WIP to account for processing time variance so that development stages don't need to wait. For example, an Agile team may find there are no user stories available in the product backlog, or a test team may run out of stories to test. Queues typically maintain upper and lower WIP limits to prevent bottlenecks and queue starvation. Refer to Reinertsen's, *The Principles of Product Development Flow*, for more information.

5.5.2 Investment Planning WIP Limits

At the start of the software development process, we don't want to plan more work than we can develop. Organizations waste hours of product management and engineering time creating detailed plans and estimates for the latest great idea, only to be replaced with a higher priority three months later. These estimates cause considerable frustration and disrupt planned work.

Many software organizations plan work that engineering never develops. In one assessment, I quantified the development effort for incomplete backlog work that had gone through a first level of planning and estimation. It would have taken their current engineering resources almost 10 years to complete the backlog, assuming no new work was added. Such a waste of valuable planning effort. We want to use WIP limits to prevent this backlog of planned work that will never be developed.

Figure 5.9 depicts the AccuWiz Investment backlog prioritized by WSJF. The grayed-out Investments can't be started within the next year based on R&D capacity.

	WSJF	
Quick Close	125	
Workflow Enhancements	105	
European Version	90	
Ui Enhancements	75	One-year
Data Analytics Connectors	60	WIP limit
Enterprise Integration	55	
Customer Support Enhancements	40	
Mobile Application	25	

Figure 5.9   Investment backlog with one-year work-in-process (WIP) limit.

Capacity may be constant, or it may be increased by adding new staff. Either way, there are a limited number of staff-hours or story points available in an upcoming year to start new Investments.

Agile development reduces wasted planning effort by adopting a "just-in-time" approach to requirements development. However, larger organizations require some level of planning before they invest in a project or release. The business case needs cost and schedule estimates.

The level of effort for estimation varies greatly among organizations with which I've worked. Estimation may involve creating an initial set of requirements or features decomposed at the user-story level. Since engineering is usually held to schedule estimates, they expend considerable effort to create the estimate, even breaking the requirements down into modules with statement counts. I've even seen cases where project managers create a schedule at the task level to produce estimates.

It makes no sense to do detailed planning for an Investment that can't be started within a year. Requirements are likely to change, or an Investment within the limit may be moved down in priority due to new opportunities. One year is a good number for an Investment WIP limit, but it can vary depending on the rate of change in your industry. The Investment WIP limit allows product managers to match their work level with software development capacity.

5.5.3 Minimizing Investment WIP

Investment WIP, the labor cost of partially completed Investments, can be minimized by placing a higher priority on completing Investments than starting new Investments. To the extent possible, work for Investments prioritized higher in backlog priority should take priority. This is not always practical because developer specialization causes resource contention that can impact the critical development path. Staff may be available, but they don't have the skills needed to work on a specific Investment.

There are two ways to look at this. The first is based on Reinertsen's, *The Principles of Product Development Flow*, where he shows that minimization of Net CoD is more important than staff utilization. In fact, queue delays go to infinity as utilization approaches 100%. So, it is not a bad thing to have some staffing flexibility for development commitments.

The second view is that since staff are available, you may as well get them started on the next Investment in line. This would presumably reduce backlog Net CoD, but it ends up being very disruptive to Agile teams. You must weigh what may be an insignificant improvement in Investment cycle times against the disruption to functioning Agile teams. Shifting staff to start lower-priority Investments has a high efficiency cost and increases WIP. It may be better to have individuals work on deferrable tasks like maintenance and remain with their teams.

The Investment model reduces WIP by being able to prioritize R&D work throughout the development organization. Prioritization of work among multiple Agile teams with interdependencies is challenging because financial value cannot be associated with features or user stories. This is especially true when functional Kanban teams support multiple Agile teams, each receiving myriad simultaneous requests from Agile teams. For example, there may be a single team to add services for database access. With the Investment approach, the priority of work of any team is based on the WSJF priority of the Investments in the backlog, ensuring that higher-priority Investments are completed before new Investments are started. This provides functional teams with clear priorities and reduces software WIP.

The ideal case is that Investment development order is not driven by developer skill availability. I know this is easier said than done. However, as the Agile community says that the business needs to be more Agile, I contend that development organizations must improve their agility to develop an Agile backlog in the order of business value. This can be accomplished by staff cross-training and layered architectures that enable teams to focus on functionality without having to know the details of lower layers.

5.6 Technical Debt Investments

"Technical debt" is incurred when engineering takes shortcuts to implement functionality in a way that increases development costs in the future. The idea was that companies should budget to retire technical debt at a future time to refactor software. For example, an engineering team may forego a layered architecture to directly build functionality to get it out quickly, recognizing that at one point they will need a layered architecture to scale.

Technical debt has long been a source of frustration for engineers. Engineers want to develop the most efficient and effective code that will provide a solid platform for scalability. Even with the best intentions, technical debt creeps into the software base because design assumptions or requirements change. Engineers can now prioritize technical debt reduction within the Investment backlog as either a tactical or a strategic Investment, but they must learn the rules of company financials.

The CoD model shows that retiring technical debt can be costly because it delays income-generating Investments. Engineers need to realize that a technical debt reduction is not likely to be a good business decision unless a direct impact

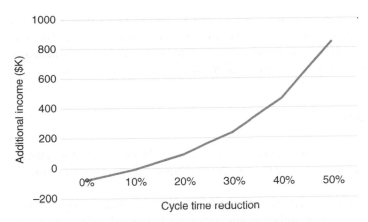

Figure 5.10 Added income from technical debt reduction.

on cycle time reduction can be justified. A general cycle time reduction has a cascading effect on Investment deployment dates and provides a significant reduction in backlog Net CoD. The example in Figure 5.10 shows additional income within a planning period of three years for a set of quarterly releases, each with a CoD of $10K per quarter.

In this case, the added effort for refactoring reduces net income by about $80K if there is no reduction in cycle time, making it unlikely that the business will approve this Investment. The Investment breaks even with a cycle time reduction of 10%. A cycle time of reduction of 30% increases income by over $200K.

The catch here is that the added income for the technical debt reduction must justify a WSJF value to be within the backlog one-year WIP limit to be further considered. The message for development is that reducing technical debt can be justified if cycle time can be reduced. A good example is refactoring a platform to release Investments on-demand to save the opportunity costs posed by large releases.

There may be other reasons other than efficiency to retire technical debt. Inability to scale is one. Quality is also often brought up. However, any case for technical debt should be justified on the basis of financial benefit for the company. For example, what is the income at stake if the system is capped at its current capacity? Would it be better to apply the money required to scale to other Investments? And what is the financial impact of poor quality caused by badly structured code? How much money are we losing from previous customers who complained about quality? Would it reduce customer churn rates? By how much? Investments provide the foundation for objective discussions for product management and engineering to make sound business decisions on retirement of technical debt.

The bottom line is that you are going to live with your technical debt unless you can quantify financial benefit for the business. Just calling it a "debt" won't get you anywhere. Technical debt retirement can be justified in cases where it significantly reduces backlog Net CoD or enables deployment of individual Investments.

5.7 Summary

1. The Investment model was created to establish software development increments that can be associated with income generation so they can be prioritized by WSJF.
2. Investment costs are based on software labor costs to prioritize software development, as opposed to initiatives and programs that include all costs.
3. Investments establish a planning element between portfolio and feature-levels.
4. P&L centers, strategies, and initiatives can be associated with Investments.
5. Investments are formed around business objectives that identify business value in terms of income.
6. Strategic Investments are those with indeterminate income forecasts or payback periods greater than three years.
7. Tactical Investments are those with projected payback in less than or equal to three years.
8. There should be separate portfolio allocations for strategic and tactical Investments to account for risk.
9. Investment effort and income estimates are called forecasts to reflect the dynamic nature of Agile development.
10. Commitments for income generation or cost reductions can be established based on a target payback period and growth profile.
11. A backlog Investment WIP limit reduces planning effort wasted on Investments that will likely change.
12. Investment WIP analogous to WIP in manufacturing organizations is based on labor costs attributed to partially completed Investments.
13. Technical debt Investments can be justified based on impact to income. The best technical debt solutions increase deployability to accelerate backlog income.

Reference

1 McConnell, S. (2006). *Software Estimation: Demystifying the Black Art*. Microsoft Press.

6

Maximizing Investment Value

The ultimate proof of Investment value is the willingness of a customer to pay for it, or by what internal stakeholders are willing to commit to in terms of expense reductions. There must be a clear link between what the Investment provides and the value stakeholders perceive.

This chapter starts with a definition of great products. What is it about a product that makes them "great"? Can we find something in common that will allow us to create great Investments? I'll share a definition of great products that I learned from a very wise person. Then we'll discuss what they have in common.

We'll then discuss three different business models that will affect how customers obtain value from your product.

The bulk of the chapter describes stakeholder value analysis, a method to maximize the value product stakeholders obtain from Investments. It is followed by a description of how user scenarios can be the common language for the business and engineering sides to facilitate collaboration and innovation.

6.1 Great Products

I often start a seminar with the question, "Who wants to build great products?" Everyone raises their hands. I then ask them how they would know if they built a great product. Typical answers are "It sells well" or "People like the product." Nobody has a good definition for something we all aspire to in software development.

Another epiphany from a Construx summit. We had Fred Brooks, the famous author of *The Mythical Man-Month* [1], as a keynote speaker at the Construx leadership summit. His book showed the industry that adding engineers to a late

Unlocking Agile's Missed Potential, First Edition. Robert Webber.
© 2022 The Institute of Electrical and Electronics Engineers, Inc. Published 2022 by John Wiley & Sons, Inc.

project makes it later. Software could not be estimated as if programmers were brick layers, where doubling resources halves cycle time. Brooks is also famous as "The father of the IBM 360," the ground-breaking general-purpose computer developed in the 1960s.

Brooks' topic was great design. He included a simple definition of "great products":

> Great products have fans.

I give this definition to seminar attendees and ask them how they would know if their products had fans. That was easy.

- People become evangelists for your product – "You've got to try this."
- Communities of users form around your product in social media.
- You can't tear the product out of their hands.

We then do an exercise where they can evangelize their favorite products. The only rule is that they need to state a specific product, not a product class like "digital cameras." It is a fun exercise where everyone starts writing down the product names so they can try them themselves. The examples of Amazon and Google always come up. The iPhone is often included.

Take the iPhone as an example. Many of you will recall the days of the menu-driven phones from the 1980s. Leading manufacturers were Research in Motion (RIM) with the Blackberry, Nokia, and Motorola. Even Microsoft had their hat in the ring with the Windows phone. I used many of them. I recall having to go through a series of illogical menus on a Blackberry to turn the phone off. Or I would have to use the Windows phone start button browser and type into the browser to get information I wanted, like how my stocks were doing, or the local weather forecast.

The iPhone changed everything. Steve Jobs challenged his engineers to come up with a single button and no menus. He did more than that. He had them focus on quick access to what users valued. With the iPhone, I can quickly access my stocks and the weather, which I do multiple times during a day. I can pull up my e-mail and calendar without having to walk through menus that I can barely read. I can roll through my contacts with a flick of my finger. Achieving value quickly and easily set the standard for the iPhone apps to follow. Unfortunately, the younger generation was never exposed to these old phone interfaces so will never truly appreciate the iPhone breakthrough.

I always ask how many people in the seminar believe that the iPhone could have been defined in a Marketing Requirements Document (MRD). Of course not.

It required a value perspective instead of the obsession with features and functionality in software development. Product definition would likely have started with menu layouts.

I love how the value provided by Amazon can be expressed in such a simple statement:

> I want to minimize the time to buy and receive something I want.

This simple value statement drives Amazon. They help you find something you want with quick search capabilities that present options in a fraction of a second. Have you ever experienced a significant delay? Amazon shows similar products that customers have purchased and their reviews. You can use the famous patented "one click checkout" to buy it. It arrives in a day or two, and sometimes even the same day. Amazon isn't stopping there. The value statement includes delivery time. They are working on drones.

I then ask the class why their companies are so focused on features when nobody lists the number of features as the reason for being fans. They get the point.

It's unlikely that this book is going to turn you into a Steve Jobs or Jeff Bezos that will change your industry forever, and I'm pretty sure that neither Jobs nor Bezos started out by writing stakeholder value statements. These insights come naturally for some people and are coupled with tenacious drive and outstanding leadership that keeps the organization focused on value.

The common trait of "great products" per Brooks' definition is they focus on something their stakeholders' value, and move it a mile rather than moving everything an inch at a time with small features and small enhancements. Companies that build great products can innovate because engineering understands the problems to solve.

Imagine your customers telling other customers they really need to buy your latest release because it's so great. Or imagine a trade show where customers love to get up and evangelize your software. Now you know the secret, and it's not about filling releases with features. It's about stakeholder value.

6.2 Business Model Value Considerations

A business model defines the products or services that a company can sell into a target market to achieve financial objectives. They are often supported by a "value proposition" that describes what customers will receive in return for purchase of your product.

There are three major classifications:

Business to Business (B–B)

Transactions are conducted with other businesses. For example, hospital information systems fall under a Business to Business (B–B) model. The hospitals buy your software to increase revenue or reduce costs. This aligns with our Investment definition. At the highest level, we can assume that the "value" delivered by an Investment in the B–B case is based on the positive contribution to the customer's financial statement.

For B–B business models, someone in the customer organization needs to demonstrate to their CFO that a software purchase can generate a positive return on their Investment.

Business to Consumer (B–C)

Consumers don't have to justify your software based on income improvement. They may buy your software because it makes them feel good, like a video game, or saves them time, like TurboTax. In this case, value is based on providing or improving something users value. Investment income is based on the willingness of the customer to pay, and market penetration.

Information Technology (IT)

Although IT departments don't build products in the traditional sense of the word, they encounter the same work prioritization challenges as product companies. IT departments are tasked with increasing productivity through Business Process Automation (BPA). This may involve purchase and customization of software obtained in a B–B model, or by internal software development projects. In either case, the IT department will need to justify an Investment by reducing operational expenses.

Investment Cost of Delay is based on income generation. The first question to ask for any Investment proposal is, "How would that Investment provide value to our customers based on our business model?" Here are some examples for the different business models:

B–B

"How will your product increase income for our customers to justify a purchase? Does it increase their revenue or decrease their operational expenses?"

B–C

"What value would be provided to users to make them want to spend money on our product versus options they have today? Why would they evangelize the product on social media?"

IT

"How will this software reduce operational expenses?"

These questions will start you thinking in terms of value. Section 6.3 explains how you can maximize the value that your customers perceive.

6.3 Stakeholder Value Analysis

This was another gem from a Construx leadership summit that enabled me to connect another dot to create the Investment model. The speaker was Tom Gilb, another major contributor to software engineering since the 1960s. Tom provided a seminar for Construx on work he had been doing on stakeholder value. Tom's son, Kai, has followed in his footsteps and is also a contributor to the software industry.

I first recognized the power of Tom's stakeholder value model to focus innovation. Technical innovation requires that engineers understand the problem they are solving, rather than just implementing requirements handed down from product management. I saw stakeholder value as a way to identify the problem to solve for engineering.

Agile was supposed to increase innovation by defining stories that represented need rather than specific functionality. However, epics and stories tend to be user-focused. Innovation requires a broader view. Value may be provided by eliminating the users who are providing input for your user stories. For example, why make a user more efficient by solving their problems when you could automate the entire process?

I developed seminars around innovating with stakeholder value. When the Investment model was conceived, I realized that it is the perfect starting point prior to any discussions on features or functionality.

6.3.1 Gilb Stakeholder Definition

Tom's point was that we develop software without understanding what stakeholders truly value. Requirements often reflect stakeholder requests, especially when discussion drops immediately to the feature and functionality levels. This is true in most Agile implementations I have seen. Features are often specified and then broken down into user stories.

Tom and Kai define stakeholders as

> Stakeholders are any person, group or system, that have or we want to have an interest in our project.

Users are obviously stakeholders. In addition, members of the technical support group that provides support services for the project are stakeholders. Salespeople who sell the product are stakeholders. Stakeholders include members of groups that may influence the project requirements, like a regulatory department.

I adapted the Gilbs' stakeholder definition by separating it into two major categories: product stakeholders and constrainers. A product stakeholder is someone who obtains value from your product. Constrainers are individuals who impose specific requirements on the product. Customers are product stakeholders. Members of a regulatory or legal department could be constrainers.

I adopted the "product stakeholder" term to distinguish it from a "project stakeholder." I found that when I discussed stakeholders with a group of engineers, they insisted that they were stakeholders, and project managers were also stakeholders. Everyone was a stakeholder. Most individuals have an interest in the outcome of a project, but do not influence whether someone is going to pay for the product. I wanted to focus on stakeholders who receive value from the product.

Stakeholder classes can differentiate groups that share a value but drive different requirements. For example, customers may be separated into younger- and older-generation classes based on their competence with modern technologies. A millennial is more likely to rely on search for help. An older employee is more likely to want a traditional user guide.

Constrainers need to be considered because they can determine the success or failure of a product. Your application may provide tremendous value for doctors or nurses working in a hospital, but it can't be sold without meeting the Health Insurance Portability and Accountability Act (HIPAA) in the United States.

The first realization is that there are a lot of product stakeholders and constrainers that may be involved in an Investment. A thorough analysis is necessary to identify the right stakeholders and what they value.

The Gilbs go one step further. They assert that stakeholder value can be measured based on a scale, and goals can be established. For example, assume a product stakeholder's value is, "I want to minimize the time to start using my software application." The scale is time. It would be possible to define a set of use cases that represent the basic functionality of the application and establish a time goal for the average user to complete them the first time they use the application. The value could be tested.

There is another valuable concept in stakeholder value analysis. Tom Gilb introduced the idea of ranges for the measures instead of fixed values. The ranges have minimum, target, and stretch values on the chosen scale. The minimum represents the measure on the scale beyond which stakeholders perceive little additional value. Basically, it is the point of diminishing returns. For example, optimizing software to reduce web-page responses below 200 ms has little perceptible change in value. "Stretch" provides an aspirational goal for a motivated team. "Target" is in the middle.

A test could be developed for the example of minimizing time to start using a software application:

I want to minimize the time from when I first log into my application until I can perform the following set of functions without having to refer to help:

- *Add a purchaser*
- *Create a purchase order*
- *Add a vendor*
- *Send a payment*

Minimum: 30 minutes
Target: 15 minutes
Stretch: 5 minutes

Note that the scale is in terms of the value provided. In this case, lower numbers represent greater value for the stakeholder.

There are some great benefits of using the scale. It provides engineering with a finite range in which to make trade-offs between implementation complexity and performance. Stretch goals help the team think outside the box. Small incremental improvements do not distinguish great products so out-of-box thinking is encouraged.

Before we move on to an example of the power of stakeholder value analysis, we'll look at a multi-million-dollar mistake that could have easily been avoided with stakeholder value analysis.

6.3.2 Ford's Big Mistake

Ford announced a breakthrough in vehicle user interaction at the Consumer Electronics Show in 2010 called "MyFord Touch," which was introduced in the 2011 Ford Edge. It was a combined effort with Microsoft to leverage touch-and-voice technology. In addition to complaints of crashing, users expressed dissatisfaction with complicated controls that caused distraction. The problem was that it introduced technology without considering how it improved stakeholder value.

A 2012 *USA Today* article [2] reported the fallout:

> Ford dropped from fifth to 23rd in J.D. Power's quality survey last summer, in large part because of this technology (MyFord Touch).

The same article stated:

> Ford will give new software to about 250,000 owners of vehicles with the often-maligned "MyFord Touch" dashboard technology in about two months to make the system easier — and less distracting — to use.

I love the optimistic quote from one of the Ford dealers:

> It can take up to 45 minutes to teach customers the MyFord Touch system, says Gary Cohen, vice president at Jerry's Ford in Annandale, VA. But he says it's "a great system once you set up your profile."

Can you imagine how the excitement of buying a new car would dwindle as you sat through a 45-minute demonstration to learn how to change radio stations?

Consider what would have happened if the design of the system started from a stakeholder value perspective.

I want to minimize the time from when I get into my car for the first time until I can experience the following without having to take my eyes off the road:
- *Listen to music I want to listen to*
- *Have a comfortable temperature in the car*
- *Have a clear windshield (no rain, ice, or condensation)*

Minimum: 10 minutes
Target: 5 minutes
Stretch: 2 minutes

Note that in this case the values are stated in terms of what the driver wants to experience, not the functionality they want to perform. For example, the driver doesn't just want to set the temperature. They value quickly attaining and maintaining the desirable temperature. They wouldn't like it if it took 30 minutes to attain a comfortable temperature. This brings the effectiveness of the heater into the value solution.

Customers don't care about turning on the windshield wipers. They want a clear windshield while they are driving. This establishes goals for the defrosters in addition to having the wipers set at a speed to keep the windshield clear. Or perhaps we can eliminate wipers completely with an innovative solution involving windshield coatings or air flow? You can see how this leads to completely different solutions. MyFord Touch could never have passed these tests.

I'm still puzzled by how far the car manufacturers are from focusing on value versus functionality. I recently drove into Canada and had to change my speedometer setting to kilometers per hour. I tried to do it while I was driving and then realized that it was unsafe, so I pulled over to the side of the road and went through several menus to finally set the scale.

Section 6.3.3 will go through an example to show you how to get to stakeholder value. It requires a shift in the way we think about defining software requirements.

6.3.3 Trucking Fleet Management Example

This is an exercise I've used in the past to demonstrate how often we start developing software without understanding who is to receive value and what they value. I explain to the seminar attendees that their company wants to create a software product that leverages the GPS unit they have sold to trucking fleets. They realize that moving to a software business model will allow them to grow faster. A typical customer may be a trucking company that delivers loads for hire.

Table 6.1 lists some of the external product stakeholders. There is a single example of what each values, but there could be more for a stakeholder type. Try to keep them to five or fewer. If you start to go beyond that, you're probably still stuck at the functionality level. Recall the discussion on great products. We want to add substantial value in a few targeted areas instead of giving a few features to everyone.

Take the safety director, for example. They may tell you that they want to reduce accidents. However, you take a broader perspective to understand their ultimate objective. It's like Amazon including the time to deliver in their target value instead of just focusing on customers finding products on their web site. Always look for how the value translates to financial benefit for the customer's company. In this case, their ultimate goal is to reduce insurance premiums. The severity of an accident may be a factor.

Table 6.2 shows the software vendor's internal product stakeholders.

Constraints imply requirements as shown in Table 6.3.

The list of product stakeholders and constrainers can get quite lengthy. You'll be surprised at how many you can think of in your own industry, and how many you typically have missed during product definition.

Note that none of the values includes functionality constraints. This is a good check to see if you are at the value level. Section 6.3.4 introduces a technique called

Table 6.1 Customer product stakeholder examples.

Stakeholder	Values	Scale
Driver	I want to set the fastest route with a highly rated truck stop available when I need to add fuel	Average time to reach truck stop rated four stars or above
Dispatcher	I want to minimize the time from when an order comes in until it is on the way	Average dispatch time reduction
Maintenance Director	I want to reduce maintenance costs	Marginal operational cost
Safety Director	I want to minimize accidents to reduce our insurance premiums	Annual insurance company premium
Accountant	I want to minimize accounts receivable	Average time from offload to invoice
VP – Operations	I want to reduce operational costs	Labor cost per mile driven

Table 6.2 Software vendor product stakeholder examples.

Your company	Values	Scale
Customer Support Manager	I want to resolve customer issues faster	Number of customer issues resolved on the first call
Trainer	I want to provide a truck driver with basic proficiency with minimum training time	Average time for a truck driver to become proficient on a specific test
Sales Rep	I want to perform an intriguing product demonstration that results in a next step with the customer	Percentage of customers requesting additional information after presentation
IT Director	I want to minimize IT hosting and labor costs	Average annual IT support costs

Table 6.3 Constraint examples.

Constrainer	Constraint
Labor Union	Our labor agreement prevents driver performance monitoring
Federal Motor Carrier Safety Administration (FMCSA)	Drivers cannot drive 60/70 hours on duty in 7/8 consecutive days

"Five Whys" for getting to the fundamental stakeholder values from functionality requests. In either event, it is a good idea to make a final pass through the stakeholder table to replace any functionality with the underlying value sought.

The product stakeholder value table will bring up questions that normally wouldn't come up during product definition. The example above includes the Federal Motor Carrier Safety Administration (FMCSA) as a constrainer. Is the product only going to be sold inside the United States? If not, who are the equivalent authorities in our target market? Are we focusing on short- or long-haul trucking companies? The regulations may be different.

6.3.4 Five Whys

The Five Whys is a good technique for getting down to stakeholder value. It was introduced in the automotive industry to determine the root causes of quality issues. A group starts with the problem and then asks why it occurred. This usually produces a superficial response with narrow impact on the problem. Questioning continues until the root cause is determined.

For example, there may be multiple customer reports of clutches failing. The first "Why" may result in, "Because a clutch spring failed." Another "Why" reveals that the clutch springs were not tensioned correctly. The next "Why" determines that the manufacturing machine was not correctly calibrated the week on which the clutches were assembled. The final "Why" might result in "There are no process controls to ensure that the machine is calibrated before each shift." That reveals the opportunity for a broader solution.

The analysis is not bound to exactly Five Whys. The team goes as far as they can to determine a root cause that they can address. In the above example, a team could go further to reveal that the company does not invest enough in quality control. However, this is likely out of the control of the group. They may make a recommendation to increase Investment in quality control, but machine calibration is within their scope.

In stakeholder value analysis, the first "Why" is applied when functionality appears in a value statement. I use an example of radio control buttons found on most car steering wheels.

Initial customer request:

I want two buttons to change the station on my car radio.

In most cases, this statement would just become a requirement:

There shall be two buttons located on the steering wheel to search for available radio stations. The first button results in a search toward stations higher in the frequency band. The other searches toward lower frequencies.

Or a typical Agile user story:

As a driver, I want to change the radio station with two buttons on my steering wheel.

Yes, this isn't a well-formed user story. It should be something like:

As a driver, I want to change my radio station to find a channel I want to listen to.

However, I usually see the user stories stated in terms of functionality that a user wants. The Agile team is just happy to get a user story defined so they can try to meet their fixed schedule!

This still includes the functionality of the two buttons. Ask "Why?".
Response:

I want to change my radio station without taking my eyes off the road.

Let's go deeper with another "Why?".
Response:

Because I like to listen to music I enjoy in my car.

Restatement:

"So, let's say that you want to minimize the time to hear pleasing music after getting in your car."

Response:

Yes!

Two value statements emerge:

1. *I want to minimize the time from when I enter my car until music I like is playing.*
   - Minimum: 3 minute
   - Target: 2 minutes
   - Stretch: 30 seconds
2. *I want to minimize the time to safely choose music I like while I'm driving my car.*
   - Minimum: 1 minute
   - Target: 30 seconds
   - Stretch: 5 seconds

I first wrote, "I want to minimize the time to locate and play music I like while I'm driving my car *without distraction*," then realized that this is imposing an unnecessary constraint. It would be fine for the stakeholder to be distracted in a self-driving car. They just want to do it safely.

Also note that the value statements do not limit scope to just the radio. The radio is just one technology to fulfill the value. The music source could be an iPhone or a USB drive. This is a lesson in making sure you have removed as many constraints as possible in the value statement. Constraints limit the ability to maximize value and preclude opportunities for innovation.

Consider the classic tree-swing example below that has been used to convey the challenges of requirements definition (Figure 6.1).

Of course, we've come a long way with Agile development. We can involve a product owner who has a clear vision of what the tree swing should look like. The swing is built in small increments, starting with getting the tire right. However, consider what your competitor introduced to the market (Figure 6.2).

How did they come up with this? They conveyed the stakeholder value to their engineering department without including unnecessary constraints, such as the tree and the tire. They realized that the stakeholder value was, "I want to relax outside." This was translated into Investment stakeholder value:

Build a device that customers rate 8 out of 10 or better in terms of relaxation.

Stakeholder value is a key for innovation. Chapter 14 further explores the relationship of stakeholder value and innovation, and provides practical ways to increase innovation at your company.

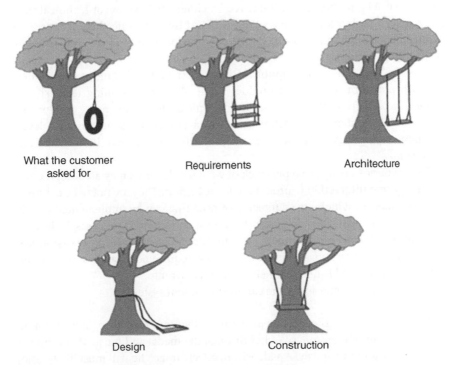

What the customer asked for   Requirements   Architecture

Design   Construction

Figure 6.1   Classic tree-swing requirements example.

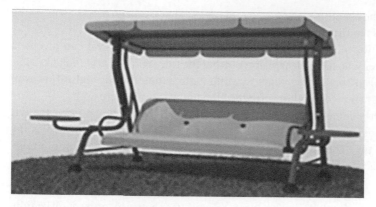

Figure 6.2   Innovative swing.

6.4   User Scenarios

I recommend an additional step before defining features and functionality. User scenarios can provide the focus for brainstorming product stakeholder value. User scenarios can be proposed and improved by either the business or technical side. They are at a higher level than user stories. And they don't need the formality of requirement statements. User scenarios can provide a fun and collaborative way to spur innovation.

A user scenario is a description of how a product stakeholder could interact with a system to obtain a product value. The brainstorming team should include people from the business and technical sides and may even include product stakeholders. The technical side can contribute solutions that leverage new technology. The business side clarifies value and illuminates any constraints.

User scenarios are a verbal playback of what would be seen by an observer during one system interaction to produce a desired result. They are not to be confused with user stories, which are statements of need that can be implemented in software within a sprint. You may also have heard the term "use cases." They are elements of a formal requirements modeling process to define every possible system stimulus and response. They can be a good requirements analysis technique, but the level of detail is not conducive to brainstorming.

Consider a user scenario for the car entertainment system:

> John unlocks his car. The entertainment system recognizes John from his key code. The system searches through the media and music that John has listened to previously. An algorithm selects music he will most likely enjoy based on his previous selections and replay frequencies. Music starts to play.

This is the "camera-eye" view of what would be observed for this one scenario. Participants can brainstorm other ideas.

> Sounds great. What if we add this? The system starts the playlist at the volume he prefers while the car is stationary. The system detects ambient road noise and employs noise cancelation, and modifies the volume to give John the best entertainment system experience.

Note that the scenarios include some level of functionality assumptions, like "recognizes John from his key code" and "employs noise cancelation." That is why engineering must participate in the brainstorming. They can contribute technologies that the business side may not be aware of.

Another example:

> It turns out that we already use facial recognition for our self-driving capability, so we know who the driver is. We don't need to rely on the key code. And this is a better solution in case someone else uses John's key.

This has come a long way from the requirement for two buttons on the steering wheel!

Some creative ideas have come out of the truck fleet management example. For example, rerouting a truck around stop-and-go traffic to minimize wear and tear to reduce maintenance costs. Or tracking truck speeds and stops to lengthen maintenance intervals to reduce cost. The safety director may get immediate notification on their phone of any driver approaching their weekly time limit with a list of available drivers who could take over. Ideas abound when the team understands the value they are trying to achieve. Engineering job satisfaction increases because they are solving problems instead of just implementing prescribed functionality.

Any decomposition technique can be applied after the user scenario brainstorming. The team may derive features or epics or go directly to user stories (remember, though, that too many features lower WSJF and may preclude the Investment).

You may be thinking that stakeholder value analysis will take more time from product managers who are already overworked. Firstly, product managers gain time by eliminating wasted planning time with the one-year Investment planning Work in Process (WIP) limit. Secondly, this is exactly what product managers should be doing. Leave the functionality details to the product owners. Product managers should be focused on value.

If you want to go deeper into stakeholder value, Tom Gilb published a more recent book [3] on the subject. I still think stakeholder value analysis is one of the most underused gems of software engineering. I've made it part of the Investment model to enable product managers to focus on value rather than functionality.

6.5 Summary

- Great products have fans that will evangelize your products – it's not about the number of features.
- Great products make quantum leaps in product stakeholder value.
- The value perceived by customers depends on your business model.
- Stakeholder value analysis drills down to what customers value rather than what they think they want.
- Product stakeholders receive benefit from a product and influence purchases.
- Constrainers impose specific requirements on your product to make it viable.
- Stakeholder value can be measured with a scale.
- Stakeholder value should not impose implementation constraints.
- Investment goals can be established by ranges on product stakeholder value scales.
- Many product failures could have been avoided by establishing and testing goals based on stakeholder value.
- The "Five Whys" root cause analysis technique can reveal the product stakeholder value behind a functionality request.
- User scenarios are a valuable tool for brainstorming innovative ways to maximize a product stakeholder value.

References

1 Brooks, F. (1982). *The Mythical Man-Month*. Addison-Wesley.
2 Jayne O'Donnell (2012). Some Ford owners to get touch-screen software fix soon. *USA Today* (8 February).
3 Gilb, Tom, *Stakeholder Engineering, Leanpubcom*, 2021.

7

Planning High-Value Investment Features

Feature definition typically occurs at the start of product planning today. Much of the frustration from missed development schedules arises from unrealistic expectations of predicting feature content within a fixed release schedule. Features even appear on multiyear roadmaps. Features are likely to stay around as a planning element despite the epics and user stories used in the Agile world. A feature is an increment of functionality that represents value for the business side. Project managers track features. Customers and sales teams expect them. Agile needs to incorporate a feature model that creates value without imposing constraints early in product planning.

The Investment model raises the level of schedule commitment above features to the Investment level. Feature-level commitments will not be eliminated but can be reduced. There are valid reasons for feature-level commitments. For example, features may be driven by regulatory requirements. Or customers may not accept your product without features provided by competitors' products, or even allow you to participate in a Request for Proposals (RFP). Feature commitments should be made on a case-by-case basis and kept to a minimum. Committing to specific features reduces engineering content flexibility needed to meet Investment timeboxes.

Product managers need to dig deeper to understand the need for a feature-level commitment. The demand for a specific feature and schedule should always be questioned. Is it because someone thinks it's a good idea, or is it necessary to sell the product? The more specific features requested, the lower the likelihood of meeting Investment schedules.

Investment stakeholder value analysis discussed in Chapter 6 provides an alternative to the feature-level planning used by most organizations today. However, at some point, an Investment is likely to be decomposed into feature work packages familiar to product and project managers. This chapter includes a method for feature content planning that provides high probability of completion within the Investment timebox.

Unlocking Agile's Missed Potential, First Edition. Robert Webber.
© 2022 The Institute of Electrical and Electronics Engineers, Inc. Published 2022 by John Wiley & Sons, Inc.

7.1 Avoiding the Feature Pit

Chapter 6 introduced the truck fleet management example I have used in seminars. For the first exercise, the group is broken down into small teams to define features. Nobody questions starting at that level because that's what most of them are used to. The point is to demonstrate that focusing on features obscures value.

The assignment results in a flurry of activity. The person tasked with writing down the feature list usually can't keep up with the flood of ideas from their team. Nobody asks for additional clarification of the scenario, like whether the focus is long- or short-haul trucks, or whether the market is domestic or international. Nobody thinks about constraints by different country regulatory authorities or unions. The teams jump into defining features with little information about the market.

I have to cut off the discussion at some point. There appears to be no end to the great ideas for features. It takes a few minutes for the buzz of the room to dissipate because they are having so much fun. I then tell them that the exercise is complete and all they need to do now is prioritize the features in a product backlog for their Agile teams. I tell them they could bring in a truck driver as a product owner to help them come up with even more features. They now suspect they've fallen into a trap. They have taken the narrow perspective of adding functionality for users of the software. Almost all the features focus on the truck driver. Then I ask if truck drivers will have a major say in the purchase of their product. The room goes quiet.

Feature examples:

- Identify the truck stops with the highest food ratings on the driver's route.
- Immediately reroute the truck to the nearest rest stop.
- A communication channel to talk with other company truckers.

Nobody would argue that these are useful features. However, are they the features that will maximize Investment value? It turns out that none of the features creates value for the key decision-makers who would purchase the application, such as the VP of operations. The head of operations is going to look at how the product reduces operational costs.

My observation is that Agile has shifted focus from value to functionality. I fully embrace the power of Agile to translate user needs directly into great software solutions with epics and user stories. However, as we now understand from stakeholder value analysis, users are often not the people making purchase decisions, and building the solution in small increments of user needs causes Agile teams to "miss the forest for the trees."

More often user stories are disguised functionality or feature requests that make teams think they're actually "doing Agile." I've seen stories like:

> As a user I want a drop-down menu to select the account.

Or even more blatantly:

> As a user I want a new feature that ...

Teams are reinforced for demonstrating user functionality in the sprint review, not for creating value. Using Investments as a first step in Agile planning ensures that value is established first and user stories relate directly to that value.

Melissa Perri in her book, *How to Avoid the Feature Trap* [1], affirms the observation that features defocus value:

> The build trap is when organizations become stuck measuring their success by outputs rather than outcomes. It's when they focus more on shipping and developing features rather than on actual value those things produce.

The Investment model quantifies "value" in terms of income. The minimum feature set to attain that value can then be defined, with a trade-off between additional functionality and backlog Weighted Shortest Job First (WSJF) rank. Adding features increases cycle time and reduces WSJF, so we want to strive to define the smallest feature set that enables an Investment to achieve its financial objectives.

7.2 Feature ROI

T-shirt sizing was introduced previously to calculate Investment WSJF. T-shirt sizing can also be used at the feature level to allow financial comparisons of features, even among different Investments.

T-shirt sizing of features within an Investment is a useful process in itself. I've found that there is tremendous value in bringing together product management and engineering for the exercise. It facilitates discussion and common understanding that can result in significant increases in value and lower development costs. Conversations go along the lines of:

> Product manager: "Why is the effort so high for that feature?"
> Engineer: "Because you wanted a completely different report layout from what our report engine currently provides."

Product manager: "I didn't think it would make that much difference. What if we went back to a traditional report format?"

Engineer: "That would reduce the effort from 'XL' to 'L.'"

The business value in traditional T-shirt sizing is subjective. It's determined by product management and can be based on numerous factors, like revenue, competitive positioning, or market penetration. Often, it's just based on strong opinions. With the Investment model, T-shirt "value" becomes more specific. It is the degree to which a feature contributes to Investment income.

T-shirt weighting points can be used to determine relative contribution of a feature to Investment income. Features should be compared within the scope of an Investment. That's much easier than trying to assign business value to hundreds of features sponsored by different product managers.

We can prioritize features within an Investment based on relative Return on Investment (ROI) contribution. Consider the AccuWiz Quick Close Investment comprised of three features as shown in Table 7.1, each weighted with a T-shirt size based on relative contribution to Investment income. Assume T-shirt sizes of XS, S, M, L, and XL correspond to point values of 1, 2, 3, 4, and 5, respectively. The "relative contribution" can be calculated by dividing the point value of a feature by the sum of the points. For example, the relative contribution of the Outstanding Purchase Orders feature in the table is $2/10 = 20\%$. Assume the Quick Close Investment generates $700K of income in the first three years. Income of $0.2 \times \$700K$ is attributed to this feature.

T-shirt sizing based on relative effort can be used to estimate feature development costs, assuming an average labor rate for the Investment. This will allow us to calculate ROI on a feature basis. Table 7.2 assumes development cost of $500K and apportions cost contribution using the same point weighting method.

Table 7.3 calculates three-year ROI for each feature.

The ROI value is meaningless as a separate value because all features are released with the Investment. If a feature could be released separately to generate income, it would be an Investment that could be prioritized by WSJF.

Table 7.1 Quick Close Investment feature income contribution example.

Feature	T-shirt size value	Weight	Income contribution (%)	Income ($K)
Outstanding Purchase Orders	S	2	20	140
Quarter Delay Scenarios	M	3	30	210
Closing Workflow	XL	5	50	350
	Total	10	100	700

Table 7.2 Quick Close Investment feature development cost example.

Feature	T-shirt size effort	Weight	Effort contribution (%)	Development cost ($K)
Outstanding Purchase Orders	M	3	30	150
Quarter Delay Scenarios	S	2	20	100
Closing Workflow	XL	5	50	250
	Total	10	100	500

Table 7.3 Quick Close Investment feature three-year return on investment (ROI) example.

Feature	Income ($K)	Development cost ($K)	ROI (%)
Outstanding Purchase Orders	140	150	−7
Quarter Delay Scenarios	210	100	110
Closing Workflow	350	250	40

The ROI calculation should be viewed as a weighting factor that indicates the relative importance of including that feature within the Investment to maximize ROI.

ROI can be used to prioritize features. Recall that we need to have feature contingency to meet Investment cycle time targets. The lowest ROI features should be dropped from the Investment if burndown projections show that all features cannot be completed by the target date.

The ROI calculation example raises the question, "Why should we include Outstanding Purchase Orders in this Investment?" The next question is, "What would the Investment income look like if we didn't include the Outstanding Purchase Orders feature?" In many cases, the marginal benefit of including a feature is not justifiable. Or perhaps there is a way to reduce the functionality of Outstanding Purchase Orders to increase its relative ROI? The feature ROI view can move us closer to the Minimum Marketable Feature Set (MMFS) and shorter cycle times.

You may be wondering why we are not prioritizing the features by WSJF within an Investment. This would require cycle time forecasts at the feature level throughout the development cycle. Features are not timeboxed, so cycle time estimates vary. The ROI method provides a way to ensure that features with the highest contribution to Investment ROI are prioritized higher without having to estimate individual feature cycle times.

We can also compare the value of features from different Investments in the backlog to determine the relative priorities of features for an entire P&L center. In this case, we compare the Workflow Enhancements Investment, which is the next Investment in the AccuWiz backlog. The Workflow Enhancements Investment will be delayed by the development of the Quick Close Investment. Therefore, the three-year income forecast for Workflow Enhancements is based only on the income that still falls within the three years. For example, an Investment with a linear income ramp that generates $300K over three years might contribute $(2.5/3) \times \$300K = \$250K$ with a delay of six months caused by the development of the Quick Close Investment. Table 7.4 shows feature three-year ROI based on income of $250K.

The ROI values of Investments 1 and 2 reveal feature priorities in Table 7.5.

The combined ranking promotes a discussion on features proposed by the Investments in the backlog. For example:

- Should the Outstanding Purchase Orders feature be dropped to accelerate the Workflow Enhancement Investment?
- Could any of the higher-value features be released as separate Investments?
- Can the effort of any of the features be reduced to increase its ROI contribution?

Table 7.4 Investment 2 feature ROI example.

Feature	ROI (%)
Invoice Reconciliation Automation	15
Exception Approvals	−25
Group Queues	−50

Table 7.5 Investments feature ROI comparison example.

Investment	Feature	ROI (%)
Quick Close	Quarter Delay Scenarios	110
Quick Close	Closing Workflow	40
Workflow Enhancement	Invoice Reconciliation Automation	15
Quick Close	Outstanding Purchase Orders	−7
Workflow Enhancement	Exception Approvals	−25
Workflow Enhancement	Group Queues	−50

These questions may lead to a decision to drop the Group Queues feature. It may be possible to release Quarterly Delay Scenarios or Invoice Reconciliation Automation as separate Investments. Or the Group Queues feature functionality may be scaled back. The focus is on releasing higher value faster.

7.3 Summary

- Product management and project management plan and track in terms of features because they represent an increment of benefit recognized by stakeholders.
- Investment feature commitments should be minimized to account for Investment estimation variance to support timeboxing.
- Product managers and engineers have long histories of moving immediately to the feature level when planning products.
- T-shirt sizing has been a useful exercise to foster collaboration between product management and engineering to define higher value with less development effort.
- Investments provide a way to relate features to financial value.
- A T-shirt sizing method can be used to prioritize feature value contribution in terms of relative ROI.
- Product management should determine what the Investment income profile would look like without lower ROI features.
- Feature ROI can be compared across Investments, allowing product management to make decisions on features to drop or resources to transfer.
- The greatest benefit of the feature ROI calculation is the questions and discussions raised to get closer to the MMFS.

Reference

1 Perri, M. (2018). *Escaping the Build Trap: How Effective Product Management Creates Real Value.* O'Reilly Media.

8

Releasing Investments

Competition for R&D capacity based on Weighted Shortest Job First (WSJF) creates incentives to plan and build smaller Investments. Planning does not begin with a release assumption in the Investment model. Income generation for bundled Investments is delayed until the release date. The first objective is to plan Investments that can be released independently. However, there are instances where Investments will need to be bundled within releases.

This chapter begins with new insights into the opportunity cost of bundled releases based on Net Cost of Delay. Quantifiable Cost of Delay allows us to calculate the income lost by delaying a completed Investment to the release date. Release trains cost the software industry billions of dollars that are invisible today. WSJF changes the economics of release planning by showing how overall R&D Return on Investment (ROI) can be increased by investing in architectural and other technical changes to simplify deployment for the organization and its customers. Many engineering organizations know how they can simplify deployment but can't justify the development costs. Organizations can now see the "opportunity cost of not being Agile." Millions of dollars are being "left on the table," some of which can be recovered with software infrastructure changes to reduce deployment time.

We examine the reasons why large releases persist despite the industry transition to Agile development. We also address why many customers won't accept releases more frequently even if a company can reduce development cycle time, and how to overcome their reluctance.

Lastly, another form of Work in Process (WIP) will be discussed that has not been considered in software development. A manufacturing analogy of inventory cost management is used to reveal the cost of capital tied up in a release, providing another financial justification for releasing Investments independently.

Unlocking Agile's Missed Potential, First Edition. Robert Webber.
© 2022 The Institute of Electrical and Electronics Engineers, Inc. Published 2022 by John Wiley & Sons, Inc.

8.1 Release Opportunity Cost

Continuous Delivery (CD) is the dream of every software company. Income can be generated as soon as an increment of business value is developed. Customers like CD because they receive value from software sooner and don't experience the effort and risk of large releases. However, CD is not widespread in the software industry, especially in larger organizations that have traditionally delivered periodic releases.

Most of the CD examples I've seen are in Business-to-Consumer (B–C) companies. Updating a website is a typical example. Another example is Google updating their search algorithm on a daily or weekly basis. Business-to-Business (B–B) companies often deliver upgrades that involve significant customer effort and changes to the way they work. Some regulated industries, like life sciences, require comprehensive validation testing after each upgrade, placing further burden on the customer. There will be cases where Investments need to be bundled into a release, but they should be justified as exceptions.

Part of the problem is that software companies have been unaware of the opportunity cost of releases. Figure 8.1 demonstrates the financial value of reducing release cycle time.

The solid line in the chart (Figure 8.1) shows cumulative income for annual releases with a Cost of Delay of $1M per month. There is no income in the first year while the first release is under development. After the first year, income of $1M per month is generated. The second release starts contributing an additional $1M

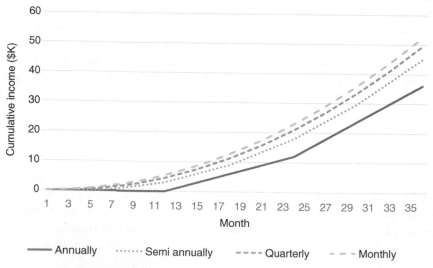

Figure 8.1 Cumulative income by relative cycle time reduction.

per month after the second year for a total of $2M per month. The solid line shows that cumulative income reaches $36M at the end of the second year for the annual release case.

The line with small dots assumes that each annual release can be split in half, each release generating half the monthly income. Since the release value is halved, the Cost of Delay is reduced from $1M per month to $0.5M per month. Income begins to flow after six months, with $0.5M per month added every six months thereafter, for a total of $45M at the end of the second year. The other lines show how the income increases within the same period based on shorter release cycles. A factor of 12 for the monthly case generates $52.5M in the same period.

Consider the question, "What software development productivity improvement would I need to achieve to increase income from the annual release total of $36M for the annual release case to $53.5M generated by the monthly release case?" Total productivity is Value Out/Value In. Assume the development costs are the same for both cases (release overhead costs are addressed later in the chapter). Productivity would have to increase by a factor of $52.5/36 = 1.46$, a 46% improvement.

Table 8.1 shows the income accumulated over the three-year period for each release cycle time reduction, with an increase in total productivity over the three-year period relative to the annual release case.

The first observation is that reducing release cycle time can substantially improve total productivity. The second observation is that the benefits of reduced release cycle times have diminishing value. Total productivity is improved by 25% going from annual to semiannual releases. Moving from monthly to quarterly releases relative to annual releases improves productivity only by $(52.5 - 49.5)/49.5 = 6\%$.

Appendix B provides a general formula that relates the fractional reduction in cycle time to equivalent total productivity improvement. Assume N is the fractional reduction in cycle time. For example, $N = 2$ for the case of moving from annual to semiannual releases. $N = 4$ for annual to quarterly releases. Appendix C

Table 8.1 Equivalent productivity improvement as a function of release frequency.

Release cycle (Annual to)	Income ($M)	Productivity increase relative to annual releases (%)	Point difference from the release case above
Annual	36	—	—
Semiannual	45	25	25
Quarterly	49.5	37.5	12.5
Monthly	52.5	46	8.5

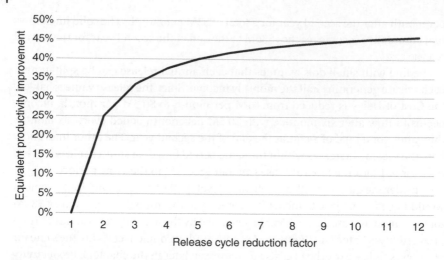

Figure 8.2 Total equivalent productivity improvement for release cycle time improvement.

derives a formula for productivity improvement as a function of release cycle reduction. The ratio of total productivity is determined by

$$\frac{P_2}{P_1} = \frac{(N-1)}{2N}$$

Figure 8.2 plots the equivalent productivity improvement for fractional reductions up to 12, equivalent to moving from annual releases to monthly releases.

Moving to CD is like splitting the release into an infinite number of release segments, each with infinitely small value. The limit of the productivity formula is 50%. The point difference between the monthly and the ideal CD release cases is only 4%.

The analysis shows that companies are losing millions of dollars today from the inability to reduce release cycle times. Money spent to reduce cycle times can provide a positive ROI.

8.2 Investment Release Bundling

Although every attempt is made to plan and develop deployable Investments, there will be times when they will need to be bundled into a release. There are three reasons for Investment bundling:

1. Investments can't be priced independently.
2. Customers reject more frequent releases.
3. Investment deployment overhead costs.

8.2.1 Investment Pricing

Many organizations have established an upgrade pricing model for their customers. Customers are charged an upgrade fee plus monthly or annual support and maintenance fees. Customers often budget based on annual upgrades. Pricing independent Investments may be a challenge in this case because it changes the customer's budgeting model; therefore, Investments may have to be bundled into releases.

Software as a Service (SaaS) has become a popular pricing model. Customers pay on a periodic basis, often monthly. Quite often, the price includes future upgrades. Features are added to releases to maintain and attract customers to grow revenue but organizations do not increase the price for individual customers. In this case, the advantage of releasing Investments independently is diminished because the income impact is based on market growth. For example, a difference of three months in Investment release dates may not justify the additional overhead costs of separate releases.

The Investment model lends itself to value-based pricing. There are several pricing models for SaaS pricing, such as user-based and tier-based pricing. The objective of each model is to relate pricing to the value the customer receives from the product. This book will not go into the many SaaS pricing options available. We will focus on a model in which customers are willing to pay more based on the additional value they receive from an Investment.

This brings up the opportunity for modular pricing, where Investments can be selectively purchased by customers. Pricing is based on the value the customer receives. Deploying independent Investments is more important in modular pricing because there is an immediate impact on income generation. Modular pricing should be the objective of companies that adopt the Investment model. It can substantially increase near-term income, providing lower payback periods at reduced risk.

The top line in Figure 8.3 represents lifetime deployment of a typical product. Growth is slow to start and then accelerates quickly as product adoption increases. Sales start to drop as the product approaches the point of market saturation. New sales diminish as the market becomes saturated. Cumulative installations follow the classic S-curve. Most companies continue to build large releases for initial installation without considering upgrades as a separate market segment.

The Net Cost of Delay depends on the rate at which customers accept modular Investments. This can be high if the customer perceives value to justify the Investment and if upgrades are seamless. Investments can provide a vehicle for planning modular upgrades of tangible value. Modular pricing for your installed base market segment can result in reduced payback periods because customers have already been acquired.

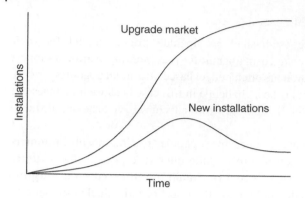

Figure 8.3 Typical product life cycle.

8.2.2 Lack of Customer Acceptance

Customer acceptance often comes up in customer discussions on reducing cycle time. "Even if we could release faster, our customers wouldn't accept more frequent releases." This may be true, but you need to think about why that is the case. Certainly, customers want to obtain value from your software as often as possible. Somehow, the customer burden of upgrading your software outweighs perceived value. This must be overcome if you are to attain the full benefits of the Investment model.

In many cases, customers have experienced upgrade quality problems that significantly impacted their operations. The potential risks outweigh any perceived benefits. High quality is a prerequisite for releasing faster. It is a difficult challenge, but software upgrades must be virtually defect-free. Don't expect your customers to accept releases more frequently if they risk disruption to operations.

Unfortunately, there is no "magic bullet" for reaching near zero-defect code quality. It requires sound software engineering quality practices. The quality bar cannot be lowered for Agile development. Even though Agile uses shorter development cycle iterations, good software engineering practices must apply, such as code reviews and automated unit regression tests with adequate coverage.

Agile development has the potential to produce higher-quality software than Waterfall does. The short development iterations can provide rapid quality feedback during release development. Retrospectives facilitate process improvement throughout the development cycle. Maintaining software in a "potentially shippable" state reduces rework and the side effects of fixes late in the release development cycle. However, in many of the organizations I've assessed, the minimalist "Agile" philosophy is believed to apply to software engineering practices. The same Waterfall quality software engineering practices need to be in place. Accept that reducing cycle time is likely to have little benefit if you can't deliver near defect-free software. Chapter 12 addresses software quality.

Feature-based planning presents a significant obstacle to reducing cycle time. Large releases today are stuffed with feature requests from multiple customers. Product managers "sprinkle" features in releases to try to quell demands. Quite often, this results in releases that contain new functionality with little or no value perceived by a specific customer. Customers must undergo a major release upgrade to obtain a relatively small fraction of features relevant to them. They incur significant costs to support the upgrade and incur changes to work procedures and documentation for little perceived value. The modular Investment model can provide a solution.

Modular Investments should be planned so that they don't impact the operation or functionality currently used by a customer. The current feature-based planning mindset neglects new modular approaches. Opportunities will appear if modular deployment is the primary goal of Investments. For example, compare the value of tweaking numerous features with providing an optional module that will reduce customer operational expenses by 20%.

Assuming customer upgrade burden can be reduced, there can still be a significant obstacle for regulated industries that require validation tests with each software upgrade. One solution is to create a suite of automated validation tests that can be executed by your customers. Validation only requires proof of successful execution, which can be documented by successful completion of a validation test suite. This shifts some expenses from the customer to the software vendor, but reduction in Net Cost of Delay will usually provide a positive return on their investment in automated validation tests.

8.2.3 Release Overhead Costs

We've discussed the need to simplify deployment from the customer perspective. There are also internal overhead costs for Investment releases that need to be considered. The main overhead costs are release regression testing and the internal cost to deploy software.

Appendix B derives a formula that accounts for release overhead costs:

$$\frac{P_2}{P_1} = \frac{(1+\alpha)}{(1+N\alpha)}\left(1 + \frac{(N-1)}{2N}\right)$$

The factor α is the current ratio of fixed release overhead costs to release development costs. Fixed overhead costs include release regression testing and deployment costs, including the cost of any field testing.

Figure 8.4 shows the productivity ratio for release cycle time reduction factors of 1–12 with release overhead cost ratios of 10%, 20%, and 30% as shown in the legend.

The top line shows that productivity is lower for release reduction factors greater than 5 if the fixed overhead cost of each release is 10% of your development cost.

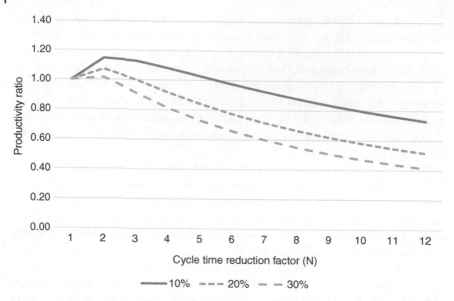

Figure 8.4 Productivity ratio as a function of release overhead cost and cycle time reduction factor.

Note how quickly the advantage of releasing more frequently is eliminated for increasing release overhead costs, stressing the importance of reducing release overhead costs to take advantage of Agile development.

Many companies' regression test suites have grown out of control. Functional test organizations are usually blamed for every defect that escapes. They typically respond by adding a regression test to prevent that specific defect from escaping again. Regression test libraries grow, resulting in major maintenance effort and costs to keep them current. The costs to automate these tests become overwhelming, and automation never gets done in many organizations. However, I'm not going to recommend automating regression tests as your first step.

You want to first reduce functional regression tests while maintaining or improving quality. This may appear counterintuitive, but you need to accept that maintaining large regression suites to debug software will not give you the result you expect. It turns out that only a fraction of software defects can be found at the functional testing level. This has been verified by a well-known software engineering metrics expert named Capers Jones, and this applies to Agile development as much as it did for Waterfall.

Capers Jones defines defect removal efficiency as the percent of defects found during a specific testing phase. He reports removal efficiencies by industry for different phases of testing. He reports that even industries with the highest reliability requirements attain defect deficiency removal rates of only 30% with functional testing [1]. His conclusion is that software defect removal should be efficient at every quality verification step, including reviews, code inspections, unit and integration testing.

Functional testing also applies in Agile development. Agile development practices include creation of user story acceptance tests prior to inclusion in the sprint backlog. These are typically functional tests that can be demonstrated to a product owner. Many organizations also perform functional testing at the feature level once a set of user stories has been completed. It doesn't matter whether you embed testing within an Agile team. Functional testing is a separate activity, and as in Waterfall, people believe that all remaining defects can be detected.

There is an explanation for the limited ability to detect software defects at the functional test level. Ask any experienced developer who has delivered highly reliable software about the fraction of his or her code executed for the success path. I get responses of 20–30%. This agrees with my experience as a developer of telecommunications software with stringent reliability requirements. The bulk of the code handles cases off the "happy path," most of which can't be simulated at the functional test level. Reasonable code coverage can be attained only with formal unit and integration testing where sets of data patterns are executed by the code. There is no shortcut.

Manual regression testing at the functional test level is expensive and time-consuming. Defects caught at this stage are more expensive to fix and are more likely to delay releases. The subject of defect prevention and early removal is addressed in Chapter 12. It shows that you will need to increase unit and integration testing to reduce rework costs. Automate unit and integration tests first. Functional regression testing should focus on requirements verification instead of debugging. This will result in fewer functional tests to automate and execute, thus reducing release overhead costs.

After addressing release testing overhead, the next issue is the cost of deployment. This is an issue whether you or the customer hosts the application. For internal hosting, your IT department incurs costs to update and verify servers. Internal installation and testing costs are incurred for customer upgrades. Many organizations live with clunky and inefficient installation procedures. I've found that engineering, IT, and field services know what needs to be done. The problem is that their ideas never get implemented because new features are always deemed more important. Deployment improvements can now be shown to reduce quantifiable release opportunity cost as Investments.

DevOps has been a positive step toward simplifying installation, but the focus is often on increasing the efficiency of development teams. Draw the boundary of responsibility for your DevOps to address customer deployment, including the processes your customers use to support and test upgrades. The reduction in Net Cost of Delay can then be reinvested in DevOps.

And if you want to make a major dent in on-site testing costs, improve the quality. On-site testing is usually extended to long periods by encountering defects. As discussed above, you need to improve the quality as a precursor for cycle time reduction.

8.3 Overcoming Modular Release Challenges

Legacy software architectures make it difficult for Agile teams to develop concurrently. New functionality may impact a slice of architecture, from UI to business logic to database. The chances of overlap in common software modules are high. This needs to be addressed with architectural improvements. Modular releases also pose configuration management challenges that need to be addressed.

8.3.1 Architecture for Modular Deployment

Service-oriented architectures (SOA) have evolved to make data from enterprise architecture more accessible. Microservice architectures have become popular in recent years. The difference is that Microservices expose application functionality and data at the Application Programming Interface (API) level. Microservices are at a lower level to provide developers with the flexibility they need to add functionality in legacy systems. Microservices can be used to implement enterprise SOA, but they are not the same. SOA are about external data access. Microservices improve development efficiency.

Most engineering departments are familiar with Microservices architectures and have long advocated them to product management. Implementation usually takes a backseat to new features. Investments in architecture to increase deployability and reduce cycle time can now be justified in terms of release opportunity cost reduction.

8.3.2 Configuration Management

Even if software functionality can be delivered in independent modules, changes to the legacy software base are often necessary. For example, new Microservices may be required to support new modules that impact the same back-end software and data schema. We want to avoid having to support multiple versions of legacy software.

The solution is a platform approach where base software upgrades can be deployed without impact on customers. Impacts from planned Investments can be collected and implemented in a new version of base software. Periodic platform releases that don't impact functionality can be seamlessly deployed to synchronize the infrastructure software base, eliminating maintenance of earlier versions. Your platform has a release cycle separate from the delivery of functionality. Again, quality is the gating attribute.

8.4 Release Investment Prioritization

You may be wondering why we want to prioritize Investments bundled within a release when they are all released at the same time anyway. We want to be able to take advantage of the agility provided by Agile development to include new opportunities that arise during the release development cycle. Developing in WSJF order ensures that releases truncated due to schedule overrun have the highest value Investments.

T-shirt sizing used for feature prioritization can be applied to Investment prioritization when individual Investment pricing is not possible. As with feature prioritization, T-shirt sizes of XS, S, M, L, and XL create a linear scale with points of 1, 2, 3, 4, and 5, respectively. Relative contribution to *release value* is calculated in Table 8.2 using the AccuWiz examples.

As we did in the feature case, income can be apportioned based on the T-shirt size. The same logic is used when assigning T-shirts sizes. "To what degree does this Investment contribute to the release income?" Relative income contributions can be calculated for an example of three-year release income estimate of $3.5M (see Table 8.3).

Table 8.4 is based on the estimated income of each Investment from Table 8.3. We assume that the Cost of Delay is proportional to the income generated by each Investment over a three-year period and use the total three-year income to

Table 8.2 Relative Investment release income contribution based on T-shirt sizes.

Investment	T-shirt size	Weight	Relative income contribution (%)
Quick Close	S	2	20
Workflow Enhancements	M	3	30
European Version	XL	5	50
	Total	10	100

Table 8.3 Release income contribution example.

Investment	Relative contribution (%)	Release income contribution ($K)
Quick Close	20	700
Workflow Enhancements	30	1050
European Version	50	1750
Total		3500

Table 8.4 Investment WSJF priorities.

	Income contribution ($K)	Cycle time (mo)	Relative WSJF
Quick Close	700	3	233
Workflow Enhancements	1050	2	525
European Version	1750	3	583

calculate the relative WSJF. We use WSJF in the Investment case rather than ROI in the feature prioritization case because Investments are timeboxed so we know target cycle times.

T-shirts sizes can be changed during release development with new information to optimize development order for Investments that are not yet completed. The relative WSJF calculation creates incentives to maximize value and minimize development effort throughout release development.

8.5   Reducing Software Inventory Costs

WIP and tie-up of capital were discussed in Chapter 5. There is another component of WIP cost in manufacturing. Manufacturing has two categories for inventory costs. The first is the WIP inventory, which is analogous to the money invested in incomplete Investments. The second is finished goods inventory, which is analogous to the capital tied up in a completed Investment that has not yet been released. Investments waiting for release are effectively "in the warehouse awaiting shipment." Inventory cost is the sum of manufacturing WIP and finished goods inventory. Even though finished goods inventory does not appear on financial reports as it does in manufacturing, software "finished goods inventory" should be tracked and minimized to free R&D capital.

Inventory costs for unreleased Investments should technically include costs outside of R&D, like the cost of labor and materials to create a training guide and marketing collateral. This would create unnecessary complexity in project accounting systems. For our purposes, we can use Investment software development labor costs, which is within the control of engineering. Software labor costs represent the majority of the "finished goods" cost.

Figures 8.5–8.7 show how a company might track inventory across multiple profit and loss (P&L) centers. Figure 8.5 is the total labor cost for Investments that have been completed in each week awaiting release. It's equivalent to putting "finished goods" in a warehouse.

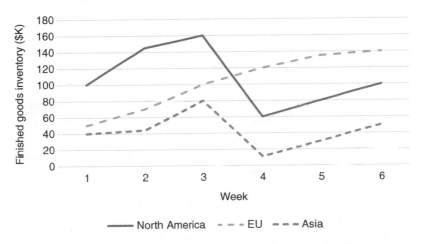

Figure 8.5 "Finished goods" inventory costs by profit and loss (P&L) center.

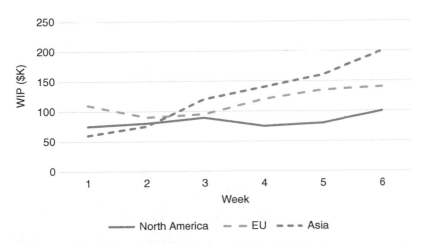

Figure 8.6 Work in progress (WIP) inventory costs by P&L center.

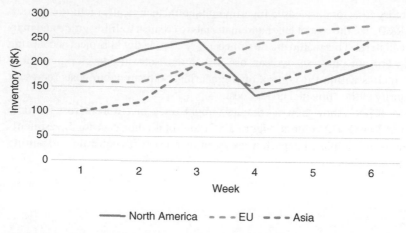

Figure 8.7 Total software inventory costs by P&L center.

Release inventory costs were reduced in week 4 in this example after release deployment for the North American and Asian markets. EU inventory costs continue to grow.

Investment WIP development costs can be added to the release inventory costs to show the total target for WIP reduction. Figure 8.6 shows an example of WIP development costs.

Figures 8.5 and 8.6 add to show total inventory costs (Figure 8.7).

Figure 8.8 shows total inventory costs as a percentage of annual R&D budget. It shows how effectively each P&L center is managing inventory. In this case,

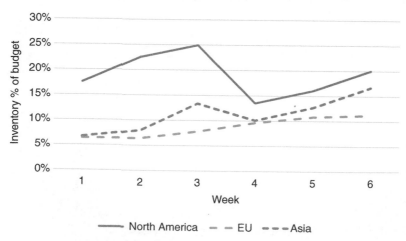

Figure 8.8 Total software inventory costs as a percent of R&D budget by P&L center.

North America should examine why their inventory is so high relative to their annual software development budget. Is it because of inability to release more frequently, or ineffective Investment development WIP controls?

The only action possible to reduce release inventory cost is to plan and deploy smaller releases, ideally at the Investment level. A reduction in release inventory frees R&D capital. Avoiding release bundling creates two wins: R&D capital is freed, and income is accelerated by a reduction in Net Cost of Delay.

8.6 Summary

- Bundling Investments within releases increases Net Cost of Delay because Investment income is delayed until the release date.
- Release Net Cost of Delay is the opportunity cost of not being able to deploy individual Investments.
- A general formula for productivity improvement as a function of release cycle time reduction is provided.
- Effective R&D productivity increases by 25% for each reduction in cycle time by 50%.
- There is diminishing productivity improvement for reductions in cycle time, reaching a limit of 50% for CD.
- The Investment model reveals release opportunity costs to justify development of infrastructure, tools, and processes to release individual Investments.
- Modular pricing and deployment for Investments should be adopted to leverage an installed base.
- Customers must be willing to accept more frequent releases if cycle times are reduced.
- Effective software engineering practices must be in place to achieve near defect-free releases that customers will accept more frequently.
- A modular approach is enabled by the Investment process by limiting impacts to current customer operations and reducing customer installation impacts.
- The productivity impact of release overhead costs can be described by a formula that demonstrates the importance of reducing overhead costs to release more frequently.
- There is a point where release overhead costs for a given cycle time reduce productivity.
- The shorter the cycle time, the greater the negative impact of release overhead costs.
- Functional regression testing can only find about 30% of defects and must be complemented by defect prevention and defect detection techniques.

- Unit and integration testing should be improved and automated to reduce the number of functional regression tests before automation.
- Functional regression tests should focus on requirements verification, not debugging, to reduce the number of functional tests to automate.
- There are technical solutions to support modular Investment releases based on Microservices and platform releases.
- Release inventory costs should be tracked and minimized to free R&D capital.

Reference

1 Jones, C. (2008). *Measuring Defect Potentials and Removal Efficiency*. Software Productivity Research, LLC.

9

Meeting Investment Targets

9.1 Meeting Commitments

Engineering has a history of missed feature commitments imposed by Waterfall planning. Estimates change or scope increases with no schedule relief. Delays impact financial predictability and create schedule surprises. Feature-level content commitments made at the beginning of release planning are expected to be met in Waterfall planning.

Investments provide a way for engineering to commit to timeboxed Investments with variable feature content, increasing the likelihood of meeting Investment schedules as discussed in Chapter 3. Feature content can vary if the income generation goals can still be attained. Income predictability is what the business really wants. We've addressed how to account for software estimation variance by including contingency for discretionary features. This chapter addresses how to meet Investment schedule and financial targets by taking quick action based on rapid feedback.

Consider an analogy of landing a plane (Figure 9.1). The pilot stays on the glidepath by making small adjustments based on real-time updates displayed on the altimeter and airspeed indicator. The pilot makes larger movements at the start of the glidepath and makes small refinements while approaching the runway. Instrumentation must be updated on the order of seconds. Imagine trying to land a plane with instrumentation that updates every two minutes! This chapter describes how Investment schedule and financial targets can be met using the rapid feedback provided by Agile development. It starts with the concept of Investment teams that collaborate to "land the Investment."

This chapter also provides a method to deal with feature requests from the sales department that pop-up during development. Product development is often forced to include new features that have little impact on income. We'll see, in fact, that money is lost in many cases when Net Cost of Delay (CoD) is considered.

Unlocking Agile's Missed Potential, First Edition. Robert Webber.
© 2022 The Institute of Electrical and Electronics Engineers, Inc. Published 2022 by John Wiley & Sons, Inc.

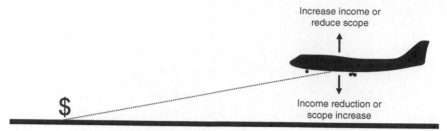

Figure 9.1 "Landing" the Investment.

9.2 Investment Teams

Who are the "pilots" for landing an Investment? Investment teams are the instantiation of product teams that most companies find so challenging to implement because of rigid organizational boundaries. Like pilots, Investment teams guide an Investment toward their financial and schedule targets by adjusting the "glidepath" in terms of development effort and income targets. It requires cross-functional collaboration.

At a minimum, an Investment team is comprised of an Investment leader, called the Investment owner, and an Investment technical owner. The Investment owner is usually a product manager, but not necessarily. Engineers can own an Investment to implement an idea they are passionate about. The Investment owner has overall responsibility for meeting the financial objectives of an Investment. The Investment owner takes a product perspective, not an engineering or product management perspective. Investments can be formed around anyone's idea and led by anyone.

The Investment technical owner collaborates with the Investment owner to help define and achieve the goals of an Investment. We've already discussed the importance of engineering contribution during the planning stage of an Investment to leverage technology. Engineers often have unique insights into product capabilities. The technical owner is usually a senior engineer.

Other people may be added to a team as long as the size doesn't exceed seven people. In my experience, teams of more than seven become committees and should be avoided. That's why Agile limits the team size. Other members may include Subject Matter Experts (SMEs), members of your support organization, IT, or field services. Team members share the Weighted Shortest Job First (WSJF) goal of income and cycle time.

Product managers need to abandon the traditional role of "voice of the customer" in this model. I've often found that engineers can complement their technical expertise with market and user needs given access to the information.

My clinical trial management software company retained a development team in Ukraine. We noticed that one of our lead developers began to display great insights into the clinical trial industry and could contribute opportunities to leverage technology. Our VP of product management had decades of experience using clinical trial management systems, which shaped our original version, and we had great respect for his knowledge. However, there were no major differentiators. The Ukrainian engineer was able to quickly learn the domain and contribute innovative solutions that allowed us to displace established players in the market. He was brought to the United States as a technical lead for our local development team. With additional exposure to the market and customers, he was soon able to shape our product roadmap with technical innovation.

This example and others have resulted in my evangelism to include an Investment technical owner from the start of planning. A major role of the Investment owner is then to educate the team on customer and market needs to facilitate collaboration and innovation, not to tell the team what to build. The concept of "voice of the customer" is outdated in this world of fast-moving technology. We've already established that direct input from customers often results in low-value features.

One hope I have is that the Investment approach enables the software industry to define a new engineering title in technical ladders called "product engineer." This is reserved for engineers who learn about stakeholder value and contribute to Investment planning without having to become product managers. Engineers can gain depth in your market opportunities while remaining in their technical roles. I believe that product engineers can be the greatest contributors of value in your organization, deserving job levels above principal engineers and architects.

The first objective of the Investment Team is to avoid Investment schedule delays that propagate to lower-priority Investments, increasing Net CoD and possibly forcing a major Investment roadmap revision. WSJF is CoD/cycle time. The team wants to avoid adding functionality that increases cycle time. It is possible to maintain WSJF with an increase in cycle time if additional income can be justified. However, this results in cascading Net CoD caused by delays of Investments lower in the backlog. This leads to the strategies described in Table 9.1 to manage Investments in the backlog.

The columns show actions the team can take to avoid or minimize financial and schedule impacts. Note that these actions are taken only after the Investment team has tried to eliminate or mitigate the change in the first place.

Investment forecasts and cycle times should be reviewed at a weekly meeting led by the head of product management or a profit and loss center (P&L) owner. The first objective of the meeting is to affirm the income and cycle time assumptions for each Investment. It's not likely that sales or operations will attend a weekly meeting, but current income forecasts can be sent to their respective VPs on a periodic basis to remind them that forecasts represent commitments to justify new development. All Investments within the one-year Work in Process (WIP) limit are included in the review, not just those under development, because planning assumptions are dynamic.

Table 9.1   Investment target remediation.

	Reduce scope	Increase staff	Increase income	Notes
Effort increase	x	x	x	Priority is to reduce scope to maintain schedule. If staff must be added, income must increase to maintain WSJF
Development cost increase	x		x	No schedule impacts. Reduce scope and/or increase income forecast to maintain the payback period and WSJF
Income forecast reduction	x			No schedule impacts but scope should be reduced to shorten cycle time to maintain WSJF

The Investment team should examine alternatives before changing an Investment target or reducing scope. Below is a checklist that can be used for collaborative problem solving at the meeting.

Added or Changed Features

1. What value is the requested change going to provide?
2. What is the relative Return on Investment (ROI) contribution for this requested feature based on T-shirt sizing?
3. Can functionality of this or other features be simplified?
4. What does the income forecast look like without this change? It may be better to accept a lower forecast than to propagate CoD through other Investments, especially for any Investment near the top of the backlog.
5. Can the feature be deferred to another Investment without major financial impact?
6. Can additional income be justified to maintain WSJF?

Increased Effort Forecasts

1. What assumptions changed and why?
2. Can the functionality of any features be simplified?
3. Can team velocity be increased to maintain the schedule?
4. Do the assumption changes impact any other Investments?

Team Velocity Reduction

1. What is causing the velocity reduction?
2. Is an ineffective product owner role causing considerable rework after stories are declared "done"?

3. Can more senior developers be used?
4. Is a high defect level causing rework?
5. Can staff be added effectively?

Changed Income Forecasts

1. Can the pricing model be adjusted to maintain the forecast?
2. Can income be increased with additional marketing support within a specific sales territory?
3. Is a reduced Minimum Marketable Feature Set (MMFS) possible? Can functionality be dropped by targeting a narrower market segment?
4. Can salespeople be added?

Development Cost Increases

1. Can the Investment or some part of it be effectively moved to an established offshore team?
2. Can we use junior developers while ensuring the ratio of junior to senior developers allows adequate design oversight?

It's extremely important to maintain a positive and collaborative environment at the meeting. The product management leader or the P&L owner needs to encourage people to come forward as soon as there is any risk of not meeting the Investment objectives. Otherwise, the changes will be revealed too late to act. It's like being hit with an unexpected crosswind just before landing. Don't pose questions in a challenging tone, and don't try to talk anyone out of a change. Thank them for bringing it up.

9.3 Managing Investment Scope

The Investment approach provides feature flexibility, and we've found a way to rank feature priorities by ROI as described in Chapter 7. How do we know when we need to drop features or reduce functionality, and by how much? Agile burndown charts can provide the answers.

In the Investment model, burndown charts are created for each Investment. This provides a lower level of granularity below the release level. Figure 9.2 shows an example of an Investment burndown chart. The vertical axis can represent story points or development hours remaining.

The burndown chart shows that the team is on the glidepath at sprint 3 to deliver all the content within the Investment timebox.

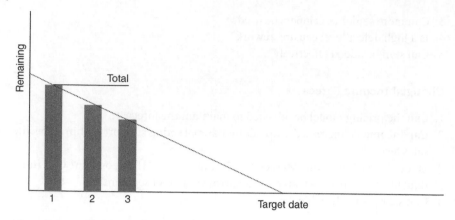

Figure 9.2   Investment burndown chart example.

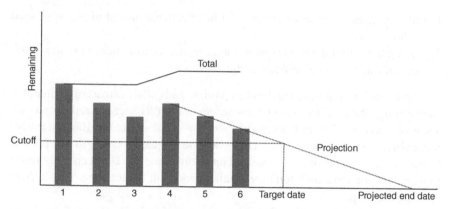

Figure 9.3   Investment burndown chart example off the glidepath.

Figure 9.3 shows that scope was increased on sprint 4 and the team was not able to increase velocity to maintain the target date.

The projection line is extrapolated using the average velocity of the last three sprints to forecast the end date if all features are to be included. The Investment must either be delayed or scope reduced. The point of intersection of the target date and the projection line forecasts the effort that will be completed by the target date.

Note that the delay in making scope changes until sprint 6 has put this team in an impossible situation. They may have been able to adjust the velocity earlier by adding developers. However, the accumulated deficit mandates a sudden and significant drop in development effort. The team should have recognized that they were not going to be able to deliver all the content within the timebox without adjusting the velocity. The issue should have been raised earlier.

Table 9.2 Investment feature status table example.

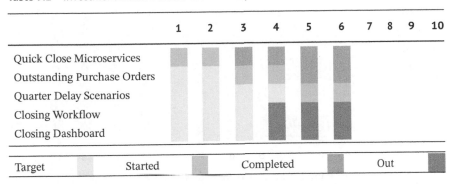

	1	2	3	4	5	6	7	8	9	10
Quick Close Microservices										
Outstanding Purchase Orders										
Quarter Delay Scenarios										
Closing Workflow										
Closing Dashboard										

Target		Started		Completed		Out	

Investment teams need to know the impact on features rather than just story points or development hours dropped. Most Agile development platforms can relate story points to features. An Investment feature burndown table can be created to facilitate quick decision-making at the feature level, as shown in the example of the features of the AccuWiz Quick Close Investment (Table 9.2).

The features still targeted for the release are within the capacity extrapolated to the target date. Each week, feature status is determined by projecting the capacity remaining for an Investment and then identifying features that likely won't be completed by the target date given the remaining capacity. The remaining features are ranked in order of relative ROI. In this case, the team will need to drop Features 5 and 6, which have the lowest ROI contribution as defined in Chapter 7. Delaying the Investment is another option. However, the team must be aware of the backlog Net CoD impact.

This looks like the feature tracking chart that was discussed in Chapter 3 on software estimation. The difference is that it can be derived directly from your Agile development platform by relating story points to features.

A downloadable Investment Backlog Net CoD Calculator spreadsheet that estimates Net CoD impact is available at www.construx.com/product-flow-optimization-calculators. You can enter specific Costs of Delay for your Investments and determine the cost impact of delaying any of the Investments by a specific number of weeks.

9.4 Managing Sales Requests

Product managers are often pressured by sales to add features. "If we don't have this capability, we'll lose the entire European market." Or, "I need these features to close a deal." Most CEOs are sympathetic with anything that could reduce revenue projections, so scope usually increases despite engineering's protests.

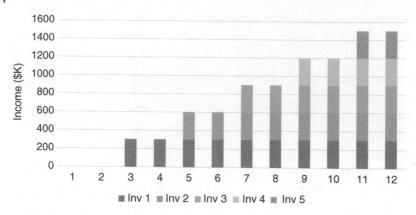

Figure 9.4 Quarterly income for five investments.

Sales requests are often justified by ROI based on development cost, ignoring Net CoD impacts. For example, committing features at a development cost of $50K to qualify for a Request for Proposal (RFP) for a sale that generates $150K of income seems obvious – an ROI of $(150 - 50)/50 = 200\%$. But these changes usually go right to the top of the backlog, so all the Investments in the backlog are delayed, increasing Net CoD.

Consider the Investment backlog of five Investments introduced in the technical debt example in Chapter 5. In this case, they could be any Investments, not just technical debt reductions. Each has a cycle time of six months and the same CoD of $100K (Figure 9.4).

The Net CoD due to the addition of feature requests can be calculated and added to the incremental development cost to determine the true cost. Assume the addition of the new features delays Investments by one month. All five Investments are generating income by the end of three years. The income shifted out of a three-year planning period for the five backlog Investments delayed by one month is $5 \times \$100K$ per month = $500K (ignoring Net Present value, NPV). The total impact of including the sales request is $50K development cost plus $500K in increased Net CoD. The ROI is really $(150 - 550)/550 = -73\%$, including the development cost of $50K.

There may be other reasons for supporting this sales request. It may be more important to get the revenue in the next quarter to meet financial commitments. Or sales could make a case for additional upgrades that can be sold to the customer to make up for the added Net CoD. In either case, product management can now see the real cost when Net CoD impacts are visible. Product management can defend their current roadmap when the CEO says, "Ken from sales told me that you're throwing away revenue by not developing a few features he wants. What's up?"

Consider a case of losing customers or a market segment. This requires what is called a defensive business case. As an example, an AccuWiz competitor in Greece has introduced an application designed specifically for the Greek market. They're a small company, but they have some traction. The international sales team is demanding more features specific to the Greek market to compete. They've told the CEO that he can forget about revenue from Greece if they don't do it. The pressure is on product management.

The first question is, "Exactly what will happen if the features aren't developed?" It's unusual to question any loss of revenue, but the Investment approach and Net CoD raise the issue. It's now a valid question from the product manager.

Product management does some research to find that they are already at 80% market penetration in Greece, and based on the projected S-curve adoption rate, they only expect a total of four new sales over the next three years with about $400K of income. Assume prioritization of the Greek features would push out the current Investment backlog by one quarter, which shifts out $1.5M from the three-year planning window. Development cost is estimated at $100K. Not a good Investment – a return of $400K at a cost of $1.6M for an ROI of $(0.4 - 1.6)/1.6 = -75\%$. This provides a convincing case that new features are not worth doing.

Continuing with our example, further research shows that customers who purchase the competitor's product are mostly interested in its customizable graphical workflow. Product management talks with engineering to see if they have any ideas on how it can cost-effectively be added to the existing application. Engineering is aware of a third-party workflow tool that can be branded as their own. It would just add $1K per sale. The development effort to integrate it and customize the UI is only about 100 hours at a development cost of $80 per hour for a total cost of $8K. It can easily be handed off to their offshore development partner with lower development costs without delaying the current Investment backlog.

Product management realizes that this capability can be sold to their current Greek customer base for $60K with a margin of 90% and can be deployed in a seamless modular upgrade without impacting customers' current operations. There are about 200 existing customers in Greece, and product management projects penetration of 80% by the end of three years, for total income of 200 customers × 80% penetration × $60K per sale × 90% margin = $8.6M.

Instead of being pushed into developing features that would cause the company to lose money, the Investment approach facilitated product management and engineering collaboration to come up with an alternative that generates $8.6M over the next three years versus losing $1.5M if they had been forced to develop the features requested by sales. Product management retains control of the roadmap.

The downloadable Net CoD spreadsheet can be used to determine the Net CoD impact for sales requests inserted in the Investment backlog.

9.5 Summary

- Investment teams share financial and schedule goals.
- Common goals foster collaboration.
- The Investment team uses rapid Agile feedback to "land" an Investment on its targets.
- Weekly or biweekly meetings should be used to expose potential changes that would put the Investment off the "glidepath."
- A list of questions is provided to eliminate or moderate proposed changes.
- Early identification of potential changes should be encouraged rather than suppressed.
- Investment teams can reduce scope, increase staff, or forecast additional income when changes impact Investment goals.
- Preventing Investment schedule slips is the team's priority because they cause a cascading Net CoD effect.
- An Investment feature burndown chart and table can project feature completions based on an Investment's planned completion date and Agile team velocity.
- The Investment feature burndown data provides Investment teams with trade-offs between feature content and Net CoD for an Investment delay.
- Sales requests often increase Net CoD that offsets potential gains. They can be countered with a Net CoD analysis.
- A downloadable spreadsheet is available at www.construx.com/product-flow-optimization-calculators to determine increases in Net CoD due to the delay of an Investment in the backlog.

10

Investment Planning Template

This chapter uses an example based on the truck fleet management system. The objective of the Investment is to reduce fleet operational costs.

A first reaction to this planning template may be that it conflicts with the Agile philosophy of less planning time to get something out there more quickly, like the philosophy of Lean Canvas. Investments constitute major expenditures in larger organizations, and it is not easy to free money for experimentation. The CFO wants to manage risk. If you are in an organization where they will fund a multimillion dollar Investment to determine if there is a market, good for you. However, most of you will need to show that your Weighted Shortest Job First (WSJF) estimate justifies priority within the backlog one-year Work in Process (WIP) limit. If you have a case where experimentation is warranted, then propose it as a strategic Investment offset by any amount of revenue that it might generate.

The backlog one-year WIP limit frees product management and engineering time to do the level of planning required to complete the template. The one-year Investment backlog WIP limit reduces wasted planning effort, and product managers aren't chasing this week's whimsical priority. Interruptions for sales requests are reduced because they must be justified based on Net Cost of Delay as well as development cost. The backlog is much more stable because it takes solid justification of a better opportunity to dislodge a planned Investment. A product manager can now leave functionality details to the product owner, allowing them to do high-value planning. The Investment template reflects exactly what product managers should be spending their valuable time on.

If you are an engineer, you may view the Investment planning template as "product management's job" and skip it. In the new world of Investment planning, engineering is involved from the start to influence the product. The information in the template provides insight for engineering into how the product is justified, which can impact functionality. A recurring theme of this book is that engineering needs to step up to understand basic financial principles that determine product success or failure.

Unlocking Agile's Missed Potential, First Edition. Robert Webber.
© 2022 The Institute of Electrical and Electronics Engineers, Inc. Published 2022 by John Wiley & Sons, Inc.

10.1 Investment Description

A name for the Investment is provided. In this case, the name is "Fleet Operational Cost Reduction." The template provides a concise description and quantification of the overall objectives. The first objective is expressed in terms of what your business expects to achieve from this Investment. It is "Increase product income by 20% within three years." The second is the value to be delivered to the customer. In this case, it is "Reduce annual fleet operational costs by 15%."

10.2 Proxy Business Case

This is likely the most valuable section for B–B companies. Put yourself in the seat of a customer evangelist that sales has managed to cultivate. At some point, the evangelist is going to have to internally justify the price.

As a CEO of a startup company developing a clinical trial management system, I found it challenging to sell into the conservative life sciences industry. I realized it was not difficult to find customer advocates for new technology. Many loved our new technology. The problem was that they couldn't sell it within their own organizations. I realized that the major focus of our sales effort should be on providing an internal advocate with the information they needed to build an internal business case, hence, the proxy business case.

It involves some time, but I would argue that one must know how the purchase decision will be made in a target market to effectively sell into an organization and to price the offering. Product managers need to know the product stakeholder values of the decision-makers and influencers because the road to financial approval goes through them. The proxy business case also provides a framework to focus marketing on what is most important to the decision-makers.

The proxy business case requires an analysis of the operational cost components of your customers. I have no experience in the trucking industry (which is probably obvious to any of you in the industry). Information was easy to find on the web. I found a report produced by the American Transportation Institute [1]. It provided the components of the marginal cost per mile in the United States from 2011 to 2019. The relative cost contributions in Table 10.1 are based on this report.

The report estimates average marginal cost per mile in the United States at $1.55. The average trucking company in this market segment incurs about $2M per year in operational costs. Information at this level of detail may not be publicly available in your industry. However, these types of reports can be purchased from industry analysts at a reasonable cost.

Table 10.1 Trucking industry marginal costs.

Component	Operational costs (%)
Fuel	40
Truck/trailer lease or purchase payments	15
Repair and maintenance	10
Truck insurance premiums	3
Permits and licenses	2
Tires	2
Tolls	2
Driver wages and benefits	26
Total	100

Table 10.2 Target annual cost reductions for new routing algorithm.

Component	Cost ($K)	Reduction (%)	Savings ($K)
Repair and maintenance	200	10	20
Truck insurance premiums	60	5	3
Tolls	40	10	4
		Total	27

The Investment team has come up with a way to reduce the cost components listed in Table 10.2 with novel routing algorithms. Stop and go traffic will be avoided where possible to reduce wear and tear on trucks. An algorithm routes trucks around high-traffic accident areas or alerts the driver to use extreme caution within areas with high accident rates. Engineering developed an algorithm to find optimal routes that account for tolls and per mile costs. Savings are based on average annual operational costs of $2M.

The Investment can reduce the operational costs for an average customer by $27K per year. This will help derive the pricing model determined as part of the Go-to-Market plan addressed in another section of the Investment planning template. How much would a customer be willing to pay to save almost $30K per year? And these savings are for an average customer. Larger customers will save more. This tells the Investment team that they may consider some form of tier-based pricing.

This example demonstrates the deeper thinking facilitated by the proxy business case. Product development has come a long way from adding features of questionable value to adding cash to the customer's bottom line. The analysis helps limit functionality because features must be justified in terms of their contributions to customer cost savings. Your evangelist is armed with the information they need to gain support for the purchase.

10.3 Product Stakeholder Analysis

Stakeholder analysis should have been completed before starting the Investment template. Hopefully, your organization has maintained a library of product stakeholders and constrainers relevant to your industry, as recommended. The template section includes only those stakeholders impacted by this Investment.

10.3.1 Customer Product Stakeholders

Table 10.3 Fleet Operational Cost Reduction Investment external product stakeholders.

Stakeholder	Values
VP operations	I want to reduce operational costs
Maintenance director	I want to reduce maintenance costs
Safety director	I want to minimize accidents to reduce our insurance premiums

10.3.2 Internal Product Stakeholders

Table 10.4 Fleet Operational Cost Reduction Investment internal product stakeholders.

Your company	Values
Sales rep	I want to perform an intriguing product demonstration that results in a next step with the customer

10.3.3 Constraints

No external constraints have been identified in this case.

10.3.4 Competition

Feature list comparisons have traditionally been used to benchmark the competition. This usually ends up with a heap of new features for engineering that "we must have, too." Huge R&D investments are often made to replicate these features without regard to value. Recall the discussion on great products. It is about a substantial increase in an important product stakeholder value, not the number of features.

Instead of a feature-by-feature comparison, we want to identify how competitors address the same stakeholder values addressed by this Investment to ensure we have a competitive or better alternative (see Table 10.5). The competitive value table will identify opportunities for significant differentiation and potential weaknesses that can be addressed by the Investment.

Table 10.5   Competitive value table.

Product stakeholder	Value	Competitor A	Competitor B
VP operations	I want to reduce operational costs	Driver utilization reporting	Does not address
Safety director	I want to minimize accidents to reduce our insurance premiums	Routing algorithm avoids high accident and high traffic areas	Alerts when driver exceeds maximum hours
Maintenance director	I want to reduce maintenance costs	Not addressed	Heavy focus on maintenance costs. Maintenance intervals based on wear and tear
Dispatcher	I want to minimize the time from when an order comes in until it is on the way	Claims that they have the most efficient dispatch algorithm	Does not address

10.4   Acceptance Criteria

An acceptance test plan is included to show how the Investment team will verify that the Investment has met its objectives. It must be an executable test plan with details on test setup, procedural steps, and data validation. In this example, it might include 10 test runs in different traffic scenarios to log brake usage, or the team may create a simulator to perform hundreds of trials based on traffic data across many different cities.

The acceptance test plan will also facilitate a deeper discussion of test functionality that may impact features and functionality. In this case, it showed that additional effort needs to be included for the simulator.

The test plan forces agreement on what "done" means for the Investment.

10.5   Go-to-Market Plan

10.5.1   Pricing Model

The proxy business case can also provide insight into pricing. In this example, the software vendor has been pricing software on a release basis with annual support and maintenance costs. The proxy business case calculated recurring financial value for the average customer of $27K per year. The Investment team decides it would be best to release this Investment as an optional modular upgrade that would create average recurring revenue of $15K per year per customer. They decided on tiered pricing levels for small, medium, and large markets of $10K, $15K, and $20K to attain the average of $15K.

10.5.2   Deployment Model

This application is hosted by the Investment team's IT department, so deployments will be internal upgrades.

10.5.3   Sales Channels

Their current sales and partner networks are capable of selling the Investment. Otherwise, this section would identify how sales channels will be developed to meet the Investment income targets.

10.6   Investment Targets

This section provides data to support the initial WSJF calculation used to determine if the Investment is within the one-year backlog WIP limit. Note that features are not expected to be broken out at this point. The Investment team will have flexibility to decide on features that contribute directly to income projections.

10.6.1 Development Cost

State the estimated development cost and the estimation model used. In this case, top-down decomposition into epics was done to arrive at an estimate of 2400 story points. The Investment team estimates 800 development hours based on a conversion rate of three story points per hour. The Investment cost target is $120K based on an average labor cost of $150 per hour.

Note that a story point to hour conversion for an entire R&D organization is not practical because each team defines its own point scale. Investments should be small enough to be developed with a single Agile team, so the story point scale is determined by a single team.

10.6.2 Cycle Time

The Investment team estimates a cycle time of two months based on a projected velocity of 300 story points per week.

10.6.3 Income Projections

Prior to getting to the Investment template stage, the Investment team would have determined the minimum sales commitment to justify a WSJF value that places it within the one-year backlog WIP limit. The downloadable Investment Income Profile Calculator was used to come up with a target based on a sales profile and target payback period. Sales is not committing to this revenue at this point. They are just saying that it appears to be realistic. The forecast is updated in Section 10.6.3.2 if it is still within the WIP limit after detailed planning, which establishes the minimum sales commitment to proceed with development.

Note that if features are added before the Investment is developed, sales would need to justify higher income to maintain the same payback period and WSJF priority.

10.6.3.1 Revenue Target

A target payback period of three years was established by the team's CFO. The team talked with sales to come up with a minimum revenue growth curve as shown in Table 10.6. The high growth rate is expected because each sale adds recurring revenue.

Table 10.6 Fleet Operational Cost Reduction Investment revenue growth profile.

Year 1	Year 2	Year 3	Year 4	Year 5
100%	150%	300%	600%	1200%

The income profile was calculated based on the estimated development cost of $120K using the downloadable Investment Income Profile Calculator spreadsheet (see Table 10.7).

Table 10.7 Fleet Operational Cost Reduction Investment income profile example.

Year 1	Year 2	Year 3	Year 4	Year 5
$22K	$33K	$65K	$131K	$262K

Note that the income from the first three years totals the development cost of $120K to achieve the three-year payback target.

At an 80% margin, the income profile required to justify the Investment is as follows (see Table 10.8):

Table 10.8 Fleet Cost Reduction Investment required revenue example.

Year 1	Year 2	Year 3	Year 4	Year 5
$27K	$41K	$82K	$164K	$327K

10.6.3.2 Number of Sales

This section estimates the minimum sales required to ensure that sales meets its revenue commitment.

Each sale adds income of $15K per year based on the recommended pricing model. There must be a minimum of 1.8 sales that start generating income at the beginning of the year to meet expected revenue. The sales will generate $27K for each year because it is recurring revenue. In general, the sales added each year must be the prior year's sales plus the difference between the years. For example, Year 2 must add $41K − $27K = $14K, which is a minimum of 0.9 sales (see Table 10.9).

Table 10.9 Minimum sales commitment.

	Year 1	Year 2	Year 3	Year 4	Year 5
Minimum sales	1.8	0.9	2.7	5.8	10.9

10.6.4 WSJF

The income difference between Years 2 and 3 is $82K – $41K = $41K. The Investment Cost of Delay based on income moved out of the three-year planning period is $41K/12 = $3.4K per month. A cycle time of two months establishes a WSJF value of 3.4/2 = 1.7, which keeps the Investment within the one-year WIP limit.

10.7 Assumption Validation

This is another gem I picked up in my career. I don't understand why it isn't used by all companies. Shouldn't you have some way of validating critical assumptions before investing millions of dollars? Investments provide a good vehicle for assumption validation.

I first heard about assumption validation when I was a director in an R&D division of Lucent Technologies, formerly the telecommunications product development and manufacturing division of AT&T. Lucent encouraged cross-division benchmarking of product development and quality practices. I visited the communication products division in Denver responsible for business phone systems. They had introduced a process where assumptions had to be "tested" before products were developed. An engineering director told me, "Engineering must do extensive testing to show that they are correct. Shouldn't product management have to do the same?" That resonated with me. Product failures can often be predicted if critical assumptions are tested.

This Lucent division had applied validation assumptions prior to investing in the development of product called "DocFon" in 1992, an interactive voice and document communications device. Among their assumptions were that the device could be sold at a price of $3000. They created a complete brochure to show to a predetermined number of customers to validate pricing. The test plan specified how the brochure would be presented to potential customers and the number of customers by region that needed to be involved.

It turned out that the price most customers were willing to pay was less than the manufacturing price of $1200. The drop-off beyond $1200 was quite severe. They wisely decided not to build the product.

One year later, HP introduced a similar product at a price of $2600. It was discontinued because sales were poor even with discounts up to $1500. Imagine the total cost of this error that could have been prevented by formally validating assumptions.

My next encounter with the concept was a great book a friend recommended to me called *Lightning in a Bottle: The Proven System to Create New Ideas and Products That Work* [2]. Here are a few quotes that resonated with me:

> Various people, including senior management, come up with ideas. Senior management lobs incoming ideas into the organization because there aren't enough good ideas coming from anywhere else.

> Ideas that flow from the top are often implemented without proper evaluation. Why? Because until now there has not been a reliable process to evaluate ideas.

The book recommended a similar approach based on testing critical assumptions.

I had my own experience with a near failure. As CEO of the clinical trial management software company, I had a "great idea" to develop "Biotech in a Box" based on Microsoft SharePoint, which was just becoming commercially successful. We would set up a biotech with all the Standard Operation Procedure (SOP) templates necessary to perform a clinical trial. It's not hard to get a lot of people to love your idea when you are CEO, and any people who question the idea are often branded as naysayers. It's not good for a career to criticize the CEO's idea in some companies.

I forced myself to put the love I had for my own idea aside to validate critical assumptions. One key assumption was customers would be willing to pay a monthly fee that would more than offset the SharePoint hosting costs. We created a test plan, including research on hosting costs and contacted a number of small biotech companies to determine how much they would be willing to pay. It turned out that the price would not cover the hosting costs. We abandoned the idea.

There is an argument that validating assumptions like this limits innovation where customers at first don't recognize the value of an idea, and if you "build it, they will come." My response is to do the analysis. Go into negative mode and encourage everyone to think of why this may not be a good idea. Validate the assumptions. Now, go ahead with what you believe is an innovative solution with an understanding of what you need to overcome. The assumption validation exercise may identify problems that you may be able to "innovate around."

Here are some assumptions that might be validated for the trucking example:

- Assumption
  - Maintenance cost reductions can justify the purchase price.
- Test
  - Obtain maintenance cost estimates from customer contacts in small (<50 trucks), medium (50–200 trucks), and large (>200 trucks) market

segments in the United States. Obtain data from at least 10 customers in each region. Average costs must be at least 80% of the estimate of $2M per year.

Note the specificity of the tests, down to the minimum sample sizes, and the regions. The objective is to not have your conclusion challenged later:

> Well, how many companies is this based on?
> What about Asia?

Yes, this is some work at the front-end planning stage, but, as we pointed out, the product manager will have more time for planning with the Investment approach. And avoiding millions of dollars from a failed product justifies the product management effort.

10.8 Summary

1. A proxy business case ensures that your product can be justified by your customers in B–B models.
2. Information for detailed planning is often available on the web. If not, studies can be purchased from industry analysts.
3. Listing stakeholder values addressed by the Investment helps focus functionality and the value contributions of features.
4. A value-based competitive analysis provides opportunities for major product differentiators for the Investment.
5. A basic Go-to-Market (GTM) can provide insight into pricing as well as other capabilities your Investment needs to include.
6. Investment income, cost, and cycle time targets are updated in the planning document to determine current position within the one-year backlog WIP limit.
7. Critical assumptions should be validated with tests to avoid product failures.

References

1 Williams, N. and Murray, D. (2020). *An Analysis of the Operational Costs of Trucking: 2020 Update*. American Transportation Institute.
2 Minter, D. and Reid, M. (2007). *Lightning in a Bottle: The Proven System to Create New Ideas and Products That Work*. SourceBooks, Inc.

11

Managing the Agile Roadmap

Why do we continue to produce multiyear roadmaps at the feature level when they're never accurate? Roadmaps are a necessary evil because customers want to see how their products will evolve. Nobody wants to get stuck with an unsupported product. Sales wants the roadmap to see what they will be selling so they can establish sales quotas. Finance wants the roadmap so they can forecast revenue, income, R&D expenses, and software capitalization for the business plan.

Traditionally, roadmaps have been published periodically at the release and feature-levels. More recently, roadmap applications that share roadmaps online have become available. In either case, roadmap changes frequently occur because of estimate changes, added work, or staffing changes. This is especially true when companies impose Waterfall planning on Agile.

Roadmap changes are not welcomed by product stakeholders who have built their plans around the roadmap. Most product and project managers avoid updating the roadmap until all hope of delivering roadmap commitments is lost. Project management still hopes the pressure of the fixed schedule and content will somehow motivate engineering to pull it off. This results in roadmap surprises for product stakeholders after it is too late to do anything.

Agile Investment roadmaps are at the Investment level instead of feature level. Timeboxing of Investments increases schedule and financial predictability. The Investment team can vary feature content and functionality as long as the Investment stays on schedule and meets the cost and income targets. Features and functionality necessary to achieve the Investment targets are within the control of the team so they don't have to commit to specific feature dates in most cases.

Of course, product stakeholders often have an interest in feature content, and in some cases, they will insist on specific features. An Agile roadmap maintains feature status in terms of "In," "Target," and "Out." As discussed in Chapter 3, specific features can be committed before development starts if there is enough feature and functionality flexibility to account for software estimation variance.

Unlocking Agile's Missed Potential, First Edition. Robert Webber.
© 2022 The Institute of Electrical and Electronics Engineers, Inc. Published 2022 by John Wiley & Sons, Inc.

An Agile roadmap relational database can provide a baseline where financial and schedule impacts can be assessed before changes are accepted. It can be used to set and maintain product stakeholder expectations.

Section 11.2.2 shows how a technology roadmap can be integrated with the Agile roadmap. Engineers are included on the Investment team to contribute solutions enabled by new technologies. Companies are always looking for new technologies that will allow them to leap ahead of their competition. This involves careful monitoring and planning of technology acquisition that must be synchronized with the Investment roadmap. The short Investment cycles of Agile development provide agility to quickly adopt new technologies with effective planning.

11.1 The Agile Roadmap Management Database

The Agile roadmap can be implemented with any relational database and presented with numerous data analytics tools available today. Tableau is used in this example. Your IT organization can probably create a simple relational database for you based on the many options available, including open-source solutions. Tableau has connectors for most popular databases, including Excel. This example will use a flat file defined in Excel, which can be created with Comma Separated Value (CSV) exports from most relational databases if a Tableau connector is unavailable.

We'll use AccuWiz as an example. AccuWiz has planned the following Investments with timeboxed start and finish dates (Table 11.1).

The relational database used by AccuWiz Investment teams relates features to Investments. Table 11.2 shows a flat-file representation.

Note that the database includes internal and external features. Microservices, for example, provide the infrastructure for software developers to access application data without requiring knowledge of the data structure. This supports layering, an architectural best practice to shield developers from complexity. The Visibility field can be used by the AccuWiz data analytics tool to filter internal data for views

Table 11.1 AccuWiz Investment backlog.

Investment	Start	Finish
Mobile Application	10/1	12/31
European Version	11/1	3/1
Audit Report Generation	2/15	6/30
Data Analytics Connectors	5/1	7/31

Table 11.2 AccuWiz Investment features.

Investment	Feature	Visibility	Status
Mobile Application	Secure Login	Internal	In
Mobile Application	Dashboard	External	In
Mobile Application	Purchase Order Approval	External	In
Mobile Application	Invoice Approval	External	Out
Mobile Application	Expense Reporting	External	Out
European Version	VAT Calculation	External	In
European Version	UK Regulatory	External	In
European Version	Germany Regulatory	External	Target
European Version	Italy Regulatory	External	Target
Audit Report Generation	Microservices	Internal	In
Audit Report Generation	Sarbanes–Oxley Report	External	In
Audit Report Generation	Accounting Exception Report	External	In
Audit Report Generation	Purchase Order Reconciliation	External	Target
Audit Report Generation	Expense Report Violation Report	External	Target
Audit Report Generation	Invoice Reconciliation	External	Target
Data Analytics Connectors	Microservices	Internal	In
Data Analytics Connectors	Basic Export Capability	Internal	In
Data Analytics Connectors	Invoice Data	External	In
Data Analytics Connectors	Purchase Order Data	External	Target
Data Analytics Connectors	Expense Report Data	External	Target

exposed to sales or customers, with the complete list limited to Investment teams and product management.

Figure 11.1 is an example of an Agile roadmap generated by Tableau from the flat file.

The status of each feature is represented by the legend in the right-hand pane. The filters change the view.

Note that the feature bars on the Gannt chart have the same lengths as the parent Investment. This representation is intended to show feature status, not the schedules of individual features. As described in Chapter 9, the Investment teams and product management have control over the Investment feature set and feature schedules.

It may be possible to represent the roadmap in a roadmap management application that you currently use with the addition of the filter fields shown. Either way,

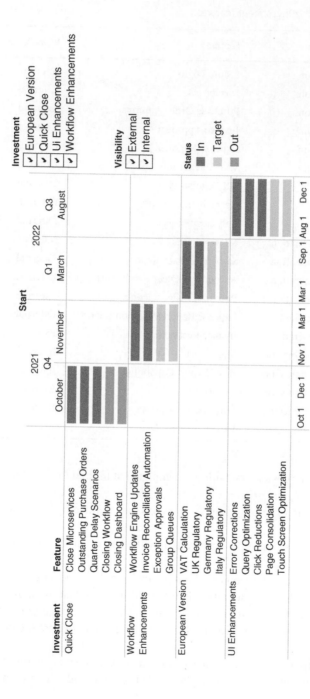

Figure 11.1 AccuWiz Tableau roadmap.

you need to provide access to a living roadmap that represents the latest development plan to maintain expectations of your roadmap stakeholders.

11.2 The Agile Technology Roadmap

Market leaders can rapidly capitalize on technologies at the point they become practical. It doesn't matter who develops the technology. The winner is the one that turns it into money and market leadership.

Apple is a good example. They bet on the availability of faster processors with reduced power consumption as well as inexpensive touch screens. They caught the technology curve at just the right time, leaving competitors in the dust. There are software examples. Lotus timed the spreadsheet with the availability of low-cost personal computers that were just being adopted in business at the time. Companies should follow new software technologies to determine when they might be integrated into Investments.

There are examples of big technological leaps in software development, such as the relational database, object-oriented development, and service-based architectures. However, there are also opportunities to leverage smaller increments of technological advancement.

Microsoft SharePoint was a key technology that enabled my clinical trial software management company to leap ahead of established competitors like Oracle Life Sciences. SharePoint was just being widely adopted in life sciences companies at the time, but its use was hampered by stringent regulatory data requirements, such as audit trails. Experimentation with SharePoint led us to a solution that synchronized SharePoint with the regulated data in our clinical trial management system to allow life sciences companies to build their own portals and integrate managed data with their Microsoft Office applications. It was all about timing. We differentiated ourselves through technology.

In many cases, hardware technologies enable new capabilities that can be delivered in software. The faster and more energy efficient processors used in iPhones is an example. Modern examples include voice recognition, higher mobile Internet speeds, and radio-frequency identification chips (RFID). A software company needs to continuously monitor both hardware and software technologies that can possibly be leveraged.

The Investment model enables organizations to quickly pivot to leverage new technologies at the right time. The challenge is the ability to implement a new technology at the right time.

11.2.1 Stages of Technology Acquisition

Based on my experience, several steps are necessary to get to the point where technology can be applied:

- Awareness
- Proof of concept
- Pilot
- Rollout

11.2.1.1 Awareness

The Agile organization should follow the progress of technologies that might be leveraged by an Investment. I saw a successful model for monitoring promising technologies in my telecommunications career. It was called the "Key Technology Program (KTP)." Many organizations depend on fundamental research groups for new technologies. However, researchers are often far removed from stakeholder value and the current internal technologies. The idea of the KTP was to involve senior developers in tracking internal and external technologies that might be applied.

Management of the program was quite simple. It consisted of a monthly meeting with the R&D VP and his directors where volunteers could present status on technologies of interest and speculate about when and how they could be applied. It was a positive experience for the presenters. Many were passionate about their technologies and loved to evangelize them.

The volunteers were called Key Technology Owners. They retained their development roles, so they maintained current product knowledge. There was no problem getting volunteers. It was a respected role that enabled engineers to move to the highest positions on our technical ladder.

11.2.1.2 Proof of Concept

Many technologies don't deliver on their promises. I learned not to trust their claims. As discussed earlier, my clinical trial management software company broke into the life sciences market with a novel solution for synchronization of regulated data with SharePoint. We had become a Microsoft managed partner, so we always looked for ways to leverage their technology. Since our customers could now access and build SharePoint portals, I had the bright idea to bundle Microsoft's InfoPath graphical form designer with our application.

Our system architect said we should do a proof of concept. Although this meant a delay, I had learned to listen to senior engineers. I found that their warnings almost always came true. The proof of concept showed that InfoPath conflicted with our workflow implementation. It would have caused major problems. We dropped the idea.

The message is not to trust the advertised capabilities of technologies. Make sure time is allowed for a proof of concept.

11.2.1.3   Pilot

This is an application of the new technology in a low-risk project. Development practices often need to be created to utilize a new technology after it passes proof of concept. For example, introduction of RFID into your product requires that a developer understand its range of capabilities and limitations. An Application Programming Interface (API) needs to be developed and tested.

11.2.1.4   Rollout

This is the rollout of the new technology for application by any developer. It involves documentation and training necessary to enable developers to utilize the technology.

11.2.2   Investment Technology Roadmaps

The rollout period must end before the start of development of the Investment in which the technology will first be deployed. In the AccuWiz scenario, a Key Technology Owner is following the latest advances in smartphones with foldable screens. Based on price drops and adoption rates, they recommended that the technology be used to provide a better interactive experience with their application, getting a jump on competition. The technology must be ready for inclusion in the Mobile Application Investment.

Figure 11.2 is a Tableau view of technology that needs to be available by the end of October.

In the spirit of Agile, this is a dynamic roadmap that can change at any time based on new information.

Figure 11.2   Technology roadmap view.

11.3   Summary

- The Agile roadmap is expected to change and should be implemented in a relational database.

- Frequent changes in Agile development increase the importance of rapid communication with roadmap stakeholders.
- A simple relational database and common data analytics tools can be used to implement the Agile roadmap.
- Net Cost of Delay can communicate financial impact of proposed roadmap changes before they are accepted.
- The short development cycles of the Investment model enable rapid infusion of new technologies.
- It's not about inventing the technology; it's about getting the timing right to adopt new technologies.
- A Key Technology Program is an effective way to transition technologies into production at the right time.
- Specific adoption stages need to be planned to align with the start of Investment development.
- Technology stages can be included in the Agile roadmap.

12

Maximizing Investment Development Productivity

I'm including this chapter because I've seen so many inefficient Agile implementations where productivity has decreased. Most of them abandoned proven software engineering quality practices because they were viewed as overhead that slows Agile development. And, "If we get it wrong, we can fix it quickly." The code created in a sprint is pretty much built and tested the same way it has been done for decades, just in shorter cycle times. Agile development should not be a step backward. Good software engineering practices can reduce cycle time and development costs.

We've shown how to get the maximum value using current engineering resources with Investment Weighted Shortest Job First (WSJF) prioritization. We now want to maximize throughput by increasing engineering productivity. Industry attempts to measure software productivity have failed. This chapter shows how "nonproductivity" can be measured. Productivity is what's left over. Nonproductivity includes testing, waste, and rework that can be measured and reduced. The traditional Cost of Quality model is updated for Agile development. This chapter shows a direct relationship between rework reduction and increased productivity.

This is followed with a way to measure software productivity in Agile. We need to be very careful here to use the measurement as a scorecard for continuous improvement and not try to compare productivity across teams. Another section shows how a minimum set of software quality metrics can be used with Agile for continuous quality improvement.

There is one other major contributor to productivity. You may have all the best practices documented in your organization, and your development organization fully trained. But what if they don't follow the practices? What level of productivity can you expect from a demotivated and frustrated development organization? How do you maximize team motivation? These questions are addressed in Chapter 13.

Unlocking Agile's Missed Potential, First Edition. Robert Webber.
© 2022 The Institute of Electrical and Electronics Engineers, Inc. Published 2022 by John Wiley & Sons, Inc.

Of course, there are many other factors that impact software productivity, such as training and tools. However, I would argue that quality and motivation have the largest impact, and both can be measured and improved. Yes, the level of motivation can be measured in your organization. Chapter 13 tells you how.

12.1 Measuring Software Productivity

For years organizations have wanted to measure software productivity. This subject came up most often in organizations where engineering consistently failed to meet schedules. Of course, they missed schedules because of being forced into Waterfall planning schedules with fixed schedule and scope. However, the rest of the organization viewed this as an engineering productivity problem.

Software productivity has been a group discussion topic at every Construx Leadership Summit I attended. Virtually all engineering leaders complained that the productivity of their engineers was often questioned by the executives. One had to go so far as to provide the executives with code check-in and check-out times by time of day to quell criticism. The executives were surprised to see that engineers were working from early morning well into the night, far harder than anyone in their departments. That stopped the snide remarks about not seeing engineers at their desks at 8:00 a.m.

Product managers usually name poor engineering productivity as their number one problem during assessments. Product management has perfect plans and only need engineering to deliver faster. I would tell them that it is not their job to question the productivity of engineering. That is a discussion between the CEO and the head of engineering. The role of product management is to determine how to produce the greatest return on finite engineering capacity.

I've asked engineering leaders what they would do if they had a perfect measure of software productivity in terms of "widgets per developer hour." Engineering leaders are usually not seeking the measure for internal use. It has been requested by the CEO or CFO because other organizations blame their failures on poor engineering productivity. In an ideal world, they would be able to use this measure to compare with industry benchmarks to show they're not as bad as everybody thinks. But nobody has found a meaningful way to measure software productivity, and measuring it as a defensive move is unlikely to change the perspective of your executives if you miss schedules.

The focus has been on "unit productivity," an attempt to measure productivity on the basis of "widgets per hour." We've all seen the meaningless measures of statements per hour. I know of one organization that even standardized story points as a measure of production. I would immediately multiply all my story points by a factor of 10! We need to accept at this point that there is no such thing as an accurate unit productivity measure in engineering. There are just too many factors that change from one software project to next. I once heard someone describe productivity as, "Statements not written."

Software unit productivity measurement would be valuable if it could be used to identify what to change to increase productivity. That's not going to happen with any software unit productivity measure. What would you do if you found that your engineers wrote fewer code statements than an industry benchmark, or if you found that one Agile team produced more story points per hour than another, assuming you could standardize on a common story point scale? Would you just ask the other teams to write code faster?

In Section 12.1.1, we'll see that while it's not possible to define a useful measure of software productivity, we can increase productivity by eliminating engineering effort that does not generate value in the end-product. We can increase productivity by reducing nonproductivity.

12.1.1 Cost of Quality (CoQ)

The concept was introduced by Armand V. Feigenbaum in a 1956 *Harvard Business Review* article [1] to determine the potential savings of process improvements. It was originally applied in manufacturing organizations to increase productivity by reducing wasted effort and material costs. It was applied within software organizations in the 1980s, including the large telecommunications company I worked for. I'll describe the model used at that time and then simplify it to make it practical for Agile development.

Our R&D budget and project cost accounting were broken into the following categories:

Appraisal

Effort and tool costs to find defects through reviews and testing

Rework

The cost to correct defects leaked from a prior development stage

Production

The R&D budget minus the costs of appraisal and rework

These categories assume that staff are creating deliverables, verifying deliverables, or correcting defects in deliverables.

People are usually surprised to find that testing is not considered as production. "Of course, we have to test to have a viable product." That is true, but what if you could produce the same level of quality with less testing? Investment in automated tests is an example. Testing effort will never be zero in software development, but it should be categorized separately as an incentive to increase testing efficiency. The separate appraisal category allows organizations to measure and reduce testing costs.

Rework is the cost to correct a deliverable after it passes to a subsequent development phase. For example, the cost to correct a coding defect during system testing would be rework. We'll address Agile rework shortly, including the issue of refactoring.

Appraisal, rework, and production total 100% of direct project software development costs. We consider appraisal and rework as non-productivity. Subtracting them from R&D project budgets shows how much effort is producing value. Reducing appraisal and rework increases productivity.

Our R&D budget had another accounting category called "prevention." This included the costs for process improvements, tools, and training to prevent defects in the deliverables (not to find them, which is covered by appraisal). For example, the labor cost to create a coding best practices document and train the developers would be a prevention cost. Our annual R&D budgets could justify an increase in the prevention budget by projecting reductions in rework. We saw rework levels drop from over 50% to just over 20% over a few years. We got there by an effective metrics program to support continuous improvement.

You're probably thinking of the project accounting method nightmare this generated. It wasn't as bad as you think because we already had detailed project accounting on an activity basis. Don't worry. I'm not going to recommend any project accounting categories for Agile development. There is a simpler approach I'll describe later.

12.1.2 Cost of Quality and Software Productivity

Before we get into Agile, let's examine the significant impact that reductions in appraisal and rework have on software productivity. Appendix D provides a derivation of an equation to determine the increase in productivity as a function of appraisal and rework reduction, assuming the ratio of appraisal to production remains the same. Further improvements are possible with improvements in appraisal efficiency, but the greatest opportunity is the reduction of rework.

The formula is

$$\frac{P_2}{P_1} = \frac{(1 - R_2)}{(1 - R_1)}$$

where P is production, and rework R is expressed as a fraction of project development costs.

Table 12.1 Productivity improvement based on rework reduction.

R_1	R_2				
	10%	20%	30%	40%	50%
20%	13%				
30%	29%	14%			
40%	50%	33%	17%		
50%	80%	60%	40%	20%	
60%	125%	100%	75%	50%	25%

Table 12.1 shows the productivity improvement gained by moving from a rework level of R_1 to R_2, assuming the same level of testing efficiency.

For example, if the current rework level R_1 is 40% and it can be reduced to 20%, the productivity improvement is 33%.

One might think that a 20% reduction in rework would provide a 20% improvement in productivity. However, there is a leverage effect. For example, if your current appraisal and rework costs are 60%, production is only 40%. Reducing rework from 50% to 30% frees up 20% of the project budget for production. Production increases from 40% to 60%, which gives a productivity improvement of 50%.

Figure 12.1 is a graphical representation of Table 12.1.

Each line shows the productivity improvement if rework can be reduced from the current level indicated in the legend. For example, the solid line is based on a current rework level of 60%.

I estimated a rework level of about 60% for a recent client using Agile development. Rework was caused by an ineffective implementation of the product owner role. Product managers were too busy to talk to product owners, and product owners had no access to customers. The product owners did not sit with the Agile teams. Requirements problems were detected during customer acceptance, causing huge levels of rework.

I believe that most Agile organizations are close to this level. I haven't seen any large product organizations that have mastered the Agile requirement process. I'm sure there are some out there, but I didn't come across them in my years of consulting. To be fair, rework levels of 60% were not uncommon in Waterfall development. The requirements process is challenging with any development framework.

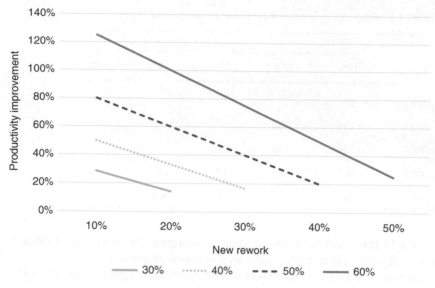

Figure 12.1 Productivity as a function of rework reduction.

12.1.3 Sources of Software Rework

Figure 12.2 has been around a long time and has been shown in many forms. I've taken this one from *Rapid Development* [2] by Steve McConnell. This is a Waterfall chart, but I will relate it to Agile development later.

Defects can be introduced in any of the four phases on the axis on the left. The horizontal axis shows the traditional Waterfall software development phases of a release where a defect can be found and corrected. For example, a design error could be caught during the design phase or in any of the following phases. Requirements errors can be detected in any of the phases on the horizontal axis. McConnell reports that the cost to correct requirements errors can be 50–200 times the cost [3] to fix it at the requirements stage.

The curve shows an exponential relationship between the phase of defect introduction and the phase of detection and repair. For example, a requirements error found during a review may be fixed in a few hours by a documentation change. The same error found in production may take hundreds of hours to fix, requiring architectural and design changes that impact software module interfaces, and even the structure of the software itself. Then there are the tests that must be rewritten and executed, plus redeployment to the field. Requirements errors are the biggest drivers of rework.

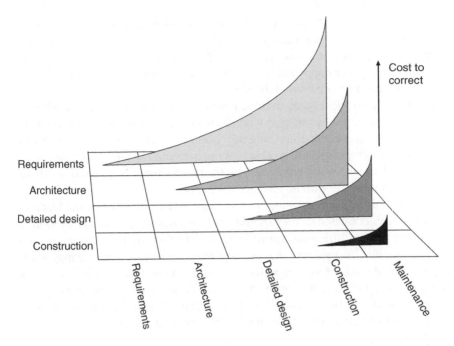

Figure 12.2 Cost of defect correction by phase of detection.

12.2 Agile Cost of Quality

Rework is a term associated with Waterfall development. Of course, Agile encourages "rework" based on feedback during development. In the Waterfall days, we created large requirements documents with UI mockups, wireframes, and screenshots and then had stakeholders sign off on them. Any changes after the approval were resisted because of the fixed schedule and content commitments. Users were told, "You signed off on it." User complaints after delivery were translated into "enhancement requests" that usually never appeared. Agile has the potential for developers to incorporate feedback during release development. I say "potential" because it often doesn't happen because of fixed schedule and content, and ineffective product owner role implementations.

Although rework in Agile is encouraged, how much is too much? What if it took six months of feedback and revision to finally get a feature to the point of acceptance? What if it took a year? How can we tell if an Agile team is inefficient, and the reason for the inefficiency? Rework is included as story points as if it were new production.

We'll use the Waterfall Cost of Quality approach that defines production as the ideal output of the development process where all documents and code could be written and approved one time. They are defect-free, so no appraisal is necessary. Of course, that never happened in Waterfall, but the model was a useful concept to continuously improve toward the ideal.

What would an ideal Agile development process look like? A knowledgeable product owner would be engaged with the team throughout the sprint to ensure that each developer knew everything they needed to build the right functionality. These ideal developers would be able to write code and release it defect free without any reviews or testing required. The user story would be marked as "done" after the sprint review with no changes necessary.

The Agile process accounts for changes necessary to incorporate the feedback from the product owner, so they should not be considered as rework. We want to encourage rework during the sprint to get it right the first time. Agile also supports refactoring, recognizing that the best way to construct software may not be apparent until after it has been written, so we don't count refactoring as rework. However, we do want to minimize changes after a story is declared "done."

Agile rework can be measured by adding a single field to the user story record in your Agile development platform with the following values:

- New functionality
- Revised functionality
- Code correction

New functionality is considered as production. It includes any rework during a sprint or refactoring. The other two categories are rework but have different root causes. Revised functionality indicates a problem in your Agile requirements process and/or an ineffective product owner implementation because stories are being approved at the sprint reviews but need to be revised later. Coding errors result from ineffective software engineering coding practices. You can define a metric called "Agile production ratio," which is the ratio of new functionality story points and total sprint story points.

You may question if revised functionality should be considered as rework if the product owner didn't have the knowledge. As in the Waterfall case, the answer is yes. The production baseline is the ideal case where the product owner has obtained the information needed to get it right. If not, the question is, "Why didn't the product owner have the knowledge?" Root cause analysis with the Five Whys can lead to improvements.

A word of warning. Do not use Cost of Quality metrics as a management tool to shame people at project review meetings to pressure them for improvements. Never show metrics at an individual level and never compare teams. Let the teams own the metrics. There's no reason for the team to share metrics with anyone unless they want to share them, and that should be for recognition. Chapter 13 explains how metrics can be used as a scorecard for team motivation. If anyone feels punished by the metrics, you will find that they are skewed, or your Agile teams will be resistant to valid changes prior to release.

12.2.1 Reducing Agile User Story Rework

The main driver of rework costs in Agile development is requirements errors. This was the case for all the Construx clients with whom I worked. Product owners were usually unavailable to teams to clarify user stories, resulting in incorrect development assumptions. Sprint demonstrations were often cursory and didn't cover all the possible cases. Product managers were used as product owners and had higher priority requests from sales, or there were product owners in engineering without market or user knowledge. If user story acceptance tests were written, they only addressed the "happy path." Product owner effectiveness must be improved to attain high productivity in Agile development. Measuring and reducing rework after "done" will put you on that path.

The relative cost to repair functionality after a user story is declared "done" is no different than the rework costs of Waterfall. Problems that escape the Agile sprint cycle into system test and beyond cause the same level of rework as we experienced in Waterfall. The difference is that Agile executes development in shorter cycles so rework feedback can be obtained more frequently.

The Agile production ratio becomes a team goal for continuous improvement. This is consistent with the Agile philosophy of using sprint retrospectives to reduce waste. Story point contributions from functionality changed after "done" should be analyzed. The team should assess causes such as the following:

- What sprint review process improvements could have detected the incorrect functionality before declaration of "done"?
  - o Additional attendees?
  - o More time?
  - o Expanded demo cases?
  - o Improved sprint retrospective meeting structure?
- What could have prevented implementation of the incorrect functionality?
  - o More product owner time with the team?
  - o Product owner colocation?
  - o Product owner with a different skill set or addition of a Subject Matter Expert (SME)?
  - o Additional product owner training?
  - o More effective communication between product owner and product manager?
  - o Improvements to product requirements elicitation process?
  - o Reduced schedule pressure?
  - o Additional cases in user story acceptance test plan?

These types of questions provide a constructive and positive environment for continuous improvement measured by reductions in Agile rework.

Steve McConnell's book, *More Effective Agile*, illustrates Agile requirements methods that can reduce Agile rework. The Investment approach helps because there are distinct roles for product managers and product owners, and the problem to solve is conveyed to engineering as opposed to detailed feature requirements.

12.2.2 Reducing Agile Defect Rework

Coding defects can also be a significant component of Agile rework costs. I've observed that software testing practices honed over decades of software development have been dropped in many Agile implementations, resulting in high defect rates. The team is focused on the near-term goal of demonstrating functionality at the end of the sprint; therefore, testing tends to be at the functionality level. Practices that were shown to be necessary to create high-quality software, like reviews, unit testing, and integration testing, have been abandoned. There is a false assumption that moving to functional testing sooner is more efficient.

Most of the organizations I worked with said they were doing reviews but really weren't. It usually meant that another developer would take a quick look at the code if they had time. I suggest you look at ways to implement effective reviews with a new understanding of the potential for productivity improvement from rework reduction. Developers often had valid complaints that the fixed schedule and content of Waterfall development caused them to skip reviews. That should not be an issue with the variable content supported by the Investment model. Application of effective software engineering practices should be a higher priority than development of new functionality.

Software organizations producing high-quality reliable software build automated unit tests that can be used for regression testing. They also mandate a minimum code coverage criterion for code, usually 70–80%. This is the only way that exception and alternate paths can be verified. Automated unit regression testing is a great way to find obscure side effects from those changes that "can't possibly impact anything else."

In many cases, engineers told their management that unit testing was no longer possible because it involved additions to legacy code that did not have existing unit tests. Obviously, creating a complete unit test regression suite for legacy code is impractical. This excuse should not be accepted. Your developers just need to be trained to design for testability. Introduce coding guidelines that limit the number of statements that can be added inline with legacy code. For example, a limit of 30 would require that the functionality be added in a new method that can be independently unit tested. Any code added in-line should be carefully reviewed.

Integration testing seems to be a lost phase in Agile development. It is usually assumed to be complete when a user story has been demonstrated successfully. This was not the original intent of integration testing. Unit testing verifies code within methods. Integration testing verifies interfaces among methods. Functional testing, which is the user story acceptance test in Agile, verifies that requirements have been met.

Integration tests were historically created from design documentation that documented the interfaces needed to be tested with drivers and stubs and break-points. All possible combinations and ranges of parameters can't be exercised at the functional-test level. Integration tests had to be developed by someone familiar with the code, hence its name "white-box testing." However, integration testing is usually not considered to be a separate testing phase in Agile.

Agile integration testing still needs to be done if you want to make a serious dent in reducing rework. Interface changes often have significant code impacts across methods. This can be challenging because separate design documentation is usually not created in Agile; however, class definitions must exist in the code.

You should be able to extract a list of new or changed class definitions for methods shared by multiple developers. Class definitions within the scope of a single developer should have been verified as part of their unit tests. Define the parameter values and combinations required to fully verify other interfaces and then check them off if they have been exercised in the user story acceptance tests. If not, either add cases to the acceptance tests or create drivers and stubs to verify them. All the interfaces must be verified.

Improving defect removal efficiency should not be viewed as overhead in Agile development. Steve McConnell, in his book *More Effective Agile*, presents a solid argument for removing defects earlier to increase software development efficiency [4].

12.2.3 Agile Cost of Quality Example

Figure 12.3 shows an example of what you would see from a team motivated to reduce rework.

The team starts out highly productive because they are not carrying significant rework from past sprints. An ineffective product owner starts to drag down production after several sprints as functional testing exposes missing or incorrect requirements. Construction defects start to rise from prior sprints. Production has fallen from 66% to 26% by the sixth sprint. Productivity has decreased by $(66 - 26)/66 = 61\%$.

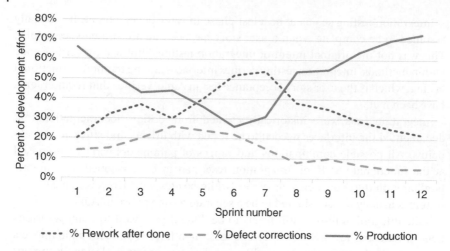

Figure 12.3 Agile production ratio metrics.

Root cause analysis is performed on the stories in the rework and defect categories to make process improvements. The detail of unit story acceptance tests is increased. The product owner now sits with the team to be 100% available. The team sets a goal of 80% for unit test code coverage. Any exceptions must be approved by the technical leader after a detailed review.

By the 12th sprint, 73% of the team's effort is going toward new production, and they are performing at a high and steady rate.

Note that this chart does not track any changes in appraisal effort per the classical Cost of Quality model. Appraisal costs require hourly project tracking, which is not likely to go over well with an Agile team. And the data accuracy would be suspect. Focus on rework after "done."

12.3   Summary

- Investment Net Cost of Delay can be minimized by improving software development productivity.
- There is no practical method to measure software unit productivity, but non-productivity can be accounted for in the form of appraisal and rework costs. Production is what remains.
- There is a direct relationship between total productivity improvement and rework levels.
- Requirements errors and missing details were the biggest drivers of rework in Waterfall development. The same effect is observed in Agile development because of ineffective product owner implementations.

- Agile "rework" is encouraged *during* sprint development. Rework is as costly as Waterfall rework after a sprint is declared "done." "Rework after Done" is a useful metric for continuous improvement to improve the product owner process and reduce software development defects.
- Agile "Rework after Done" can be measured by adding a user story field in your Agile development platform.
- Rework from construction defects can be reduced with improved reviews and testing.
- There are three distinct phases of testing, whether testers are embedded in the Agile team or external. Unit testing verifies code coverage, integration testing verifies interfaces, and functional tests verify requirements.
- Continuous improvement based on rework reduction metrics can more than double software development productivity.
- Metrics should be owned by the team and never used by management to judge performance or compare teams.

References

1 Feigenbaum, Armand V. (1956). Total quality control. *Harvard Business Review* (November–December), p. 34.

2 McConnell, S. (1996). *Rapid Development: Taming Wild Software Schedules.* Microsoft Press.

3 McConnell, S. (2001). An ounce of prevention. *IEEE Software* 18: 5–7.

4 McConnell, S. (2019). *More Effective Agile: A Roadmap for Software Leaders.* Construx Press.

13

Motivating Agile Teams

This chapter relates Agile development team motivation to established organizational behavior principles. I've included this chapter because Agile development has the potential to significantly increase motivation, but it is squandered by the persistence of Waterfall planning. Organizational behavior principles can explain why and what you need to do to establish highly motivated Agile development teams.

The chapter begins with the experience that led me to this conclusion. It reveals six principles of organizational behavior that enable you to measure and maximize motivation in your organization. It ends with a discussion of the myriad books on motivation, and why the advice usually doesn't work in your organization.

If you're an engineer like me, you are probably skeptical at this point about the application of psychology in a technical environment. I was. I took Psychology 100 as a required humanities course for engineering students. There were lots of theories, but psychology lacked what I valued in science – the ability to predict outcomes based on foundational principles. For example, I could predict the orbits of the planets with an understanding of the laws of gravity. I learned basic organizational behavior principles that help engineers understand, and even predict, how people behave in their organization. Behavior can be predicted and changed with an understanding of the consequences in your organization.

13.1 Background

You're probably wondering how an engineer like myself is qualified to talk about organizational behavior. I'll start with a true story.

It began in the large telecommunications company I worked for. I had just been promoted to director by a new VP who was appointed because of the division's recent history of quality issues and late software deliveries. To be fair, quality and reliability expectations were extremely high in telecommunications, and the quality levels were much higher than what you find with most software developed today.

I had started out as a software engineer at the start of a project developing a revolutionary digital telephone switching system using the latest technologies. This involved digital switching of encoded voice samples, the latest communications technology at the time. We also employed dozens of new Intel 8086 processors throughout the system. I know we were on the cutting edge because we couldn't get the 8 MHz parts we needed at the start of the project and had to initially test with 6 MHz parts. For comparison, today's processor clock rates exceed 2 GHz! I experienced the challenge of working with hundreds of software engineers on a massive project under tight deadlines. The time squeeze made engineers skip software engineering quality practices, only to bear the consequences later.

Soon after my promotion to director, I heard that the new VP had hired someone to focus on quality processes. She had a PhD in psychology. Of course, my first reaction as an engineer was skepticism. What does psychology have to do with software development? I was sure this was a big mistake.

I learned what the connection was. Execution of quality processes involves behaviors. A behavior is an action you can observe. For example, you can observe an engineer writing or executing test plans. You can observe someone doing a code review. Getting our culture back to one of process discipline involved behavior changes. Within three years, our organization attained national recognition for quality because engineers followed processes. The division became successful. Schedules were met. Engineers were motivated to follow processes.

The woman who opened my eyes and changed the company's culture became my wife, Susan. She has been my teacher and consultant. What I will share with you is based on learning the fundamentals of behavior and applying them successfully throughout my career.

13.2   Why You're the Only Smart One in Your Organization

This is a facetious title for explaining the mystery of organizational behavior. How often have you heard things like?

> Why doesn't my product owner realize how important it is to be available to the team so we build the right product?
>
> Or
>
> Why isn't my product manager attending sprint reviews? This is their chance to provide input.

I can give you a real example. I did an assessment for an organization that was rebuilding their platform from scratch. They wanted to make sure they obtained input from their product stakeholders, so they created cross-functional teams to participate in requirements development. Their software was used by internal operations. Operations had criticized the existing product, so this was their chance to provide their input. "If they don't provide feedback, they can't complain later." It sounded like a great plan.

The problem was that the operations people assigned to the teams weren't showing up for the meetings. I heard engineers say, "Why don't they understand that this is their opportunity to shape the product? They can finally change the things they've complained about for years."

Whenever I hear, "Why don't they understand?" or "How can they be so dumb?" I recognize it as a behavioral problem. There is a good reason for the disconnect if you understand the consequences the person anticipates for the desired behavior, and there is a systematic way to analyze consequences. The problem was solved by a PhD holder in psychology named Aubrey Daniels, a pioneer in the application of organizational behavior principles in the workplace.

Susan was smart enough to recognize that the root cause for not following quality processes was an issue of consequences. Even when engineers had time, they often skipped code reviews or unit testing because they found it laborious, and it lacked any recognition for the reviewer. She contacted Aubrey Daniels and brought in his organization to help us.

If you're uneasy at this point because behavior change sounds like some kind of mind-control or manipulation, I assure you it's not. Everyone in the organization, including the engineers, was taught the principles. It was embraced by all because the solution requires overcoming negative consequences with positive consequences. What's not to like about an organization where people feel sincerely recognized for their achievements? Manipulation is when you fool someone to do what you want.

Aubrey's organizational behavior principles provided a structured way to predict behavior. I had believed in self-motivation in professionals earlier in my career. It was just a matter of getting more self-motivated people on your staff by getting rid of the unmotivated and replacing them with the self-motivated. Of course, I soon realized that you may be able to do this for a team with a handful of people, but not a department of hundreds of engineers. When I realized that Aubrey offered an analytical model of organizational behavior, I became hooked. I realized my responsibility as a leader was to motivate the unmotivated, which comprised most of my department. These were the average engineers who came in every day, did what was asked of them, and then went home. Fewer than 20% were the superstars that did whatever it took to achieve their goals – the so-called "self-motivated."

An understanding of organizational behavior made me realize that as a leader my primary responsibility was to manage behaviors to motivate the unmotivated to achieve business results.

13.3 Consequences and Behavior

I recommend Aubrey's book, *Bringing Out the Best in People* [1], for those who want to gain a deeper understanding of organizational behavior. However, I will summarize the principles I have applied to create highly motivated teams.

Principle 1

> The probability and strength of a behavior depend upon the consequences anticipated by the individual.

Consider this example of the same requested behavior but two completely different outcomes. You ask someone on your staff to present their idea to the executive team. They give the presentation and receive different consequences. In the first case, the executives praise the idea. In the second case, they criticize – even saying, "Why are you wasting time on this when we're behind schedule?"

Two weeks later, you ask the same person to present another idea to the executives. What's going to happen? In the second case you're going to hear, "I don't have the time." In the first case with positive recognition, the engineer was already bugging you to get another opportunity to present an idea. In the first case, the individual is motivated to provide a presentation. In the second, they are not. Behaviors are not driven by what you ask people to do, they're based on perceived consequences.

Principle 2

> Anticipation of a consequence is based on how consistently, and how soon after the behavior, the consequence is experienced.

People build a history of consequences from behaviors in the past. Immediate or near-term consequences are taken more seriously, especially if they happen frequently. For example, if an engineer is thanked almost every time they move their task on a Kanban board in a standup meeting, they are more likely to volunteer for another task. Consider if that has only happened once for the last 10 task completions, or if the engineer receives recognition two weeks after they moved the card on the board.

The perceived probability of a consequence is also a factor. For example, if a manager were to continually threaten people with being fired for missing schedules and never followed through, the consequence of being fired would have little impact. However, if the manager were to say it once and others observed an empty office the next day, they would take it seriously.

I'm not recommending threatening people with being fired as a good way to manage people. I will explain later why positive consequences lead to higher performance (see section 13.3.1).

Principle 3

Either positive or negative consequences increase behavior.

A positive consequence is where an individual experiences something they want after performing a behavior. The team recognition received by the engineer for completing the task on the Kanban board is a positive consequence. A negative consequence is the case where someone performs the behavior to avoid punishment. For example, fearing being called out at the next project meeting for having late deliverables is a negative consequence.

I have worked with engineers who don't like public recognition. There are cultures where people are embarrassed by public recognition. This is an important point about positive reinforcement. Positive or negative reinforcement is based on the perspective of the individual performing the behavior, not what you would personally experience.

There is an important distinction between negative reinforcement and punishment. Punishment occurs as a result of the behavior. People can be motivated to perform a behavior to avoid punishment. Think about the carrot and the stick in the horse and cart analogy. If the stick is used, that's punishment. If the stick is made visible to the horse under the threat of punishment, that is negative reinforcement. The horse will walk (the behavior) to avoid being hit by the stick. However, they must have been hit with the stick previously, and probably several times, which was the application of punishment.

13.3.1 Performance and Organizational Culture

I have always been a positive leader trying my best to recognize people for their contributions. I observed cases where a department or project continually missed schedules. The leader was then replaced by someone known to be tough. They didn't accept excuses. People who were late on schedules were "called on the carpet" at 7 a.m. meetings. Managers were threatened with being fired if they couldn't meet schedules. Suddenly, schedules were met.

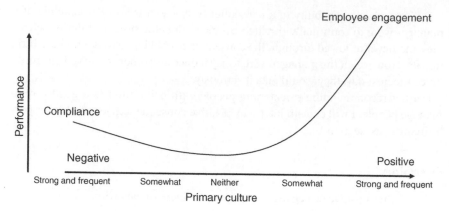

Figure 13.1 Motivation curve.

This was a mystery to me. Should I be the tough leader or the positive leader? With the new insights of organizational behavior, I was able to create the chart (Figure 13.1) to explain what was happening.

The vertical axis represents the degree to which desired results are produced by a department. Individual behaviors create the results. The horizontal axis is the extent to which individuals experience positive or negative reinforcement. We know that either positive or negative consequences drive behavior. Why use one over the other?

Aubrey had a good answer. You only get results for what you can measure with negative reinforcement. For example, project task tracking can provide the basis for punishment in project reviews. Quality metrics are another good example. How many engineers look forward to the project quality metrics review? The other consideration is that people will do the minimum to get by under negative reinforcement, and, of course, there are other side-effects like finger-pointing to avoid blame.

Positive reinforcement on the right-hand side of the chart leads to higher performance. People with a history of positive reinforcement in an organization will seek ways to obtain positive reinforcement. For example, they anticipate recognition from the team when they volunteer for an extra task on the Kanban board. They will put in extra effort to complete their user stories on time in anticipation of recognition.

A culture of positive reinforcement results in what is called today the mysterious "employee engagement." HR departments conduct annual surveys with hundreds of questions to analyze how they can increase engagement. The answer is simple – incorporate positive reinforcement in the work of the people. Think back to a job where you were totally engaged. I'll bet that you were receiving frequent and timely recognition for what you were doing.

Let's talk about the middle of the chart where there are no significant positive or negative consequences. I call this, "being nice." You can provide all the great benefits you want, and even provide the gourmet lunches and on-site dry-cleaning, but they will not create a high-performance culture. Startups have none of that, yet they have some of the highest performing engineering teams because people are getting frequent reinforcement for their contributions.

Aubrey's principles disprove the adage that "happy employees work harder." I can think of companies that have great benefits and terrific social gatherings but low performance. There is no pressure. People are happy. They do some work every day and go home at 5 p.m. They miss schedules with no consequences. It's not a high-performance culture. The relationship between happy people and performance is that we observe happy employees in high-performance organizations. They are happy because they are getting positive reinforcement from their work. It's the positive reinforcement built into their jobs that makes them happy and engaged.

People often ask me the question, "Does that mean we need to be positive all the time?" The answer is "no." There are times when negative reinforcement can be used effectively. The good thing about negative reinforcement is that it gets results quickly. People will usually respond immediately to a threat. I believe it's based on human survival instincts. However, people require a history of reinforcement to anticipate positive consequences so it takes time to become effective. You can use negative reinforcement to get a desired behavior started immediately that you can then positively reinforce. Remember this is not about being nice. It's about effectively applying consequences in your organization. However, you want to shift to the engagement side of the motivsation curve in Figure 13.1 as quickly as possible to maximize performance. Avoid the middle of the curve.

As an example, perhaps you have an Agile team continuously missing sprint goals even though you have encouraged them to adjust their velocity. You have looked at other potential factors, like sprint backlog instability caused by new work being added during the sprint. You feel the team has been trained and is capable. It looks like a motivation problem. Perhaps the engineers are frustrated by having to implement software on top of an unstructured and poorly documented software base, or they are consistently being told that they built the wrong thing in sprint reviews. Either way, you need to motivate the team.

If you have exhausted external influences, it is fine to apply negative reinforcement to make the team realize you're serious. You might have everyone make a personal commitment to you to complete their tasks to meet the next sprint, and anyone not completing their tasks can join you in a 7 a.m. meeting after the sprint to explain why they didn't.

Turn to positive reinforcement as quickly as possible. Give them recognition when they meet their first sprint, perhaps even a lunch with the team at a local restaurant. It's not about the free lunch. It's about the social recognition you provide during the lunch by showing them you value them enough to sacrifice your time. Ask them how they did it and recognize individuals for their specific contributions.

You may be thinking that the immediate effect of the negative reinforcement will result in a very conservative estimate of the stories they can complete in the next sprint in this case. This will create angst for those of you who use negative reinforcement where, "It's better to set the goal high so we get closer to what we want." In fact, you want them to initially establish a conservative goal they can meet to receive the recognition. You either believe in the motivation curve in Figure 13.1 or not. If you do, accept the fact that frequent and positive reinforcement will create the engagement to maximize performance, or be the tough leader that everyone fears. Let the team set goals they can meet.

Based on my experience, most software organizations are in the middle on the chart. Software managers find it difficult to confront people to enforce accountability, and managers have not been trained to instill positive consequences into the work of their people. The good news is that Agile enables management to establish this motivational environment. Can you think of a software development framework where engineers can work in teams and set and accomplish visible goals every two weeks? Just don't screw up Agile with Waterfall planning where engineers can't meet goals.

Principle 4

> You don't have to reinforce the desired behavior every time.

As you can read in Aubrey's book, there are reinforcement schedules to instill a behavior as a habit. The essence is that you use frequent reinforcement to increase a specific behavior, and then reduce the reinforcement schedule. It turns out that the most effective reinforcement schedule is when the individual receives reinforcement after a variable number of behaviors. Think of slot machines. People are willing to spend hours pulling the handle with no result. Social media companies like Facebook are very skilled in effectively applying reinforcement schedules, as is the video-game industry.

Principle 5

> Don't confuse reward with recognition.

Rewards have tangible value. Recognition is an expression of gratitude. Recognition is positive reinforcement. The problem with rewards is that the tangible value is often associated with the value of the work itself. Consider an example of an engineer returning from a meeting with her manager with a $10 Starbucks card in hand. "I worked the last four weekends to meet our release date and all I got is this $10 card."

However, rewards can be vehicles for recognition. Consider an example where a manager takes time over the weekend to purchase a set of golf gloves to recognize an employee for a significant accomplishment. "Ken, I really appreciate the extra effort you put in to meet the sprint goals. The team and I appreciate what you did. I know you're an avid golf player, so I stopped off and picked these up for you." In this case, it's not the value of the gloves. It's the recognition, made more significant by the manager's willingness to invest their own time to provide the gloves.

Given everything above, I highly recommend not using rewards like certificates and plaques. The fact is that you don't need them to motivate engineers, and they can backfire. For every engineer who receives a plaque, there are 10 others dissatisfied because they didn't. Not only that but who do we give the awards to? The self-motivated.

It's actually very simple to provide motivation in the engineering workplace, and it doesn't cost anything. I've found that engineers require only one of two prompts.

Show me what you built.

Or

Tell me what you know.

The first is especially powerful. Why do you think engineers work long hours eating stale pizza at a hackathon? Do you hear the buzz in the room? It's the peer reinforcement they are receiving for what they create. "That's cool. How did you think of it? Let's show the rest of the team how you did it."

There is an important point here that leads us to the motivational environment of Agile. The most powerful reinforcement is from peers, not an occasional "great job" from a manager. Agile has removed management from the details of software development so they are less likely to know what to reinforce. Developers spend most of their time with peers. This leads to our last principle.

Principle 6

The most important role of engineering leadership is to establish work environments where frequent peer recognition takes place.

One of the best ways to establish the environment of peer recognition is the Kanban board. Even if you're doing Scrum, make sure the team has a physical Kanban board they can gather around to recognize each other for progress. Don't, as I have sometimes observed, put the Kanban board online to make updates "more efficient." There will be no opportunity for social recognition.

Charts and graphs that demonstrate progress can be used as opportunities for positive reinforcement, the so-called "information radiators." A burndown chart prominently displayed can provide opportunities for reinforcement. A written comment of appreciation for meeting the last five sprint goals will go a long way. Encourage teams to display their quality metrics to show improvement.

If you find your team does not want these charts posted, it's because they associate them with negative reinforcement. "I don't want to be criticized when we don't meet our sprint goals." If that's the case, you haven't built up the anticipation of positive consequences needed to sustain high performance. Once you do, they will embrace quality charts. This happened at the telecommunications company where I learned about the power of positive reinforcement. Engineers would even recommend their own metrics and start using them within their teams. Metrics became scorecards for success, not opportunities for punishment. You'll know "you've arrived" when this happens.

I'll end this discussion with sports analogies that often come up to challenge the behavior model of motivation. People give examples of very tough football coaches who yell at their players, and rarely provide positive reinforcement. Professional sports teams recruit players with strong histories of success. They are selecting players from champions. The players have built up a history of positive reinforcement to become "intrinsically motivated" to play their sport. This is not your situation at work. You have new people struggling to learn their jobs and fit in. You have people taking on new jobs who lack confidence. You probably have over 50% of your employees in the "OK" zone who rarely receive positive reinforcement. You will only bring out the best in them with positive reinforcement. You are not selecting champions. You are growing them. That requires positive reinforcement.

13.3.2 Behavior and Software Quality

I previously told the story about how our organization's desire to increase software quality led to the behavioral approach. I'll give an example of how it increased design and code review effectiveness.

In our behavioral assessment of our quality issues, Susan identified that there were mostly negative consequences for code reviewers. The review meetings tended to be formal with very little recognition for identifying defects. Spending time on a review of someone else's work put at engineer at risk of not meeting their own deliverables, and it was time away from what engineers love to do – develop code.

Prior to understanding the importance of timing and frequency of consequences, we had encouraged engineers to do code reviews for reasons that impacted them far in the future, if at all:

- "Finding defects later in the development cycle costs more to fix."
- "It's more likely that we will meet our schedules."
- "Customers will receive a higher quality product and be happier."

Some were at a personal level, but again they were future and uncertain consequences:

- "You won't risk your vacation because you have defects that are delaying testing."
- "You won't have to work long hours and weekends to fix defects."

I'll relate my personal experience with code reviews as an engineer. As a team lead, part of my responsibility was reviewing the code of other engineers. It was even spelled out in my job description. I much preferred developing code myself. When I ran out of things I liked to do, I would finally start wading through pages and pages of code that had piled up.

I had a reputation as a great system debugger, for which I received a lot of peer recognition. As I was finally going through my pile of code to review, I would overhear someone talking about an obscure problem holding up testing on our system prototype. I would jump out of my cube and run downstairs to be a hero and get the immediate social recognition I anticipated. When my manager would ask me why I was late on code reviews, I would answer, "You don't schedule enough time for code reviews."

The solution was to establish more positive immediate consequences for reporting defects at reviews. Something as simple as counting defects provided the opportunity for positive reinforcement. A review leader could take the team out for lunch to celebrate an effective review. We established the positive environment for code reviews and effectiveness improved significantly. Good reviews became part of the culture.

In general, we found that the most effective reinforcement was based on results as opposed to specific behaviors. We let teams create weekly goals at all levels in the organization. There was lots of peer recognition when the goals were met at the end of the week. Our development model was Waterfall, but we broke it down into small goals, similar to sprints in Agile.

We noticed something interesting when teams were consistently meeting their goals. They were willing to set higher goals for themselves, and, more importantly, they would engage in grassroots process improvement to achieve the goals. They would improve software engineering practices themselves to meet the common goals. They would engage in root cause analysis to identify what limited their ability to meet their goals. Quality soared to new levels.

13.3.3 Intrinsic Motivation

I often get the response from engineering that they don't need external reinforcement. "As professionals, we're self-motivated." Let's define "intrinsic motivation" as the willingness or desire to continue to perform a behavior without extrinsic reinforcement. We see intrinsically motivated people working with extreme dedication and "engagement" to complete long-term tasks. They just get it done. What made them intrinsically motivated? Were they born that way?

I use the example of a fisherman in my discussions on motivation. Consider a fisherman who takes his entire vacation in a remote cabin by a fishing stream. The weather is terrible, but every day he skips breakfast and gets out early to stand in hip waders in the freezing stream. He flings his fly rod back and forth for hours without result. He comes back the next day and does the same. He may catch no fish during his vacation, yet he reserves the same cabin for next year.

We can consider the fisherman to be intrinsically motivated because they are willing to execute the behavior of throwing the fishing line without the desired result of catching a fish.

I then ask if anyone has taken a child fishing. Some hands go up. If you put a fishing rod in a child's hand, they will soon ask where the fish are. Shortly thereafter, the fishing rod is on the ground and they are down the beach throwing rocks. Can we agree that humans are not intrinsically motivated to fish? Something happened to the fisherman between childhood and now to make them intrinsically motivated.

The answer is that they became intrinsically motivated through a history of positive reinforcement from fishing. They have been successful enough to build up a history of positive reinforcement, and fishing has the variable reinforcement schedule of slot machines. Do you think they would have become intrinsically motivated if they had never caught a fish?

The secret of self-motivation can be explained by dopamine in our brains. Dopamine is a type of neurotransmitter that acts in association with the brain's reward system that produces pleasure. Dopamine creates pleasure that makes an individual want to repeat a behavior. In fact, you can explain "getting something you want" in our definition of positive reinforcement as the effect of dopamine on your brain.

The most startling fact is that when you have a history of positive reinforcement for a behavior, your brain will create dopamine whether the reinforcement is experienced or not. The behavior itself will increase dopamine. Interestingly, dopamine is even created when a pencil is held in the mouth when the brain recognizes it as a smile [2]. People who smile usually receive smiles in return, which makes them feel good. The act of smiling itself produces dopamine. Of course, if the person never received a smile in return, they would stop smiling, but that interval will depend on the extent to which the behavior has been reinforced in the past.

In our behavioral approach to software quality, we found there were engineers who were recognized as outstanding code reviewers. They would take the time to study the code and identify many defects at the review meeting, as opposed to others who would glance at the code 15 minutes before the meeting. It appeared these great reviewers did not need extrinsic reinforcement. These "self-motivated" engineers had received recognition for their talents over time. They had a history of positive reinforcement for finding defects in reviews.

13.4 Agile and Motivation

Agile can provide the frequent positive peer reinforcement needed to maximize performance. The founders of Agile innately understood the motivational power of a team frequently setting and meeting goals. They become winners. The founders were familiar with the demotivational aspects of Waterfall development. In the Waterfall days, engineers were given assignments and may work alone for weeks to finish a piece of functionality. Many times engineers felt they were "cogs in the wheel." There was no immediate reinforcement. In fact, they were called out at project meetings when their deliverables were late!

Amazingly, software management can establish highly motivated Agile teams with advice expressed in one sentence – "don't screw it up!" I have seen many cases where Agile teams almost never meet their sprint "commitments." The word "commitment" itself infers negative reinforcement. Teams are pushed to add stories to the sprint to meet feature and schedule commitments, and then chastised when they don't. Work is added during the sprint with no relief for "committed" functionality. These Agile teams feel like losers.

I've seen cases where an Agile transition has occurred without redefining the role of project managers. What do project managers do? They continue to perform the tasks that they were reinforced for in the past, which has little value in Agile. I've seen project managers tracking story completions! It's not the fault of the project manager. They weren't taught the valuable role they can play in Agile development by proactively managing external dependencies and performing risk management, becoming an asset for the team.

Sprint reviews can often be a punishing experience for engineers. I've seen cases where product managers do nothing but criticize a demonstration without a hint of recognition. Often, the product managers have provided little or no direction to the team or product owner during development but take the opportunity now to tell them how they got it all wrong. It's sometimes an opportunity for an arrogant product manager to show how much smarter they are than the engineers on the team.

Much of what I see in Agile is based on attempts to perpetuate the negative reinforcement used to drive most software projects. "Stretch them so we get most of what we want." These organizations have observed that setting lower goals allows engineers to "slack off," and, of course, that's true. You are using negative reinforcement, and if you let down on the negative consequences without a complete movement to the positive reinforcement side of the motivation curve in Figure 13.1, performance will indeed decline. It's a self-fulfilling prophecy.

Principle 6 stated, "The most important role of engineering leadership is to establish work environments where frequent peer recognition takes place." If you don't see the excitement and engagement in your Agile teams, you have failed. It's not the fault of the people. You have not set them up for success.

Strong and effective leaders establish umbrellas around their teams where positive reinforcement takes place. The leader needs to deal with all the politics and shield them from others who persist in using negative reinforcement. Your teams should be able to set sprint goals they can achieve at least 90% of the time. Encourage them to forecast fewer story points in their sprints until they obtain a rhythm of success. Once they do, performance will increase well above anything you might have attained through negative reinforcement.

Let's use the motivation model to consider the current trend of working from home. Most of the studies I've seen try to make a case that working from home is as effective as working in the office, or perhaps more so. The problem is that most companies have not established an environment of frequent peer reinforcement so working remotely doesn't make much difference. However, these organizations are missing the opportunity to create high-performance teams.

I don't believe working remotely can be as effective in terms of Agile team motivation because it diminishes spontaneous peer reinforcement, and there is the loss of spontaneous collaboration to be considered. What can you do if you have no choice, as in the case where working remotely has become company policy? Standup meetings can still be interactive over video, but the positive reinforcement and information exchange from daily collaboration are missing.

It may help to establish core hours where people are expected to be accessible for spontaneous video meetings, say three or four hours in the day. Also, ensure that engineers can move from messaging to a video meeting with one click. Schedule a group meeting during the week where engineers can volunteer technical challenges they are encountering. This invokes the "tell me what you know" positive reinforcer that is so powerful for engineers. At the same meetings, ask engineers to volunteer what they've learned that week that may be useful to their teammates. Create an environment of active discussion where peer reinforcement can take place.

Investments establish good discussion topics for peer reinforcement. Have an Investment team present where they currently are in terms of translating stakeholder value into a software solution. Have the team go through the user scenarios they've come up with and let people volunteer improvements. Ask for suggestions on how technology could be applied in a solution.

Just remember that the purpose of these meetings is motivation. If done right, the meetings will not be viewed as just another one of those time-wasting administrative meetings that engineers are forced to attend. If people aren't showing up for the meeting, you know you have not created the right environment and/or you are not holding these sessions frequently enough to make a difference in their weekly consequences. If you are still using schedules as negative reinforcement, don't bother adding these meetings. The negative consequences will outweigh any positive consequences you are able to provide at the meeting.

13.5 Measuring Motivation

I use a survey as part of an organizational assessment to benchmark motivation. I always like to get a read on the organization's level of motivation because nothing will really change without motivation to do so. The motivation curve in Figure 13.1 can be used as the basis for a simple survey question to find the position of your organization on the chart. It's based on the single question below:

Choose the word that best describes how you feel about your work:

1. Pressured
2. Frustrated
3. OK
4. Motivated
5. Excited

People who choose "pressured" are experiencing negative reinforcement. They are doing their work to avoid punishment, like being put on the spot in a project review for a late task. "Frustrated" means that the individual is trying to get work done but experiencing obstacles. This also usually indicates negative reinforcement. Under positive reinforcement, people will take obstacles in stride and overcome them rather than use them as excuses. We want people to at least indicate they are motivated, and excited is even better. These are people who can't wait to get to work to accomplish something.

"OK" is not OK. These are people "in the valley" of the motivation curve in Figure 13.1 who lack effective negative or positive consequences in their daily work. They do what they're told but nothing above the minimum. With one exception, the motivation index has been below 50% in all the companies I surveyed. The exception was an employee-owned company in the corporate tax software business where everybody focused on putting out a new release each year with the tax year changes. I don't believe the high motivation was due to the financial benefits of employee ownership. A dividend check once a year is not a near-term, frequent consequence. Performance was high because peer reinforcement was generated by aligned goals in the organization supported by an enlightened management team that provided positive reinforcement throughout the year.

Unless you have consciously decided to use negative reinforcement as your main motivation tool, you want to avoid the performance curve valley (Figure 13.1) and maximize the scores in the "Motivated" and "Excited" categories. This is arguably the most important Key Performance Index (KPI) for the effectiveness of the leadership team, and the productivity of your organization.

Viewing survey results separately for management and individual contributors has given some interesting insight into the ineffectiveness of negative reinforcement in software development organizations. There is typically little pressure on the engineering staff. All the pressure is on the management, especially first-level management. The management is working under negative reinforcement to avoid missing delivery schedules while new work is piled on. The negative consequences for job performance are not passed down to individual contributors because engineering managers don't like to apply negative reinforcement to their staffs, especially these days when companies are trying to recruit and maintain engineering talent.

Figure 13.2 is an example of two surveys for a large medical device company taken five months apart.

I helped this organization make a transition to Agile development. The management contacted me with a concern that they had "reached a plateau"

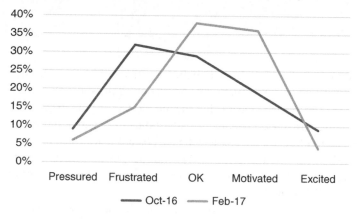

Figure 13.2 Motivation survey example.

and weren't improving. Investigation showed that the management was still applying schedule pressure to the teams, from the top down. I had stressed to the executive team that they were moving to self-directed teams that needed to be motivated through positive reinforcement. They all nodded, but changing from negative to positive reinforcement is a challenge because it has worked for most executives.

It's very difficult to convince leaders to replace negative reinforcement with positive reinforcement. Anyone who has successfully applied negative reinforcement to get results is certain that it gets results – because it does. These leaders get what they want when they apply negative reinforcement, so it is positive reinforcement for them. As you would expect, it increases the behavior of applying negative reinforcement. A history of effectively using negative reinforcement instills the behavior. The higher up you go in organizations, the more likely that negative reinforcement is applied. A good leader can work under negative reinforcement while creating the positive reinforcement environment for their staff.

I found product management was dictating sprint content in this company, often making changes during the sprint. Teams almost never met sprint objectives. Standup meetings had become status meetings where a manager would go around the room asking each person what they had accomplished. Project managers applied pressure for task completions. The inherent motivational environment of Agile was destroyed.

I went through a round of training for the management and coached managers on how to support the team instead of trying to control them. The result was an increase in the motivation KPI (percent motivated or excited) by about 40% over six months. The client was extremely happy with the improvement in the motivated category and said they could see visible improvement in employee engagement.

A word of advice if you are going to use this survey. Don't set up focus groups to ask people why they don't feel motivated. Answers will be all over the board, like poor benefits, low salaries, and possibly because you don't provide gourmet lunches on-site. People will not really understand what makes them motivated in terms of organizational behavior principles expressed in this book. Look at why they are missing frequent reinforcement. Do they have frequent short-term goals they can meet so they can receive recognition?

13.6 Motivation Advice?

I'll end this chapter with treatise on motivation books. I've found that any motivation advice in motivation books can be explained in terms of consequences. The behavior model explains why sometimes it works, and sometimes it doesn't.

Do a web search on "secrets of motivation" to see page after page of advice. My question is, "If all the secrets have been revealed, why are there so few organizations with highly motivated teams?" The problem with most of the motivation books I've read is that they are based on anecdotal evidence. "I observed this at company X, and therefore you should do the same." Some examples:

"Engineers who receive more training are more likely to be motivated."
"Opportunities for growth increase motivation."
"Flexible work hours increase motivation."
"Empowerment increases motivation."

You can now recognize that the above do not generate the frequent consequences required to increase motivation. They may increase retention, but they are not primary drivers of motivation.

Daniel Pink is brought up during most of my talks on motivation. I'm not going to contradict Pink, because I believe his "autonomy, mastery, and purpose [3]" can be observed in many organizations where people are motivated. "Autonomy" refers to the human desire to lead a life of one's own. "Mastery" is the desire to improve something that matters, and "Purpose" is the desire to serve something greater that oneself.

Pink refers to scientific studies that demonstrated rewards do not necessarily increase motivation and may even decrease motivation. I have no disagreement with these conclusions. The pitfalls of using rewards for motivation were discussed earlier in this chapter. Remember Principle 5, "Don't confuse reward and recognition." The problem is that Pink does not distinguish between rewards and recognition.

It is the frequent peer recognition in Agile that motivates the team, not an altruistic sense of purpose. Take two theoretical Agile teams and imagine there is no frequent peer recognition on one. Replace recognition in that team with dramatic statements of the higher purpose, like "Customers will benefit from your software." Or, "Shareholders will be richer as a result of your work." Do you really think that both teams would be motivated to the same extent? It would result in the stale work environments where negative consequences are necessary for motivation, as opposed to the high level of engagement possible with Agile development.

I believe Pink's theory of motivation has been embraced by professionals because it makes them feel good about themselves. They are the self-motivated people who can apply themselves to any goal they want to accomplish. They believe they are above requiring the extrinsic reinforcement needed by nonprofessionals. Those who have become intrinsically motivated through a history of positive reinforcement will believe that everyone should be just like them, but as we discussed earlier, the objective is to motivate the unmotivated in your organization.

I'm not going to say that Pink is wrong. He's not. It's just that his definition is not useful as management advice. Autonomy certainly helps as we see in the self-directed teams of Agile development, and I agree that there is a high degree of mastery in many software developers. But these won't make much difference unless the frequent positive consequences exist.

Let's examine "purpose." The *Merriam-Webster dictionary* defines it as follows:

Something set up as an object or end to be attained.

Pink presents a cyclical argument. Having purpose means that someone is already motivated to attain something. The question is, "How do you create the motivation to achieve the purpose, especially when the desired result is far in the future?"

Consider my code review example. I certainly understood the purpose of code reviews, and even evangelized the purposes to other engineers in my team. I had autonomy to schedule my time to review the code. I had mastery. Yet, the opportunity to receive immediate recognition for system debugging overrode everything. All the touted benefits of code reviews were in the future. Everyone understood the purpose, but behavior was driven by near-term consequences.

I am not going to argue that there aren't people who embrace a higher purpose beyond personal benefit and who make personal sacrifices. People of strong faith are examples. But you don't have many of the people working for you who are going to develop software with the conviction of the faithful. The problem is that most software developers are unlikely to commit their lives to increase corporate profits. They must receive frequent positive reinforcement from their work.

The takeaway is that even though you may empower a group with mastery and a purpose, motivation may not happen. I've observed Agile teams where all three exist, yet they are demotivated. The importance to the company for meeting the release schedule has been fully communicated. They have been trained and have mastered the skills necessary to do Agile development. They have autonomy because they are given a backlog and empowered to divide the work among the team in any way they choose. However, there is no recognition from peers or anyone else because they never meet their sprint goals. They are still unmotivated.

Go ahead and read management books on motivation but use the organizational behavior model to understand cause and effect. Advice based on anecdotal evidence is unlikely to work in your organization unless the same behaviors are reinforced in your organization. Motivation is generated by a system of consequences in one company that may not exist in yours. Using anectodal evidence is like putting wood together and expecting a fire to break out.

Finally, a true story about creating motivation. I was leading a project to develop a new smart antenna system that reduced cellular interference. It was a small team of about 15 engineers with development skills that spanned software, digital hardware, and RF hardware. The team was highly motivated and collaborative because there were frequent points of integration where functionality could be demonstrated. I maintained an environment of positive reinforcement, which included team celebrations when milestones were achieved.

The project included specialized signal processing software that used a Digital Signal Processor (DSP). Completion of the software presented a critical path for the project. There was only one engineer who had the specialized skills. He told me he needed to take a few days off because his family was about to move into a new home that needed to be painted before the furniture could be moved in. There was no way I could deny him the time as he had already gone above and beyond to get us to where we were.

The team volunteered to paint his house over the weekend, so the DSP engineer didn't have to take time off work! The team, myself included, spent the weekend painting the interior of the house. That is the type of engagement that stems from positive reinforcement and supportive management, especially considering that these engineers were already voluntarily working long hours to meet their project goals.

Of course, this is much easier to do with a small team focused on a new project. Enabling leaders to create motivation within larger established organizations is the objective of this book. Common goals are clearly defined for Investment teams that will thrive in an environment of frequent positive reinforcement, and Investments allow you to leverage the inherent motivational environment of Agile by letting teams set and meet their own goals.

13.7 Summary

1. Motivation is the desire to perform a *behavior* to obtain a result. Therefore, organizational behavior principles can explain motivation.
2. Anticipated consequences drive behavior – not what you ask people to do.
3. Consequences during or immediately following the behavior consistently applied increase anticipation of the consequences, hence behavior.
4. Negative or positive reinforcement will increase behavior. Behaviors will occur to avoid punishment or to receive desirable consequences.
5. A culture of negative reinforcement is limiting because people will do just enough to avoid the punishment.
6. A culture of positive reinforcement creates "employee engagement."

7. Avoid the lowest performance state with neither positive nor negative consequences.

8. Frequent and immediate positive consequences must be built into the daily work to reach high-performance levels. Agile provides such a vehicle if implemented as envisioned.

9. Waterfall planning with fixed schedules and content reduces opportunities for positive reinforcement.

10. The Investment model supports the variable content necessary for teams to continually set and meet goals.

11. Investments create common goals for product management and engineering that promote peer reinforcement.

12. Effective engineering leaders and product managers establish umbrellas of positive reinforcement around their Agile teams.

13. Look more deeply into common motivation advice given the insights of the behavior model of innovation. Advice based on anecdotal evidence will likely not translate to your organization.

14. Working from home will likely limit motivation in your organization because it reduces opportunities for frequent positive reinforcement. Video calls can be scheduled where peer recognition will take place.

References

1 Daniels, A.C. (2000). *Bringing Out the Best in People: How to Apply the Astonishing Power of Positive Reinforcement*. McGraw-Hill Education.

2 Kleiman, K. (2012). *Try Some Smile Therapy*. Psychology Today.

3 Pink, D. (1995). *Drive: The Surprising Truth About What Motivates Us*. Penguin Group (USA) Inc.

14

Innovating with Investments

This chapter builds on two pillars of this book: The Investment model and the behavioral model of motivation. Investment stakeholder values focus innovation by providing engineers with the problem to solve instead of telling them what to build. However, innovation is scarce in most organizations even if the problems are identified. We'll show how the behavior model provides insight into why so few organizations are innovative, and how you can measure and increase motivation.

Let's begin with a vision of an innovative organization. You can think about whether this scenario would likely happen in your company. The chapter will then reveal what it takes to create a culture of innovation.

Ken loves to go to work each day. He woke up at 3 a.m. with a great idea about how to significantly increase the stakeholder value on which the team has been focusing – enabling their product stakeholders to set up their system in hours instead of days. He learned about the opportunity from a discussion with their product manager where this challenge was presented. He's been thinking about it for days.

Ken thinks it will be a major differentiator for the company. He gets his team together the next day to build on the idea. They love it and enthusiastically contribute improvements. They do a critical review the next day and make some tweaks to make it practical. It goes on the team's innovation Kanban board.

The team suggests that Ken put a demonstration together for the next weekly team "Innovation Fest." Ken's manager, Sharon, suggests they add some "innovation story points" to their next sprint to give Ken and the team time to create the demonstration. He presents at the Innovation Fest and receives a lot of great ideas for improvement, as well as recognition for his creative solution. The VP of his department told Ken how valuable the idea is to the company.

Unlocking Agile's Missed Potential, First Edition. Robert Webber.
© 2022 The Institute of Electrical and Electronics Engineers, Inc. Published 2022 by John Wiley & Sons, Inc.

Sharon tells Ken that she is going to elevate it directly to her VP-level Kanban board and ask one of her directors to sponsor it. Sharon is also going to ask the product management department head if he can provide a product manager to work with Ken to help shape the idea into an Investment.

My guess is that this scenario is not likely to occur in your organization, unless you are one of the few companies that really does prioritize innovation, like 3M or Apple. For many of you, your engineers are under schedule pressure, so innovation is a rare topic.

This book has shown you how to define Investments that increase one or more stakeholder values that focus engineering on innovation. The Investment timebox approach with variable content can reduce schedule pressure that overrides innovation. However, the Investment model alone will not increase innovation. You can implement all the Investment practices to focus innovation without seeing any.

In addition to implementing the Investment model, organizations need to somehow create the nebulous "culture of innovation" in which ideas flourish and individuals translate their ideas into software that creates business value. This chapter builds on our organizational behavior model to provide the answer by addressing the question, "What motivates an individual to propose an idea at work and be willing to spend extra time to develop it into something useful for the organization?" The chapter will make a strong case that frequent positive reinforcement must exist for *behaviors that lead to innovation*. For example, volunteering an idea is a behavior. Creating a demonstration is a behavior.

Appendix E includes a survey based on an organizational behavior model of innovation. You'll be surprised at how a handful of questions can predict whether you are, or will ever be, an innovative organization.

This chapter ends with practical methods to create a "culture of innovation" in your organization.

14.1 Innovation – A Working Definition

Innovation is often discussed in the context of new products that revolutionize an industry, like the iPhone. Taking risk is a major topic because these big innovations require major Investments. The ideas and practices in this chapter can lead to revolutionary innovation, but most software organizations are just looking for ways to differentiate themselves from their competition with incremental innovation. Most companies today want to be the first to leverage leading-edge technologies, which come from the engineering side.

There are other forms of innovation from which companies benefit. Process innovation is an example. Someone comes up with an innovative process or tool that reduces code defects by 30%, or a junior engineer figures out how to save 5000 lines of code by using an existing class library. These are innovations.

I usually start my talks on innovation by asking the group to volunteer their definitions of innovation. Responses vary:

- A good idea
- Something useful
- A new product

Innovation definitions abound:

> *The introduction of something new.*
>
> *Merriam-Webster Dictionary*

> *A product, process or service new to the firm, not only new to the world or marketplace.*
>
> M. Hobday

> *The sequence of activities by which a new element is introduced into a social unit, with the intention of benefiting the unit, some part of it, or the wider society. The element need not be entirely novel or unfamiliar to members of the unit, but it must involve some discernable change or challenge to the status quo.*
>
> N. King

No wonder we find innovation such an abstract concept. We don't even have a uniform definition of what it is. Recall that great products were recognized for substantially increasing or adding value for a product stakeholder. Great products often spring from innovation where stakeholder value can be "moved by a mile."

I use this definition for innovation:

> Innovation is a non-obvious improvement provided by a product, process or solution that results in a notable increase in product stakeholder value.

We learned how to determine stakeholder value in Chapter 6, and we found that stakeholder value can be measured on a scale.

There is a legal definition for "non-obvious" used for US patents.

> A patent for a claimed invention may not be obtained, notwithstanding that the claimed invention is not identically disclosed as set forth in section 102, if the difference between the claimed invention and the prior art are such that the claimed invention as a whole would have been obvious before the effective filing date of the claimed invention to a person having ordinary skill in the art to which the claimed invention pertains. Patentability shall not be negated by the manner in which the invention was made.[1]

---

1 35 U.S. Code §103 – Conditions for patentability; nonobvious subject matter.

We certainly don't want to resort to legal arguments to define innovation, but the U.S. Supreme Court recognizes that is possible to determine non-obviousness. I prefer the "slap-test." Do you slap yourself on the forehead when you first see the innovation? We certainly recognize innovation when we see it.

Now that we know how to define it, how do you make it happen in your organization? It turns out that it's not that easy. It requires innovation processes and a top-down culture change. You can't get there by just putting up innovation posters and having an annual innovation awards dinner.

14.2 Investments as an Innovation Vehicle

An article from *USA Today* reports the results of research by Accenture [1]:

> Specifically, many employees think they have a good idea, but their managers won't listen to them. In their defense, managers say these ideas often are out in left field with no real focus or value to the company.

> But Accenture research also finds that corporate leaders find it difficult to channel the entrepreneurial enthusiasm to the right areas with 85% reporting that employee ideas are mostly aimed at internal improvements rather than external ones.

> Some of the problem is because managers may pose, "What do you think?" queries to workers without clearly defining what the problem is and what they're seeking in terms of innovative ideas, he says. If managers put up "guardrails" clearly defining their needs, workers would understand the limits and provide better solutions.

This agrees with my experience. Engineers are "kept in the dark" by building small pieces of functionality with prescriptive requirements. They can't see the big picture. I've seen cases where engineers who thought they had an innovative idea were ridiculed by the business side because the idea showed a naïve perspective of the market and customers. Some product managers designated as "the voice of the customer" jealously guard their special knowledge.

The Investment model defines a problem to solve for engineers. How can the software create product stakeholder value? Where are the opportunities for innovation where we can "knock a product stakeholder value out of the park?" Give a group of engineers a problem, and they will pour their energies into a solution. That's what they love to do, and what they were trained to do. They were reinforced for solving complicated problems every day in their engineering college curricula.

I know companies that try to increase innovation by teaching engineers problem-solving skills. There's nothing wrong with learning good problem-solving skills. They can be useful, but it's not the answer. Engineers know how to solve problems. It would be more effective to educate them on what their product stakeholders value.

After you have completed stakeholder value analysis, form a small innovation team comprising creative engineers and product managers. Ask them to identify values from key product stakeholders that provide opportunity for innovation – an "out-of-box" solution that will create a quantum leap in value. Consider having them go off-site for a day or two with a facilitator skilled in brainstorming techniques like story boards. Let them run wild with the possibilities of new technologies. Their output can be a set of user scenarios that innovatively integrate new technologies. An Investment can then be defined to establish specific goals.

There is also a "simmer approach." Create an internal innovation website open to anyone in the organization. Create discussion topics around stakeholder value. Anyone can contribute ideas and user scenarios to deliver significant stakeholder value. Someone will need to moderate the discussions and select those worthy of further review.

We still need the "culture of innovation" to create the motivation to contribute ideas. Adding comments or user scenarios to the website are behaviors. Discussion groups do have some level of positive reinforcement built in. Have you ever wondered why people contribute to discussion topics? They anticipate recognition for how smart they are. Innovation discussion groups leverage the strong engineering antecedent, "Tell me what you know."

An intermediate approach is hosting periodic brainstorming sessions around a particular stakeholder or value. This could be hosted by an engineering leader, or a product manager. What a great way to demonstrate that your organization is serious about innovation!

Investments have the potential to increase innovation because they focus creativity on product stakeholder value. However, you can do all the above and find that there is little or no innovation. What is different about innovative organizations, and why is innovation advice not likely to work in your organization? For that, we need to turn to the behavior model of innovation.

14.3 Why Your Organization Can't Innovate

Source: DILBERT, 2011 Scott Adams, Inc. Used by permission of ANDREWS MCMEEL SYNDICATION.

I'll start with the same argument that was used to introduce the motivation topic. Do a web search on "secrets of innovation." Again, pages and pages of "secrets" come up. If the secrets are out, why are so few companies innovative?

One clue is found by asking executives how often innovation is discussed in their weekly staff meetings. The answer is usually, "Not much." What do they talk about? Problems and issues, like how to recover from a potentially late delivery or budget cuts.

My next question is, "Why would anyone in your organization think that innovation is important if you never talk about it?" I then ask executives what they actually do to support innovation. Typical answers are the following:

- We have posters on the wall that say that innovation is important.
- We have a great annual awards banquet where we honor the "Innovator of the Year."
- We provide a $500 patent award.
- We have a suggestion box.
- We hand out little light bulb figures to put on people's desks to remind them of how important innovation is at our company.
- We encourage employees to spend 20% of their time on innovation like Google.
- We have objectives on performance reviews to submit at least one innovative idea each year (yes, I've seen that).

I then ask them if they consider themselves to be an innovative organization. The answer is "not really." In fact, only a few large corporations are known for innovation. They are the 3Ms and the Apples of the world.

We'll see that organizations with strong cultures of innovation have been able to establish frequent positive reinforcement for the behaviors that lead to innovation. Innovation is a result of a series of behaviors that we can define, and innovative organizations have been able to reduce negative reinforcement that overrides any positive consequences for innovation. Innovation is a flickering flame that needs to be fanned with positive reinforcement, or it will die out.

Yes, we do see the "intrinsically motivated" innovators in our organization and should consider ourselves blessed to have them. The same question we asked of motivation applies, "What makes someone intrinsically motivated to pursue an innovation over a long period of time without positive reinforcement?" I preclude negative reinforcement because I don't think there are many examples of innovation under threat (we'll talk about Steve Jobs later). Innovation is a discretionary gift provided in anticipation of positive reinforcement.

I have studied the background of many famous inventors. I find they built up a history of positive reinforcement during childhood. There appears to be a common personality characteristic of extreme curiosity, but something happened to them along the way to make them pursue an invention, often with blood, sweat, and tears and many failures along the way. I typically see that they received positive reinforcement for behaviors that led to innovation when they were young.

Henry Ford is a good example. His parents let him put a workbench in their living room where he could tinker with and repair watches [2]. Can you imagine the recognition he would receive from his parents when he showed them a watch he had fixed, or something interesting he had discovered about watches? He received frequent positive reinforcement that resulted in intrinsic motivation to innovate with mechanical devices.

The conclusion is that organizations need to establish frequent positive reinforcement for behaviors that lead to innovation. Reinforcement that occurs only for the result of innovation is too far in the future to have any significant effect on day-to-day behaviors for most people. If you can increase these behaviors, innovation will happen in your organization. The first step is to identify behaviors that lead to innovation.

14.4 An Organizational Behavior Model of Innovation

I have observed that the following steps in Figure 14.1 are necessary to move innovation to the point where it gains support in an organization.

An individual needs to be aware of opportunities for innovation that will produce value to stakeholders and the company. The stakeholder value analysis discussed in Chapter 6 can provide the focus. An innovator in your organization needs to learn about what stakeholders value, as well as up and coming

Figure 14.1 The three steps of innovation.

technologies that could be leveraged. If the information is out there but nobody takes the time and effort to learn it, nothing will happen.

Ideas for solutions need to be generated. We want to gather the ideas of multiple people. Linus Pauling, the Nobel Prize–winning chemist, is noted for his statement, "The best way to have a good idea is to have a lot of ideas and throw the bad ones away." Volunteering an idea is a behavior. Encouraging and building on ideas are behaviors. And we want the ideas focused on product stakeholder value.

Nothing happens if we stop there. The idea must become a proposal to gain support. Creating and giving a demonstration are behaviors. For example, preparing a presentation for management to gain support is a behavior. It may start with a presentation to one's own manager.

As with motivation, there must be a system of positive consequences established for these innovation behaviors. A few "great ideas" tossed around or a patent award will not work. Certainly, a response of, "That's great, but we have a schedule to meet" is going to extinguish innovation behaviors. In fact, schedule pressure in engineering is the biggest factor in a company's inability to innovate. I have yet to see spontaneous innovation from an engineering group that is constantly under negative reinforcement for production.

It is possible to increase innovation in your organization where a limited level of schedule pressure exists. It's about offsetting any negative reinforcement to meet schedules with a higher degree of positive reinforcement for innovation behaviors. Practices to positively reinforce innovation behaviors are included at the end of this chapter. But first let's review the common practices in organizations today that "pay lip service" to innovation that have little impact.

Posters and Trinkets

I have seen the most beautiful and eye-catching posters along the halls in some organizations with captions like "Innovation is the lifeblood of our company." Some just have the word "Innovate" and a light bulb. These general statements are unlikely to spur innovation. Recall that behaviors occur given anticipation of consequences. The behaviors leading to innovation will not happen unless people anticipate short-term positive consequences. It's about what they experience, not about what you tell them is important.

My favorite is when companies make statements about accepting or embracing failure. That's great until someone really fails. Did it really end up with gratitude for trying and what they learned? Likely not. It's unlikely that the innovator will have another chance to take a risk in that company. Besides, we have defined innovation as significantly increasing a product stakeholder value, not necessarily a revolutionary new product justifying substantial company Investment and risk. We want continuous innovation as part of the work people do.

Awards and Banquets

Awards and ceremonies can become opportunities for recognition. They also demonstrate exemplary behavior in your organization and show that innovation does receive some attention. However, any consequences are usually far in the future and have no real impact on behaviors that lead to innovation. I doubt that anyone really innovates to attend an awards banquet.

The other problem is that the award is given based on achieving innovation, not the steps that led to the innovation. Therefore, awards are given to those wonderful intrinsic innovators you may be lucky enough to have in your organization. You are motivating the self-motivated. And, as with motivation, for every innovator you reward, there are 10 others disappointed because they didn't receive an award.

Many companies use financial patent awards. I received several of them as an engineer in the telecommunications company for which I worked. The monetary award was never a factor in the innovation. I innovated because I loved to solve problems and to demonstrate how smart I was. I was a good problem solver, so I had built up a history of recognition for solving problems. I had become intrinsically motivated to solve tough problems.

There was one impact of the patent award, however. It motivated me to go through all the boring paperwork and discussions with our patent attorney to complete the application. I guess the money was a bit of an incentive, but I mostly wanted the nice plaque that went along with it to hang on my wall to get recognition every time someone walked into my office. I wouldn't have admitted this to myself at the time.

Suggestion Box

Don't waste your time. A suggestion box may yield some ideas for process improvement because people are knowledgeable of their own processes. However, most people don't know enough about their product stakeholders to innovate. The exceptions are companies where engineers are also stakeholders for the products they develop. Apple is an example where iPhone is used by engineers. Microsoft has been successful developing products used by engineers in their work. Visual Studio is a good example. SQL Server is another. Consumer products? Not so much.

But the main reason suggestion boxes don't work is that any potential positive reinforcement is long delayed after the idea is submitted. Submitters may get form e-mails like, "Thank you very much for your idea. Our selection committee meets at the end of each month and your idea will be considered. We will get back to you if your idea is selected for further discussion." In either case, there is little or no recognition for submitting an idea. And, if there is, it is long delayed.

Dedicated Innovation Time

This is one of the best examples of anecdote-based innovation advice that is not likely to work in your organization. I've heard from engineering management who told people they should use a portion of their time to innovate, but few actually did. There's a simple answer. Any positive consequences for innovation behaviors are outweighed by near-team negative consequences in these organizations. I found that schedule pressure was the culprit. Nobody is going to spend 20% of their time on work that might lead to an innovation when they fear being called on the carpet for missing a schedule at the next project review meeting. And many of these companies set aggressive schedules to "motivate the team" to at least come close to an acceptable schedule, resulting in demotivated losers.

Dedicated innovation time can work in a production-oriented environment that uses negative reinforcement for motivation. Your only option is to take people out of their daily work environments and put them on an "Innovation team" with positive reinforcement for innovation behaviors. The downside is that you don't get innovation from everyone in your organization, and people removed from the development environment for long periods of time become stale in terms of their knowledge of technology and the software base. But if you can't address the negative consequences from schedule pressure, this is your only option.

Performance Reviews

I have come across this several times. For example, "Submit an innovative idea each quarter that results in an improvement in our development process." Setting innovation goals at least demonstrates that innovation is important. The bad news is that performance reviews don't have much impact on day-to-day performance.

My wife Susan was a VP of HR at several high-tech companies in the Seattle area. Performance reviews were considered a way to document poor performance to avoid legal issues after someone is fired (since then, HR has realized that performance reviews often have the opposite effect where nice managers have completed reviews with platitudes and acceptable performance ratings come back to bite them).

HR people understand that the consequences for achieving performance review objectives are long delayed and therefore not very effective in improving day-to-day behavior. Exceeding your objectives might make the difference between a 2% and 3% salary increase. However, performance reviews are a way to communicate expectations.

Susan explained that mandating performance reviews was the only way she could be sure that a manager sat down with an employee to give some feedback on performance at least once a quarter. That's why HR trains management to provide timely feedback. They understand that just setting objectives is not going to have much impact on day-to-day motivation. But face-to-face feedback is not a strength for most engineers, so it doesn't happen frequently.

14.4.1 An Innovation Tale of Two Companies

Consider two well-known mobile phone manufacturers, one that out-innovated the world, and one that fell from grace. The first is Apple. The second is Research in Motion (RIM), maker of the once-ubiquitous Blackberry phone.

Many people believe that Apple was innovative because Steve Jobs relentlessly drove people until they produced something he liked. Actually, Steve Jobs was proficient in applying consequences in his organization to foster innovation. He understood human behavior to the point where you may call him a manipulator. We've heard the stories of people being chewed out by Jobs. However, he also established a culture where positive reinforcement took place for behaviors that led to innovation.

The yelling and drama? Jobs understood that he could use negative reinforcement to encourage a behavior – stretching oneself beyond what they thought they could achieve. "Go back and try again." However, innovation would not have thrived at Apple if the culture did not nurture innovation behaviors with frequent positive consequences. RIM will be our counter example.

Business Week posted an article on Apple's design processes in 2008 [3]. It included examples of how Apple used positive reinforcement for innovation behaviors. The article referred to Apple's paired design meetings:

> This was really interesting. Every week, the teams have two meetings. One in which to brainstorm, to forget about constraints and think freely. As Lopp put it: to "go crazy." Then they also hold a production meeting, an entirely separate but equally regular meeting which is the other's antithesis. Here, the designers and engineers are required to nail everything down, to work out how this crazy idea might actually work. This process and organization continue throughout the development of any app, though of course the balance shifts as the app progresses. But keeping an option for creative thought even at a late stage is really smart.

Apple recognized that ideas flourish in a positive environment. Criticism was left for a separate meeting where the practicality of the idea was assessed. Imagine the positive reinforcement in a meeting where engineers can be recognized for their ideas without fear of being shot down. I've been involved in brainstorming sessions where a card on the wall alternates between "creative" and "critical," but the combination of positive and negative in the same meeting fails to build excitement in the room.

Innovation is reinforced at all levels at Apple. Here's an insight from the same *Bloomberg Businessweek* article on "Pony Meetings."

> This refers to a story Lopp told earlier in the session, in which he described the process of a senior manager outlining what they wanted from any new application: "I want WYSIWYG... I want it to support major browsers... I want it to reflect the spirit of the company." Or, as Lopp put it: "I want a pony!" He added: "Who doesn't? A pony is gorgeous!" The problem, he said, is that these people are describing what they think they want. And even if they're misguided, they, as the ones signing the checks, really cannot be ignored.
>
> The solution, he described, is to take the best ideas from the paired design meetings and present those to leadership, who might just decide that some of those ideas are, in fact, their longed-for ponies. In this way, the ponies morph into deliverables. And the C-suite, who are quite reasonable in wanting to know what designers are up to, and absolutely entitled to want to have a say in what's going on, are involved and included. And that helps to ensure that there are no nasty mistakes down the line.

Executives at the top positions of Apple take an interest in innovation. I believe these "Pony Meetings" would have been positive to foster innovation behaviors. Otherwise, they would have found that fewer and fewer engineers brought their ideas to them.

Take RIM as a counter example of positive reinforcement for innovation behaviors. A 2013 article in the Canadian news publication, *The Globe and Mail*, provided a synopsis of the rise and fall of RIM in the mobile phone industry [4].

In 2009, Fortune named RIM as the world's fastest growing company. Much of RIM's innovation is credited to an engineer named Mike Lazaridis, a founder of the company and company co-CEO. Blackberry was a breakthrough technology at the time that incorporated a keyboard and LCD screen into a mobile phone. It was positioned as a mobile phone with e-mail capability.

RIM executed a powerful marketing strategy. They focused initially on the business segment by providing company CFOs with a secure device that could be managed by their IT organizations. Blackberry then became one of the most popular consumer mobile phones. They continued to dominate the market after the initial breakthrough with incremental improvements in technology and design. It evolved from an e-mail device to include web access via a custom browser, albeit buried within a maze of menus.

Then the iPhone happened. RIM sales plummeted. Their stock price dropped from $144.56 in June 2008 to $6.46 in September 2012. The company struggled along after introduction of the iPhone with forgettable "me-too" versions of their smartphone, but there was no innovation to differentiate themselves from the rest of the mobile phone manufacturers. Apple continued to out-innovate them by quickly productizing leading-edge technologies, like higher capacity memory chips and faster processors.

The Globe and Mail article provides evidence that RIM had a culture dominated by negative reinforcement. Larry Conlee was the RIM chief operating officer (COO).

> The split company also lost a major unifying force when Chief Operating Officer Larry Conlee retired in 2009. Mr. Conlee was a whip-cracker who held executives to account for decisions and deadlines, establishing a project management office. Many insiders agreed that after he left, a slack attitude toward hitting targets began to permeate the company. "There was a gap" after Mr. Conlee's departure, Adam Belsher, a former RIM vice-president, told The Globe last year. "There was no real operational executive on the product side that would really get teams to hit deadlines."

Note that once the pressure was removed, performance dropped in the company as described by "a slack attitude toward hitting targets." This is a good example of the peril of operating on the negative reinforcement side of the motivation curve introduced in Chapter 13. Strong employee engagement didn't exist. When negative reinforcement was reduced, RIM moved toward the valley of the motivation curve.

It appears from *the Globe and Mail* article that the negative culture was established by co-CEO Jim Balsillie, and Conlee was the enforcer. Some quotes from the article:

> Mr. Balsillie was brash, competitive and athletic, and wore his reputation for being aggressive, even bullying in meetings, as a badge of honour. If anything, he viewed that outward toughness as a job requirement, not unlike tech CEOs such as Steve Ballmer at Microsoft Corp. or Apple's Steve Jobs. "Show me how else you build a $20-billion company," he once confided to a colleague. "If I was Mr. Easy-going, they would kill BlackBerry."

I'm not sure why he would use Ballmer as an example of a leader of innovation. And he obviously didn't understand the positive culture Jobs established to nurture innovation at Apple.

The behavior model of innovation would have predicted RIM's failure to innovate after their initial win based on a single idea from their cofounder, Mike Lazaridis. They failed to scale innovation by having a controlling culture and top-down negative reinforcement.

There were other factors that made Apple successful. The smart marketing deal with AT&T. Betting on future technology advances, but there is a strong argument that these resulted from a strong sense of engagement and common goals throughout the organization.

14.4.2 Creating a Culture of Innovation

"Culture" is also one of those nebulous properties of organizations. As with innovation, I'll start with the dictionary. There are several definitions for "culture" in the *Merriam-Webster Dictionary*, most relating to sociology. There is one definition relevant to corporations.

> A set of shared attitudes, values, goals and practices that characterize an institution or organization.

I can support that. But what would you observe in an organization to know it has "shared attitudes and values?" It's based on the behaviors you would see if you were an observer in the organization. How do these behaviors come about and persist in organizations? That leads to my behavioral definition of culture.

> Organizational culture is the set of behaviors that are frequently positively reinforced throughout the organization.

It doesn't matter what you claim your culture to be. It's based on behaviors people observe.

Organizational culture usually starts at the top with the CEO. The CEO establishes consequences for their executives, who do the same for their managers, who deliver consequences for their people. We can use RIM as an example, Balsillie as co-CEO established the negative reinforcement culture. Conway, his COO, enforced the negative culture. I can't imagine a case of Conway receiving positive reinforcement from Balsillie because someone in the organization came up with a good idea, especially if schedules were being missed. A story from Conway about putting someone on the carpet or firing someone because of a late release would more likely have resulted in recognition from Balsillie.

Many of you reading this book are not CEOs so you may be disillusioned at this point because you don't control the top-level culture of your organization. The good news is that you can build a culture of innovation within your scope of control if you can shield your team from negative reinforcement. This takes strong leadership. My definition of strong leadership is

> A strong leader is willing to accept frequent negative consequences to support an environment of positive consequences for their team.

These are the engineering leaders who tell product management and their bosses that they are not going to apply pressure to their developers even though they themselves are under intense pressure. They will use positive reinforcement to increase motivation and innovation. How did they get there? These are leaders who have built a history of success.

14.4.2.1 Learning about Opportunities for Innovation

This is the first step in the innovation model. People need to understand opportunities for significantly increasing stakeholder value. I don't limit this to "product stakeholder value" because we also want innovation for internal processes that significantly increase a value for internal stakeholders. For example, a developer might create a "nonobvious" class library that reduces development effort of their department by 50%.

As a leader, you need to create the opportunities and provide the time and priority to learn about stakeholders. Some examples:

- Periodic team meetings with a product manager who leads the discussion on a specific stakeholder value followed by brainstorming of ideas or user scenarios.
- Ask for volunteers to follow new technologies they are interested in that may be applicable to your product, solution, or process. Take a portion of the weekly staff meeting for technology update presentations where they can receive recognition for their research. If you don't get volunteers, you haven't created the positive reinforcement.
- Send engineers to customer sites to shadow users of your application. Give them an opportunity to present to the department when they return.

Note that the positive reinforcement occurs during or soon after the desired behaviors in the examples above. I'm sure you can think of other ways to do this in your organization.

You first reaction may be "OMG, this is going to take some time away from production." If this is your reaction, don't bother trying these methods. Accept that you are a product organization where innovation is not a high priority. There's nothing wrong with that. Just set the expectations of the people who work for you, but accept that innovation posters and trinkets are not going to change anything.

There is another important point to be made here that also applies to the idea generation and proposal stages. We know that managers must establish the environment for frequent positive reinforcement. This involves behaviors on the part of a manager. Therefore, managers must receive positive reinforcement for behaviors that create the environment in which positive reinforcement for innovation behaviors takes place. In other words, if you want your manager to find ways to motivate their teams to innovate, the manager needs to be positively reinforced for implementing systems of positive reinforcement for innovation.

Managers may receive some recognition from their teams for supporting innovation, but there also needs to be positive reinforcement from their managers. This applies all the way up to leaders at any level. At some point, you are likely to reach a high management level where negative reinforcement prevails. This requires strong leadership to overcome, as we defined it.

One simple approach is to use at least 15 minutes of your staff meeting for open discussion on what your management team has done this week to build an environment of positive reinforcement for innovation behaviors, or how they have done something to reduce negative consequences that may override the positive consequences. For example, a manager may have asked a product manager to attend a team meeting to improve insight on product stakeholder value, or perhaps they even invited a real customer.

Don't go around the table and ask each manager to report what they've done. This feels like typical status reporting used for negative reinforcement. Just open the discussion, "What have we done this week to establish positive recognition for innovation?" No volunteers at first? Give it a chance. If still nothing, you may give them a serious talk to remind them of the importance you place on innovation. Perhaps give examples where you have promoted innovation. Eventually, a flame will flicker that can be fanned with positive reinforcement.

You have a manager who never contributes? Have an individual discussion with them to find out why and to stress that you consider this to be a major part of their job responsibilities. As soon as you observe a hint of the desired behavior, move to positive reinforcement.

If you are at the director or VP level, you may experience even more angst at the thought of having to dedicate precious time to innovation instead of more "important things." If so, you're not ready to try this. Innovation is actually not a priority for you.

14.4.2.2 Generating Ideas

This one shouldn't be difficult because most engineers like to contribute ideas. Remember "Tell me what you know" from the motivation chapter. Again, it's just a matter of leadership providing the opportunity for positive reinforcement for ideas focused on stakeholder values.

Create an internal collaboration site organized by product stakeholders. Include their values as topics and encourage engineers to submit innovative ideas.

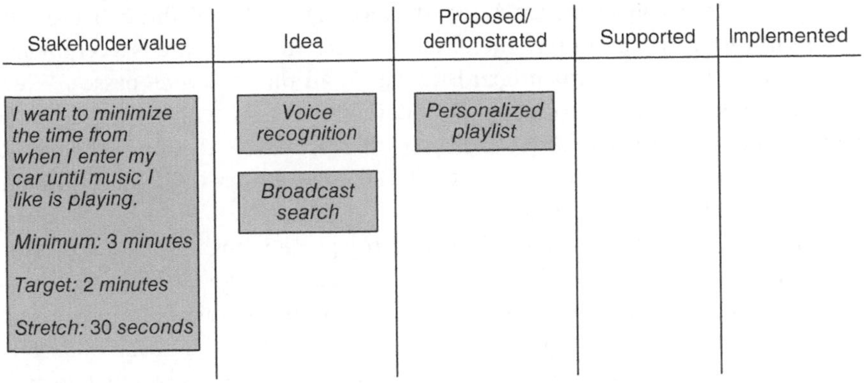

Stakeholder value	Idea	Proposed/ demonstrated	Supported	Implemented
I want to minimize the time from when I enter my car until music I like is playing. *Minimum: 3 minutes* *Target: 2 minutes* *Stretch: 30 seconds*	*Voice recognition* *Broadcast search*	*Personalized playlist*		

Figure 14.2 Innovation Kanban board.

Engineers will provide positive comments for ideas if positive reinforcement dominates in your organization. You can also schedule meetings with people who can contribute ideas to a specific stakeholder value. Use separate creative and critical meetings as Apple does.

At some point, the ideas need to be filtered to determine which should be submitted to the next level of management to garner support. My recommendation is a physical innovation Kanban board at each level in the organization like the example in Figure 14.2.

A first-level manager facilitates updates to their team's board each week. Again, no status reporting. People volunteer ideas and update progress in anticipation of positive reinforcement. Why would the manager be motivated to maintain the board? Because he or she gets to volunteer success stories at their manager's weekly innovation discussion. They also could pitch for support from their next level of management if implementation is beyond their control. For example, it may require departmental funding. Once support is gained at the next level, they can move the idea to the "Supported" column, with positive reinforcement from their team and boss.

The ideas supported by the next management level appear on their Kanban boards. Their boards show the progress of innovations that have reached their level of support. The board is reviewed weekly at each management staff meeting, with recognition for helping move a card across the board. What message do you think that sends about the importance management assigns to innovation? You're no longer just paying lip service to innovation.

If you are an engineer, you're probably already thinking about how the Kanban can be implemented in a relational database. Don't do it. You now know that the social interaction surrounding changes in Kanban card positions provides the opportunities for positive reinforcement. I guess you could put the Kanban online and update it from a video screen during the meeting, but I don't think that results in the same team recognition as the physical cards. Moving a card is a ceremony. Better yet, post all the Kanban boards along a wall that everyone passes. What a strong message it sends to see a VP updating the board with an enthusiastic group of directors! You can see in the survey in Appendix E that one of the most significant questions that determines the level of innovation is, "My department encourages and supports good ideas."

Think of other ways to communicate and recognize innovation at the department level. Start "tweeting" on innovation and recognize good things that happened that day or week. Recognize your managers in the tweets for what they have done to contribute to innovation in the department. The innovation itself is not the basis for reinforcement. It is the behaviors of your managers that created the environment from which innovation was born. Always ask them what they did to make the innovation happen. It's an opportunity for reinforcement as well as to share effective methods among your managers.

Go ahead and invite an innovator to a higher-level staff meeting to present their idea to receive positive reinforcement. It can be an effective reinforcer if the presenter perceives it as a positive meeting. However, I would argue that the same meeting would be better spent having a manager present on how they established the environment that led to the innovation. You will only reinforce a single innovator in the meeting. Reinforce the manager for the environment they have created, and this will motivate multiple potential innovators.

14.4.2.3 Innovation Proposals and Demonstrations

This is the final step before implementation for many innovations. Many good ideas are within the control of the individual or manager, and it only takes a "let's do it!" Others may require significant commitments of resources and money. Creating a proposal may involve negative consequences for those who must take the time away from their work or something else they enjoy. You need to establish the opportunities for reinforcement for creating and pitching the proposal.

Hackathons are excellent vehicles for innovation reinforcement. There is excitement in the room as engineers huddle around a workstation to recognize something cool. It generates peer recognition from "show me what you built." Try to do one each month. Walk around and select a few near the end of the session for presentation to the entire group.

Establish innovation demonstration stations in well-traveled areas. It doesn't have to just be engineers. Catch product managers or operations people on their way to lunch. Engineers will thrive with positive feedback for their demonstrations.

Give someone a week off to create a presentation or demonstration. You say you are serious about innovation? Show it.

I'll end this chapter with the same subject discussed at the end of the motivation in Chapter 13. Does working from home impact innovation? I've seen many articles that acknowledge the possibility of losing spontaneous ideas from incidental contact in the workplace. The behavior model of innovation shows that these articles miss the real impact to innovation – the environment of positive reinforcement for behaviors that lead to motivation. It is possible to recreate some of the innovation reinforcement methods over video, but they limit opportunities for reinforcement to scheduled meetings.

The sad truth is that most companies will not see a decrease in innovation because they have been unable to create that nebulous, "culture of innovation" in the first place. Refer to the preceding motivation chapter about working from home. You will need to schedule weekly video meetings where people can be reinforced by their peers for innovation.

It should now be clear now why so few organizations are innovative. It takes more than innovation posters or great award dinners. It takes the full commitment from management to stoke innovation behaviors every week. This level of commitment must come from the top. Most engineering organizations are driven by pressure that starts at the CEO level. Executives spend virtually none of their time supporting innovation.

Of course, business schedule and financial commitments must be met. However, find a way to apply positive consequences for both production and innovation. Investments are a good start to get innovation flowing because they provide your engineers with problems to solve. Address behaviors that lead to innovation with positive reinforcement to create the culture that produces innovative products.

14.5 Summary

- An Investment facilitates innovation by providing engineers with the problem to solve.
- Involving engineers in Investment planning gives them an opportunity to innovate.
- Innovation is a nonobvious improvement provided by a product, process, or solution that results in a notable increase in product stakeholder value.
- Innovation is a result of a series of behaviors.
- Culture is defined by the behaviors observed in your organization.
- Innovation can be increased through effective positive reinforcement of behaviors that lead to innovation.
- Many companies apply ineffective methods to increase innovation because they lack near-term positive consequences for behaviors that lead to innovation.
- Schedule pressure is the antithesis of innovation.

- There are three phases of corporate innovation
  - Identifying stakeholder value
  - Generating ideas
  - Creating proposals
- Near-term positive consequences can be established for behaviors that support the innovation phases.
- Innovative organizations balance production and innovation through positive reinforcement.

References

1 US Government (2014). Is America losing its innovation edge? *USA Today* (5 January).

2 Curcio, V. (2013). *Henry Ford*. Oxford University Press.

3 Apples design process. *Bloomberg Businessweek* (March 8 2008).

4 Sean Silcoff, Jacquie McNish and Steve Ladurantaye (2013). Inside the fall of Blackberry. *The Globe and Mail* (27 September).

15

AccuWiz Gets It Together

Recall that product manager Pete, and Tom, VP engineering, had become disillusioned with the company. Customers were no longer seeing the innovation that first attracted them to AccuWiz. Customers were promised features that didn't show up in releases. Releases were packed with features that didn't appeal to every customer. Even if the release contained features customers wanted, they experienced long delays because of long release cycle times and schedule slips.

The founders certainly didn't achieve the revenue growth or predictability necessary to position the company for a public offering or acquisition. Charles, the COO, responded by increasing his attacks on Tom at the program reviews. In Charles' opinion, everything would be just fine if Tom could just be harder on his engineering teams to make them deliver all the features that have backed up.

Tom approaches Lauren, VP of product management, because he believes they share the same concerns about what has become of AccuWiz. He introduces her to the Investment model. He hopes it will allow his team to go back to real Agile development with variable content and improve collaboration between product management and engineering. Lauren likes the idea of being able to manage the expectations of the sales department instead of being buried under a cascade of features she can never deliver. The positive Investment approach is also more in-line with her management style.

They decide to make a pitch directly to the founders because they believe Charles is stuck in his big company ways. He's unlikely to support the positive environment they know is necessary to get the most out of the Investment planning method. They both have nothing to lose at this point because they will leave AccuWiz if nothing changes.

Unlocking Agile's Missed Potential, First Edition. Robert Webber.
© 2022 The Institute of Electrical and Electronics Engineers, Inc. Published 2022 by John Wiley & Sons, Inc.

15.1   The Founder Meeting

Tom still has a relationship with the founders, Ken and Brett, from the early days, although they have become a bit more distant since Charles came in. Tom calls the founders and asks if they can meet with him and Lauren on the weekend. Tom tells them they have information that may ultimately determine the success or failure of AccuWiz. Ken and Brett agree to meet.

Ken and Brett open the meeting by saying they are open to change. The status quo is not working. Tom and Lauren explain that the organization has fallen into the feature pit. It's not about value. Product management has been relegated to taking feature orders from sales as they chase every opportunity. There is no end to the requests. At this point, there is a backlog of over 200 features. It would take over two years of development to complete them at the current development rate.

Tom says the company has lost the ability to deliver real value for customers. Engineering was closer to customers before the product management department was established. The product managers now create detailed feature requirements, leaving little opportunity for engineering to add value, and there is also a lot of confusion between the roles of product manager and Agile team product owners. Some of the product managers like to wallow in design details, even to the point of creating UI drawings.

Tom and Lauren go over the Investment planning approach at the meeting. Ken and Brett like the visibility and control they would have below the release level, and they like the idea of sales committing to income before risking their money on new product development. Ken and Brett understand how they can increase financial predictability by timeboxing Investments with feature flexibility if income forecasts are maintained.

At this point, the conversation turns to the changes required to successfully implement the Investment model. Investment teams are mini-product teams that need to be empowered to achieve financial targets. Teams must be trusted to achieve their targets without pressure and control from project management. Project management can play an important supporting role, but they are no longer the schedule enforcers.

The meeting ends.

15.2   The Announcement

Charles is not present when Lauren, Tom, and Michelle show up for the next staff meeting. Only the founders are there. They explain that they have asked for Charles' resignation, and he is returning to his old company where he can use his old playbook. They believe his style is not a fit for the entrepreneurial organization they envisioned and built. Lauren, Michelle, and Tom will report to the founders, but their roles will change. They will be supporting empowered virtual product teams created around the Investment model. Michelle is concerned because she's not sure what project management will do. They were Charles' enforcers.

The founders note the concerned look on Michelle's face and explain how project management still plays a significant role. Project management is still responsible for project budgets and schedule predictability, but now for smaller projects at the Investment level. Project management's role is to support empowered teams to achieve Investment schedule and development cost targets.

Project management will use the time they previously spent on tracking and status meetings to break down barriers beyond control of team scrum masters and identify and manage Investment team dependencies. The founders also want them to assist the teams with Investment planning with top-down software estimation techniques. The founders also want project managers to spend more time on risk management.

Key Performance Indicators (KPIs) are discussed next. The founders like the motivational survey questions used in the Investment Model where people rate the way they feel about their work by choosing "Pressured," "Frustrated," "OK," "Motivated," or "Excited." The founders recognize that empowered teams must be motivated by their work to eliminate project tracking. Initial survey results will not look good, but they want to support their executive team to make improvements each quarter until they have at least 70% in the Motivated or Excited categories.

The founders want to add one question to the quarterly survey for the Innovation teams: "Our project manager helps us meet our goals." They acknowledge that the original scores will be disappointing based on the prior role of project management. It will require that Lauren set up opportunities for positive reinforcement for the alternate desired project manager behaviors, like removing obstacles and performing risk analysis. The founders say they will support Lauren to make gradual improvement in the project management value KPI.

The next step is for Lauren and Tom to do an assessment of the current backlog to determine which features might be formed into Investments with quantifiable value and which still need to be delivered. They will produce an Investment roadmap that can be reviewed with sales and eventually communicated to customers. Tom will have to work with his team to determine which features can be delivered in upcoming releases, taking estimation uncertainty into account. The founders want to go to their customers one time with changes, and expect that Lauren, Tom, and Michelle will put in Investment planning methods to make sure they make commitments they can meet.

Table 15.1 Key stakeholder values.

Product stakeholder	Values
CFO	• I want to maximize cashflow for the organization • I want accurate data that complies with accounting rules • I want to increase accounting staff productivity to reduce operational costs
Accounting director	• I want to minimize the time between the close of a financial period and reports to satisfy my stakeholders • I want to reduce the application training interval to quickly fill staffing vacancies
CIO	• I want to minimize my application support costs
General manager	• I want rapid notification of projected budget variances so we can react quickly to maintain budgets

15.3 Product Stakeholder Analysis

The product management team goes offsite for a day to identify their product stakeholders and their key values. They think this will give everyone better insight into how to screen for value within the current feature backlog. It turned out to be a great team building event.

Everyone is surprised at how many stakeholders they identified. This was the first time they considered internal organizations like customer support. They acknowledged that customer support has been crucial in retaining customers despite the late releases. Features requested by support never made the roadmap because of the constant flow of feature requests from sales and customers. That needs to change.

They identify the key stakeholders that make or influence purchase decisions (Table 15.1).

Many other stakeholders were identified as users and managers in specific accounting areas. They found that many of their values correlated with how performance was assessed for their roles and generally supported the values of their management. A repository was created with all the stakeholder information available to all Investment teams. Anyone can add stakeholders to the library.

15.4 Creating the Investment Backlog

Lauren and Tom, with the help of some key staff, went through the feature backlog to separate them into Investments. The "Five Whys" method was used to dig

Table 15.2 AccuWiz feature backlog categories.

Category	Number of features
1. Contingent Sales Commitments	5
2. European Market Penetration	25
3. UI Improvements	20
4. Enterprise Integration	15
5. Workflow Enhancements	15
6. Regulatory Mandates for Current Market	10
7. Miscellaneous Enhancements	110

down from feature functionality to the value they are expected to provide. For example, would this feature increase customer revenue or increase market share? Why would customers pay for it? What is the approval process and who are the approvers?

They categorized the current backlog features as shown in Table 15.2.

Contingent sales commitments are features promised to customers to close a deal. Sales can't renege on the features, so development effort will be subtracted from the tactical Investment portfolio. Lauren asks for product management volunteers to form Investment teams around categories 2–5. The regulatory mandates are nondiscretionary, so headcount will be reserved and removed from the Investment portfolio allocation. Lauren asks for another volunteer to review the miscellaneous enhancements to determine if any represent significant product stakeholder value worthy of an Investment.

The European Market Investment team finds that the number of required features is so large because sales wants to offer the product to all the countries in the European Union (EU) to increase the chances of gaining traction in any country. This involves development of regulatory features specific to each country. The team estimates a duration of about nine months to complete all the features. They ask sales for the income profile for the first three years. The downloadable Investment Income Profile Calculator spreadsheet is used to determine income required to meet the company's payback period goal. The third-year income is $1.2M. Cost of Delay (CoD) is estimated at $1.2M/12 = $100K per month using the Third-Year Income Slope CoD Method. Weighted Shortest Job First (WSJF) is estimated at $100K/9 months cycle time = $11K per month per month of delay.

They understand that Europe is a strategic target for AccuWiz, but they still want to maximize WSJF to obtain as much funding as possible from the tactical portfolio allocation. They determine that Germany, France, Italy, and Spain represent almost 60% of the EU market, but only 20% of the requested regulatory features apply to them. These features could be developed in three months. The CoD would be reduced to $100K \times 60\% = \$60K$ per month, but the cycle time has been reduced from nine months to two, establishing a WSJF of $60K/2$ months $= \$20K$ per month per month of delay, almost double the previous value. It places the investment within the one-year Investment backlog Work in Progress (WIP) limit.

The other Investment teams strive to maximize WSJF for their Investments. The engineering technical owners contribute ideas on how to modify functionality to reduce development effort and reuse existing software. They also identify ways that the Investments could be released as modular packages. There is a lot of recognition among the team for new ideas.

The UI improvements are difficult to associate with increased revenue. The Investment team reviews customer churn rates and doesn't see a significant trend. They find that the inside sales team always records the reason for leaving. There aren't any comments about UI. Most of the churn was caused by undelivered features, late releases, and problems experienced during complex upgrades. The Investment team decides that there are about five UI features that would have the greatest impact on customer satisfaction, down from the original 20. They propose the reduced UI improvements as a strategic Investment with no associated revenue.

In addition to their assigned categories that represent potential Investments, Lauren asks the teams to review the stakeholder value information in the repository to determine how their Investment might relate to the values of key stakeholders. Lauren asks them to consider every stakeholder regardless of the level to determine how they could possibly benefit from their Investment implementations.

Lauren sets up a meeting in two weeks to let each team pitch their proposed Investments. Tom and Michelle are also there to assist with prioritization. It's a very positive meeting where each team is excited to present the ways in which they have been able to increase value and reduce cycle time. The product managers are thrilled with being able to do real product management instead of taking orders for features.

Pete was the product manager who was very disappointed when he just became a cog in the feature factory. He expected that he would be the "voice of the customer" to tell engineering what customers needed. Pete now realizes that this is not his role in the new AccuWiz. He finds that many of the senior engineers have gained amazing customer insights by developing accounting software over the years, and their knowledge has been aggregated from multiple customers. The engineers are quick to point out to Pete things that are often done differently in other countries.

The engineers also have great ideas on how to add value and reduce development effort. Pete now realizes that his role is to allow every member to contribute and to do as much as he can to expose engineers to the market so they can become more effective. He loves his new responsibilities. The engineers love the new insights to the new market. Some have even been able to job shadow accountants in customer organizations. It really opened their eyes.

The teams present their critical assumptions and the validation results to support their Investment proposals. In some cases, the VPs ask for additional validation tests.

Lauren, Tom, and Michelle meet a week later for the review of the initial backlog prioritization (see Table 15.3). The shaded Investments are beyond the one-year WIP limit.

The Quick Close Investment was proposed with insight into the key product stakeholder values. It maintains the end of quarter financial statements in real time, so everyone knows exactly how they impact current financials. Closing the books at the end of a quarter has been reduced from three weeks to one. The Investment also satisfies the General Manager value for rapid response to potential budget variations. He can now see how any variation will impact the financial reports and take quick action.

The review of the miscellaneous features revealed many reporting enhancements. AccuWiz has its own reporting engine, but adding all the requested features would require significant effort. Someone from engineering suggested that it would be better to provide data connectors for the new data analytics tools on the market. The customers can then drag and drop data to make their own reports and dashboards. They estimate that a connector to support the most popular analytics tools could be sold to customers for about $60K. The Investment team was able to validate the price point with a test of the assumption.

Table 15.3 Initial AccuWiz Investment backlog.

Category	WSJF
1. Quick Close	125
2. Workflow Enhancements	105
3. European Version	90
4. UI Enhancements	75
5. Data Analytics Connectors	60
6. Enterprise Integration	55
6. Customer Support Enhancements	40
7. Mobile Application	25

Features necessary to meet regulatory requirements were identified. There are also some technical features required to maintain browser compatibility. These features will be funded out of the support and maintenance portfolio allocation because they are nondiscretionary.

The new Investment backlog, executed in the priority order, will increase revenue and income by about 25% without any additional engineering resources, resulting in a significant improvement in R&D Return on Investment (ROI). The product management team has added additional Investments to the backlog to create a three-year sales forecast. It wasn't difficult. Product managers came forward with great Investment proposals they had wanted to implement for a long time. However, they never got done because of pressure to add features. They now have an Agile roadmap to maintain expectations among all roadmap stakeholders.

The sales VP has agreed to the new plan and committed to the aggregate three-year revenue profile. He and Lauren understand that the Investment backlog will now be more dynamic, but changes will be based on new opportunities to improve the forecast. Lauren and Tom assure him that they will be able to meet the baseline three-year Investment deployment plan by using timeboxing and variable content to stay on target.

The product managers dug into Investment planning with enthusiasm. The one-year WIP limit gave them time to do a great job of planning for the Investments that can be started this year, and they weren't pestered with whimsical feature requests because they could be evaluated in terms of the increase in backlog Net CoD.

15.5 Customer Management

The next step was to create a road show to introduce the new AccuWiz to their customers. It would involve telling them that some of the features published in prior roadmaps will not be available. Sales felt that based on their recent experiences of late releases and missing features, the roadmap had little credibility anyway. They believe the new plan will be well received because of faster delivery of value customers will recognize. Sales also believes that Quick Close will be a game changer for customers and AccuWiz. Nobody has anything like it.

The meetings went well. The founders attended the meetings with major customers to show their support, and to maintain old business relationships. There were some complaints about missing features at some of the meetings, but they were mostly forgotten when Quick Close was introduced. They saw the same level of innovation they had recognized in AccuWiz when they selected them. The customers were also thrilled that they would be getting smaller release increments with seamless upgrades.

15.6 Investment Development

AccuWiz met the one-year Investment schedules that had been given to customers. The Investment teams had been sure to reserve contingency because they knew they had to rebuild credibility with customers. The Agile teams were highly motivated by experiencing the frequent positive reinforcement of Agile development. Nobody questioned how hard they were working to meet the Investment goals.

Additional features were requested by sales during development, but product management was able to quickly calculate the Net CoD impact on the Investment backlog to show they had a negative financial impact. The teams were able to accommodate a few feature requests when they were convinced that they would significantly contribute to Investment income. However, they kept the Investment within the timebox by reducing functionality of other features or discarding those rated with the lowest Investment ROI contributions.

These decisions were made in a weekly review where teams presented their feature burndown charts to compare current and planned glidepaths. Teams off their "glidepaths" always included alternatives to get back on track by reducing Investment effort or, in some cases, adding additional staff. Maintaining Investment schedule was the number one objective to prevent cascading schedule delays on the roadmap.

The environment for the Agile teams has completely changed. They are able to choose their own sprint objectives based on their velocity. The teams initially made very conservative estimates because of the history of being called out by project management. They also had a history of work piled on during the sprint, and people being pulled off the team for other priorities. Tom and his management team encouraged the teams to adjust velocity to meet their sprint schedules. They found that the teams were willing to set more aggressive goals after a few weeks of achieving sprint objectives.

Some interesting new dynamics were observed in the teams. Their confidence in achieving schedules had increased. They now acted like a winning team, increasing collaboration and mutual support to achieve the sprint goals. The desire to meet their goals resulted in ground-up process improvement. All became highly engaged in sprint retrospectives and contributed ways to increase efficiency to achieve their goals.

15.6.1 Project Management

Michelle, the head of the project management office (PMO), had been concerned about how her project managers would adjust to a role of support versus control. She received training on the behavior model of motivation, which gave her some ideas on how to move forward. She first hosted sessions with her project managers to introduce them to their new roles and the behavior model. She wanted to be completely open with them about why new processes would be implemented. Some of the project managers were skeptical. Her response was, "Tell me what could be bad about an environment where people receive frequent and sincere recognition for their work?"

She also went over the new quarterly KPIs for the department, a rating for supporting the Investment teams. Many were concerned at their performance being measured. They associated metrics with punishment. Michelle assured them that she did not expect positive results for some time given the past culture and their enforcement role, and her intent was to coach them to gradually improve scores. She not only stressed patience but also said that accountability for their most important job responsibility was unavoidable. This was a good use of negative reinforcement to get the desired behaviors started.

Lauren understood that she needed to establish reinforcement systems for the new project management behaviors. She identified the following behaviors:

1. Removing project obstacles elevated by scrum masters
2. Performing risk management
3. Managing project dependencies among the Investment teams

For the first behavior, she asked her project managers to set up their own Kanban boards to accept and track obstacles escalated by the teams. The boards were to be updated during the Agile team daily stand-up meetings. This was an opportunity for the project managers to be recognized by the team members for helping them. In addition, Lauren walked through each project manager's Kanban board on a weekly basis to elicit success stories. She also asked what she could do to support the project manager during each meeting.

Lauren set up a weekly project review meeting dedicated to the subject of risk management. The separate meeting sent a message about the importance in the new organization. She also provided risk management training. Most project managers were unaware that there are so many great structured methods for risk management. Project managers got to present their risk management plans and present success stories. Lauren was good at asking questions to recognize specific behaviors that led to success stories.

A separate meeting was set up for review of Gantt charts that captured Investment dependencies. Schedules included new tools, upgrade procedures, documentation, training material, and marketing collateral, as well as sales training. Investment interdependencies were a major focus. The meeting provided an opportunity to recognize behaviors that led to success stories. Project managers could also present challenges that were often solved in the meeting through collaboration with other project managers. They enjoyed coming to the meeting.

Lauren instituted one additional ½ hour weekly "coaching" meeting for individual feedback. The agenda was simple:

1. What you did well this week
2. Opportunities for improvement
3. What can I do to help you be more successful in your job?

She always tried to give immediate feedback during the week, but this meeting was a synchronization of mutual expectations. The project managers liked the meeting because they didn't have to keep wondering how they were doing. Lauren's willingness to provide frank feedback assured them that communication was completely open and the recognition they received from her was sincere.

Lauren identified a few project managers who were struggling. She pinpointed examples where she felt that the project managers could have handled a situation better. She identified specific training courses in cases of deficient skills. There was one project manager identified after six months who just couldn't adopt the personality traits necessary for the supportive role. He had gotten by in the past by just marking off tasks and blaming individuals for project failures. He enjoyed the control. He had been unable to develop any of the new skills or desired behaviors. He had to be replaced. Lauren developed behavioral interview questions that required candidates to give specific examples of the behaviors she was looking for in her new PMO.

Soon Lauren's job had changed significantly. The project managers were much more engaged, rarely having to come to Lauren with specific issues. They looked forward to telling Lauren what they had done to resolve the issue themselves. Lauren's support was still needed in some cases, but their needs were nicely summarized in the weekly meetings for quick decision-making.

15.6.2 Managers

The role of middle management had become cloudy with the transition to Agile. Their role, as defined in Agile, was to keep out of the way. This was difficult for many managers who had been promoted after a successful technical career. They often tried to contribute to the teams, but it was clear it wasn't welcome. They were told by the team that their job responsibilities were staffing and career development and to focus on them. There's certainly no frequent positive reinforcement for these responsibilities. Like everyone else, managers want to "play in the game" and be recognized for their contributions.

Tom recognized that a key role for managers was to establish and maintain the environment in which positive reinforcement could take place for the Agile team. He was quick to recognize managers for actions taken to support the positive environment. However, that didn't involve any measurable results that can serve as opportunities for frequent reinforcement for the managers. Tom realized that managers had a major influence on the quality produced by Agile team members who reported to them. Measurable quality improvement trends could be used for positive reinforcement.

In their matrix organization, teams were essentially organized by the development process. Architects reported to one manager, and product owners responsible for requirements analysis to another. There was a UI manager, several development managers, a database manager, and a functional test manager. Managers were responsible for the practices and tools used by teams on which quality depended.

The quality metrics could serve as a scorecard for a manager's success. Fortunately, Agile development provides the opportunity for frequent quality metrics at the sprint level. He decided to have each manager focus on defect leakage from their responsible areas. Even though the team members were distributed among Agile teams, defect reports could be assigned to individuals associated with managerial departments. It wasn't difficult to provide reports on a managerial basis.

Defects found in user story acceptance tests could be summarized by the manager. Defects were also reported from feature-level tests. Tom didn't want to put a burden on the team by having to report defects during the development process. Defects could be allocated to managers based on the individual who fixed the problem. Defects associated with the testing group were defined as test plan errors that caused a defect to be reported incorrectly, which had been wasting a lot of development effort and causing frustration.

Tom recognized that he had to use these metrics as a source for positive reinforcement based on continuous improvement. Negative reinforcement would result in finger-pointing. The weekly quality reviews became positive meetings where managers could be recognized for steps taken to reduce defect leakage. Actions might include training courses provided for their engineers, new tools, and process improvements. The Agile teams recognized them for the value the managers added.

15.6.3 Executive Team

The nature of the weekly executive team staff meeting changed. The founders recognized that they must build reinforcement systems to recognize their direct reports for establishing positive recognition for their direct reports. The founders held weekly meetings with the VPs to hear success stories on what they had done to promote an environment of positive reinforcement for their managers. They also adopted Lauren's weekly coaching sessions. They looked back at how much of their time had been previously wasted on issues that were now taken care of willingly by their VPs. The change freed more than enough time for the coaching meetings. They now considered the coaching meetings to be the most important meetings of the week.

15.7   Innovation Is Revived

The founders knew that the ability to introduce new technologies like graphical workflow had differentiated AccuWiz from the entrenched competitors. Innovation had disappeared with transition to the high-pressure, production organization that Charles instituted. Innovation Kanban boards were now implemented at each level of the organization to facilitate positive reinforcement for behaviors that move ideas through to proposals.

A technology roadmap was put together identifying key technologies that they may be able to leverage ahead of their competitors. For example, deep learning looked like something that was maturing to the point where it could have a practical application in accounting. A key technology program was established where volunteers could research technologies in which they were interested. An entire wall visible in a hallway was used for a new technology introduction Kanban board. The founders stood in front of the board every two weeks to reinforce the volunteers for progress. Engineers looked forward to telling them and the other engineers what they had learned or done to move their technologies forward. The Kanban made it clear to everyone that innovation was important, and introduction of new technologies would likely receive positive reinforcement.

15.8   Synopsis

The changes at AccuWiz may seem fantastic to the reader. However, every one of the new behaviors is supported with systematic and frequent positive reinforcement. You can implement systems of positive reinforcement within your own work environment and see the results.

In effect, AccuWiz attained the culture described in the classic management book, *The One Minute Manager* [1] by Kenneth Blanchard, PhD. The book describes three management techniques to foster employee engagement to achieve goals without the need for management control:

- One Minute Goal Setting
- One Minute Praising
- One Minute Reprimands

Look familiar? The only difference is that the book you are reading recommends that reinforcement systems be established within the work process. If you have ever observed the undeniable power of gamification, you'll understand why. Fortunately for the readers, Agile development as envisioned can create the frequent recognition provided by games.

Reference

1 Blanchard, K. and Johnson, S. (1982). *The One-Minute Manager*. William Morrow and Company Inc.

16

Getting It Together in Your Company: A Practical Guide

Your head is likely spinning at this point with the daunting challenge of implementing the teachings of this book in your organization. For those lower in an organization, the AccuWiz vision may seem like an impossible dream. Change can be implemented with the aid of an incremental project plan that builds on small successes using the organizational behavior model to influence and sustain change.

There are eight steps to implement your Investment roadmap:

1. Organizational support
2. Stakeholder value analysis
3. Stakeholder research
4. Stakeholder interviews
5. Investment candidates
6. Initial roadmap
7. Investment planning
8. Consequence alignment

The objectives are to establish an initial Investment backlog and roadmap and then instill the practices necessary to manage it. The initial steps can be accomplished without risk and minimal use of resources to establish credibility and support for the overall initiative.

16.1   Step 1: Organizational Support

There are three key decision-makers in your organization who must come onboard. They are the product management leader (VP/director of product management), engineering leader (VP/director engineering or CTO), and your PMO leader if you have one (head of program or project management). If you are

Unlocking Agile's Missed Potential, First Edition. Robert Webber.

lower in the organization, there may be several management levels that you need to get on your side before getting to these higher-level positions.

Everyone is suspicious of the person who has just experienced an epiphany from reading a book or attending a seminar. Most people can't contain their excitement and overwhelm others by condensing what they learned over days or weeks into sound bites. You can take a strategic approach to influence decision-makers with your new insight into organizational behavior principles.

Some say that people are naturally resistant to change. I disagree. If I were to give someone one million dollars, would they be resistant to that change? Of course, not. People resist change when they anticipate negative personal consequences. We know that positive consequences can be used to reinforce the desired behaviors necessary to support change. So don't expect that just evangelizing in terms of general and longer-term nebulous consequences is going to get you anywhere. You want to identify the frequent consequences for the key decision-makers.

I recommend you start by understanding and addressing the organizational consequences for product management, engineering, and project management leaders from whom you will need support. The key point is that whenever you are "selling" the idea to anyone, it should be in terms of the consequences they experience on a daily or weekly basis, not how the idea benefits you or the organization.

Although you may not like the term "selling," this is what one must do to gain support for a major initiative. We know from marketing that people will buy when a product or solution provides a benefit or reduces a pain point. You can now recognize that benefits create positive reinforcement, whereas pain points are negative reinforcement.

Pain points tend to work better at higher levels in the organization because losing one's position is the overwhelming negative consequence (sadly, this often means that the best management tact is to lie low and do nothing!). I also think people react more quickly to reduce pain points. It's probably related to our strong survival instincts. The ability to reduce a significant pain point will spur purchasing behaviors.

Table 16.1 provides typical pain points for individuals in a product development organization and how the Investment model addresses each of them. They also provide an example of how the organizational behavior model can be applied to roles within your organization to understand and change behavior.

16.1.1 Influence Strategy

I hope the pain point exercise provides insight into how consequences drive behavior of product leaders in your organizations, and why they are unlikely to change if Waterfall planning persists. You may be able to think of other pain points, but the

Table 16.1 Organizational consequences by role.

Pain point	Frequency	Investment approach
Engineering leader		
Pressure from product management to add features beyond development capacity	High – saying no often results in escalation and pressure from the CEO, often with career implications	WSJF prioritized backlog and roadmap managed collaboratively by product management and engineering
Criticism for missed schedules	High – often occurs in every project or program review and executive staff meeting	Investment planning with fixed schedule and financial objectives and variable scope
Complaints from staff of pressure from product and project management	Medium – engineers express frustration by fixed schedule and content that precludes Agile the way they were taught	Agile with flexible content allows engineers to set and meet their own sprint goals
Product management leader		
Saying no to sales	High – in organizations still using Waterfall planning	Investment backlog prioritized by WSJF with one-year WIP limit
Product managers complain of no time to plan	Medium – product management leaders often express this frustration	Separate planning and implementation roles for product management and product owners. Investment model provides framework for planning
CFO, CEO, or PMO criticism for missed schedules	High – often occurs in every project or program review and executive staff meeting	Investment planning with fixed schedule and financial objectives and variable scope allow schedules to be met
Project/program management		
Missed schedule, content, and/or budget	High – takes blame from CEO and CFO for being off target at project or program reviews	WSJF prioritized backlog and roadmap managed collaboratively by product management and engineering. Engineering and product management are accountable for achieving Investment objectives

analysis will suffice to develop your strategy. Either way, the reason leaders in product development behave the way they do shouldn't be a mystery any longer.

There are some key observations. The first observation is that most of the behaviors in larger organizations are driven by negative reinforcement, which becomes more significant as job levels increase. Most actions take place to avoid punishment. On the other hand, positive consequences are usually uncertain and long delayed and do not outweigh negative reinforcement.

The second observation is that the engineering leader has the most severe and frequent negative consequences and has the most to gain from introducing the Investment approach. The engineering leader is the ideal executive-level sponsor for the change. Unfortunately, they usually have less political power compared to their product management and PMO peers.

The next most likely ally of engineering is the PMO, if you have one. They are usually frustrated by being in the difficult position of trying to deliver feature-level predictability with Agile development. They will welcome a solution that allows them to achieve predictability.

The product management leader can be a major obstacle. Many product managers have found a comfortable position with little accountability. Most are not accountable for profit and loss (P&L) results because there are so many factors that change by the time releases are widely deployed, and schedule surprises are always the fault of engineering and project management. Your most substantial leverage occurs when your product management department is driven by an insatiable, hard-charging sales department. I've been there as a VP of product management. Focus on that consequence. Product management will likely welcome a way to manage their sales stakeholders.

The last potential influence strategy is the "nuclear option." The CEO and CFO are usually frustrated by the lack of visibility and predictability of software development relative to the predictability of manufacturing or operations. The CEO or CFO is a last resort because it may increase resistance from people below. However, the CEO and CFO have the power in the organization to initiate change. Ideally, the heads of product management, engineering, and project management jointly pitch the new planning methods to the CFO and CEO, but alignment can be achieved from the top if necessary to get product management onboard.

Now, you know how to gain support for change in your organization. The next step is to recommend a low-risk, low-effort exercise to demonstrate the relevance and value of the Investment approach for your organization.

16.2   Step 2: Stakeholder Value Analysis

A preliminary stakeholder analysis is a low-effort, low-risk next step. It will likely show that product management is so deep in functionality that they miss customer value. You can facilitate this yourself if you are a product manager. If not, propose a morning or an afternoon session that can be facilitated by a product manager. Product management can learn a useful technique for getting down to core customer value. The process enables product managers to get above mundane feature-level requirements to generate customer value as professional product managers. It's a small investment in time with the potential for very high payback. The benefits of focusing on value should become apparent.

The facilitating product manager should read Chapter 6 of this book. Study the examples and use the same categories and stakeholder table formats (e.g., internal versus external stakeholders). Invite senior engineers to let them contribute to Investment planning.

Start the meeting by creating a complete list of product stakeholders using the categories in the examples. The rules are the following:

- A product stakeholder is a role that gains benefit from your product.
- Include constrainers who can influence or impose requirements.
- Define stakeholder classes for those with the same role and different requirements.
- More is better at this point. Stakeholder roles can be collapsed if the values and requirements turn out to be the same.

The initial experience will reveal that engineers and product managers are challenged to think in terms of value instead of functionality. Most of the initial value suggestions will be functional requirements. Here are some examples from sessions I have facilitated:

- "I want additional reports to see late invoices."
- "I want a stable system to integrate with."
- "I want faster response time to get my work done."

The flag here is that they all imply functionality. They are not at the level of value. Further discussion and application of the "Five Whys" lead to the underlying values:

- "I want to reduce outstanding cash balance to meet or exceed my performance objectives."
- "As a partner, I want to maximize our integration profits."
- "I want to achieve higher throughput to meet or exceed my performance objectives."

The above are good examples of the difference between user stories and epics. Value statements are higher level than user stories. They are like epics, but they relate to business or individual performance objectives – the root driver of organizational consequences.

The key to successful facilitation is to continually screen value statements in terms of the following characteristics to know when you have reached the underlying value:

- Not a feature or requirement
- Does not imply or constrain implementation
- Supports business or personal performance objectives
- Is measurable

It takes some practice, but persistence and continuously cross-checking with the above-listed criteria will get you there.

My experience is that participants are initially struck by the sheer number of job titles to which their product adds value. They usually find that the values of internal stakeholders who support the product were not being considered. They also see that the values are different at each job level and are usually supportive of the next highest level. Satisfying the value of an influencer can create customer evangelists for your product. However, the attendees recognize that product success depends on ultimately addressing the values at the executive level with a proxy business case described in Chapter 10.

Focusing on the values of each stakeholder guides a deeper level of discussion and leads to common understanding. You will likely hear many comments of, "I didn't know that." Product managers are often surprised by the stakeholder values contributed by senior engineers who have worked on the product for years. Engineers often feel that a veil of secrecy has been lifted with new access to market and customer information.

The stakeholder value exercise results in a concise picture of opportunities to add value for which customers will be willing to pay. Just as importantly, the exercise reveals information that should be known but isn't. This provides the basis for stakeholder research and interviews described in the following sections.

The session output can be shared as a living document for engineers and product managers. Stakeholders and their values don't change frequently within a market segment. What a great way to onboard new product managers and engineers to rapidly sensitize them to your market and customers.

The last word of advice is that you should consider using a professional facilitator and provide them with the stakeholder value criteria to lead the discussion.

16.3   Step 3: Stakeholder Research

This step involves more resources. The work can be done on a part-time basis without impacting business commitments by using effective positive reinforcement. Presumably, stakeholder analysis has produced sufficient intrigue to gain support from above. Presenting the results of the stakeholder analysis to the key decision-makers can garner executive-level support to provide the resources.

The stakeholder analysis will likely identify large gaps in customer and market knowledge. As opposed to general untargeted market research, a product manager can now focus on specific stakeholder values. Most product managers are surprised at how much information can be mined from the web with focused searches. The trucking proxy business case used earlier in the book showed that I could quickly find detailed data on US trucking operational costs. Credible data can often be found on the web, or reports can be purchased from market analysts. Start with the Key Performance Indicators (KPIs) and stakeholder values of the key decision-makers.

You may want to pair each product manager with a senior engineer who has product interest beyond implementation. Doing this sets the tone for business and technical collaboration fundamental to the Investment model and demonstrates the value of technical input early in product planning. Recognize that being involved at the business level will not be of interest to many engineers. Many want to remain technical. You can usually find senior engineers who view involvement in planning as career development or have just been dying to have their product ideas heard. Market awareness and business involvement can be criteria for your technical ladder. Engineers can grow in both business and technical directions without having to become product managers who soon become technologically stale. You may even consider a title of "Product engineer."

The other purpose of this research stage is to prepare for stakeholder interviews in the next step. Interviewers should be able to show that they have done their homework before taking a stakeholder's valuable time. Preparation of questions to fill in the gaps will result in a more concise and effective interview.

This section began with the importance of effective positive reinforcement to engage product managers and engineers. Set up weekly review meetings where the teams can present what they have learned about stakeholder value. Be sure to recognize incremental progress.

16.4 Step 4: Stakeholder Interviews

Identify a subset of product stakeholders who can provide insight into how a specific value impacts their success. Prepare a set of questions based on the research done in the prior step.

Drill down with the "Five Whys" technique to the point where value can be measured. Steer the discussion to value when functionality comes up. You've reached your objective when you can recite a few simple value statements that do not constrain functionality. Stakeholders will usually respond with an enthusiastic "yes" when you hit the mark.

16.5 Step 5: Investments

This is the fun part – an opportunity for creative brainstorming. A half-day meeting is set up with the participants in the stakeholder value exercises and anyone else you feel could contribute ideas. Again, business and technical fusion is important. Consider inviting others outside of product development, such as operations, support, or IT. The only requirement is that they have reviewed the stakeholder value analyses and the stakeholder interview presentations.

There are numerous brainstorming techniques that can be used, like storyboarding and mind mapping. There may be a common approach used in your organization. If not, bring in a professional facilitator for the meeting. I'm always impressed by how a good professional facilitator can lead a group to creative results without being familiar with the domain.

The purpose of the meeting is to identify opportunities to significantly increase stakeholder values. It starts at the top with the decision-maker values and then proceeds to the influencers. Recall our definition of great products introduced in Chapter 6:

> The common trait of "great products" per Brooks' definition is that these organizations focus on something their stakeholders' value and move it a mile rather than moving everything an inch at a time with features and small enhancements.

The best possible case is that you move a key decision-maker value by a mile to differentiate your product. However, that's not always possible. The next best thing is to provide a quantum leap in value for one or more influencers. For example, spreadsheets weren't originally justified based on bottom-line savings. They provided a leap in value beyond methods currently available to create a groundswell of support.

Each value should be examined for the potential to "hit one out of the park" to encourage out-of-box thinking. You may not find one, but the ideas generated will often lead you to solutions with value customers will pay for.

16.5.1 User Scenarios

User scenarios provide the vehicle for business and technical collaboration and lend themselves well to brainstorming. Clarify the definition of user scenarios at

Table 16.2 ATM use case example.

Prior state	Stimulus	System action	Final state
Start	User inserts card	Request PIN	Waiting for PIN
Waiting for PIN	User enters correct PIN	Displays transaction options	Waiting for transaction selection
Waiting for transaction selection	User selects withdrawal	Requests withdrawal account	Waiting for account selection
Etc.			

the beginning of the meeting to avoid getting into user stories or use cases. Again, a professional facilitator can help.

User scenarios are descriptions of what one would observe a stakeholder doing for one transaction with the system. You can consider them as a description of a success path use case from the initial state to the final state without the alternate and error cases.

Let's make a distinction between use cases and user scenarios. Use cases are broken into small steps between stable system states. The system waits for a stimulus to move from one stable state to another. The stimulus is an event triggered by a user, or a system timer.

For example, Table 16.2 shows ATM use cases for the first few transactions of a successful withdrawal.

You can see that use cases are very detailed, so the big picture is often missed, and the example above doesn't include error or alternate cases yet. A group creating use cases for an Investment will spend their time debating minutia instead of coming up with innovative approaches.

A user scenario is a paragraph describing an end-to-end transaction without considering intermediate system states. For example:

> The bank customer inserts their card into the ATM. They enter their PIN. The system displays the customer accounts to select. The customer enters the withdrawal amount. The system returns the bank card. The user removes their card, and the system disperses the cash.

Use cases have their place in requirements analysis, but user scenarios are a useful brainstorming tool to produce a high-level description of system functionality. Scenarios can rapidly be improved through brainstorming.

User stories have their place in Scrum to break down epics into what can be demonstrated within one sprint. In theory, epics and stories are supposed to describe the problem to solve and not constrain functionality. In contrast, user scenarios introduce innovative functionality at this early stage that can be suggested and vetted by the business and technical meeting attendees. Ideas for leveraging technology are welcome.

16.5.2 Feature Definition

It is possible to move directly from user scenarios to epics and user stories. However, most organizations use features as increments of functionality that convey benefit. Investment burndown charts can be at the feature level to forecast those that will be included in the Investment by the target end date.

Feature definition can be another group exercise using the user scenarios as input. However, feature discussions don't center around what someone just thinks is a good idea. Features must be justified in terms of how they contribute to the income generation goals of the Investment. T-shirt sizing, where business value represents contribution to income, is used to prioritize features and determine a reasonable cutoff point. The team is incented to minimize features because adding features increases cycle time and lowers Weighted Shortest Job First (WSJF) priority.

16.5.3 WSJF Screening

Rank the Investment candidates based on WSJF considering potential income and cycle time. Development effort can be used as a proxy for cycle time at this level of planning. Allocate 200 points that each attendee can use to assign across all Investments. They can spread 100 points separately for three-year income and 100 points for cycle time. Allow them to explain their reasoning for their allocations, followed by group discussion. Let them make any adjustments.

Sum the points for three-year income and cycle time separately for each Investment and divide three-year income points by cycle time points to estimate WSJF. Order the list by descending WSJF. Continue to score and truncate the list until you have a manageable list.

Look for large deviations in the scores among Investments. This often reflects different assumptions by the scorers. Discuss why they are so different and make any adjustments. Take some time on each Investment to brainstorm how income could be increased and development cycle time reduced. The value of this ranking exercise is the discussion and common understanding it generates, not to arrive at exact numbers.

For example, assume four participants allocate their points to three-year income as in Table 16.3. Points are proportional to estimated income.

Table 16.3 Three-year income point weighting example.

Investment	Score 1	Score 2	Score 3	Score 4	Average
Investment 1	30	25	15	30	25.0
Investment 2	20	15	10	25	17.5
Investment 3	0	15	0	30	11.3
Investment 4	10	0	10	0	5.0
Investment 5	0	0	30	0	7.5
Investment 6	10	15	10	5	10.0
Investment 7	30	20	20	10	20.0
Investment 8	0	10	5	0	3.8
Total	100	100	100	100	

Table 16.4 Preliminary investment WSJF ranking.

Investment	Income	Cycle time (weeks)	WSJF
Investment 7	20.0	3.5	5.7
Investment 1	25.0	5.2	4.8
Investment 3	11.3	5.5	2.0
Investment 2	17.5	20.0	0.9
Investment 5	7.5	12.5	0.6
Investment 6	10.0	20.2	0.5
Investment 8	3.8	7.7	0.5
Investment 4	5.0	25.4	0.2

The shaded rows are examples of significant deviation among the scores that should be discussed. Don't try to convince anyone to change their score, but make sure that everyone is working from the same assumptions.

The exercise is repeated for cycle time. Income contribution points have been divided by cycle time points to calculate WSJF in Table 16.4.

Don't pare the list at this point. Schedules will be estimated in Section 16.6. That will allow you to establish your Investment backlog one-year Work in Progress (WIP) limit to determine the subset for detailed planning.

16.6 Step 6: Initial Roadmap

The initial roadmap is a challenging step because resource availability for Investments must be reconciled with current business commitments. Your sales and operations stakeholders should be involved because trade-offs will need to be made between current roadmap targets and the Investment candidates. There will likely be pressure to include all the Investments as well as current commitments. This is where the value of the Investment approach is demonstrated. Your stakeholders will realize that they can benefit more from shorter development increments with higher value.

Start by making any changes in rank based on the updated WSJF values determined during Investment planning. Establish a payback period target if one doesn't exist. Two years is a good starting point to minimize risk. The downloadable Investment Income Profile Calculator spreadsheet can be used to calculate the annual income profiles based on Investment payback periods and development costs for each Investment.

16.6.1 Resource Allocation

The initial Investment roadmap will be based on current resource availability. There will likely be current commitments to be delivered in the next planned release, so work on the Investment backlog can't start immediately. However, the features in the release should be evaluated in terms of Net CoD impact on the Investment backlog. Reducing the size of the release will move quantifiable Investment income forward in time.

Some will be hard customer commitments that can't be changed. Other features can be assessed in terms of the Investment backlog Net CoD reduction relative to income lost if they are not included in the release. Upon careful evaluation, you will find that many of the discretionary features can be dropped to increase overall income.

The downloadable Investment Planning Schedule Calculator spreadsheet available at www.construx.com/product-flow-optimization-calculators can be used to forecast Investment schedules based on Full Time Equivalent (FTE) profiles. It should not be used at this time to fix Investment schedules. The spreadsheet does not account for resource specialization, so results should be viewed as the best possible case where engineering staff is interchangeable. Investment timeboxes should be reforecast by engineering after the initial Investment backlog prioritization. The spreadsheet allows you to quickly adjust FTE profiles to recalculate the Investment schedules. The Investment Backlog Net CoD Calculator is available in the same location. It allows you to calculate changes in Net Cost of Delay based on Investment delays.

16.7   Step 7: Investment Planning

Investment planning starts only for Investments that fall within the Investment backlog one-year WIP limit. Planning involves completion of the Investment planning template introduced in Chapter 10. The key is to break it down into small increments as weekly goals for Investment owners. For example:

Week 1

- Proxy business case

Week 2

- KPIs
- Stakeholders
- Constraints
- Competition
- Acceptance criteria

Week 3

- Go-to-Market plan

Week 4

- Financial and development cost targets
- WSJF update

Week 5

- Assumption validation

Establish a weekly meeting with the Investment owners to allow them to present. Provide feedback and recognition.

Investment WSJF values are then updated based on the knowledge gained from completing the Investment templates. Investment timeboxes can be updated to provide reasonable schedule targets that incorporate sufficient feature contingency, as described in Chapter 7.

16.7.1   Agile Roadmap Alignment Meeting

The Agile roadmap is managed with the stakeholder alignment cycle depicted in Figure 16.1.

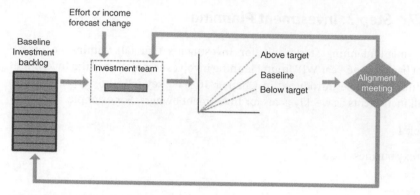

Figure 16.1   Agile roadmap alignment cycle.

This is the basic cycle used to achieve schedule and financial targets. The meeting should be weekly, or at least biweekly. Any changes that would impact baseline schedule and/or financial targets are identified by the Investment teams. They must present a comparison of any financial impacts with the baseline target. The team may be asked to go back and look at alternatives, such as dropping or simplifying features to stay on target.

The meeting is an important synchronization point to maintain roadmap stakeholder expectations. Even if change doesn't occur weekly, it's good to verify that assumptions are still valid. This is also an opportunity to raise risks that can be addressed proactively. The meeting would typically be led by the product management leader or P&L owner, and attended by project management, sales, and operations leaders.

Investment owners also present their feature burndown projections and financial forecast at each meeting. The following presentation template can be used:

Slide 1: Investment Summary

- Changes from last week
- Financial impacts

Slide 2: Mitigation

- Actions taken to minimize impacts

Slide 3: Alternatives and Recommendation

- Feature content or functionality reduction?
- Additional resources?

- Increased income?
- Investment delay?

Slide 4: Assistance

- Support required outside of team authority

Each alternative should include overall roadmap impacts, including cascading delays and associated Net CoD to facilitate decision-making. A recommendation may be accepted or a recovery plan initiated. Any changes will be incorporated into the baseline roadmap only after the stakeholders agree on the changes and the financial and/or schedule impacts for the next review.

16.7.2 Program Review

There should also be a biweekly or monthly program review meeting at the release level. The objective of the meeting is to synchronize expectations for department-level deliveries necessary for release deployment. It is also an opportunity to present ways in which release size can be reduced by releasing Investments on-demand. In most large organizations, a project or program manager will be assigned to each release. They can take a broader program-level perspective now because they are not involved with administrative task and feature tracking. The Investment schedules and release assignments are based on the baseline roadmap.

I use the term "program manager" instead of project manager to reflect the higher-level focus on release business objectives. Program managers present their project plans showing all the dependencies necessary to take the release through commercial availability, including any planned field verification. Responsibilities are assigned at the department level. For example, the training department is responsible for creation and delivery of training for Investment stakeholders. Marketing is responsible for delivery of marketing collateral and sales training. Operations may manage the first deployment and verification.

Most mature organizations know how to do this. The difference is that current program reviews typically dwell on the software development minutia, often down to the task level. In this approach, Investments are the lowest-level product development planning element, increasing focus on critical departmental-level dependencies and risk management.

In addition to the program plan review, each program manager presents current obstacles to releasing each Investment separately. Reducing release cycle time by being able to deploy Investments independently is a major objective for the program managers. Cross-functional management attending the review can contribute ideas and support to release Investments independently. For example, an Investment-level pricing model may be introduced instead of being bundled within release pricing. Or perhaps additional development effort can be justified based on Net CoD savings from being able to deploy an Investment independently. The main objective is to maintain organizational focus on reducing release opportunity cost. Release bundling is a last resort.

16.8   Step 8: Consequence Alignment

Most organizations include "alignment of recognition and rewards" in their change management plans. Unfortunately, this usually just involves individual performance plans. We know from the behavior model that performance reviews have limited impact because consequences are long delayed. The Investment approach has been designed with an understanding that frequent positive consequences must be built into the work itself.

You will recognize that the roadmap alignment meeting incorporates a rapid consequence feedback loop. Additional features must be justified in terms of positive financial impact relative to the cascading roadmap Net CoD impacts. Dropping lower-value features will shift income forward in time. For the first time, you can demonstrate how sales and operations can increase income by reducing features and functionality, moving closer to the illusive Minimum Marketable Feature Set (MMFS).

The roadmap meeting should be a collaborative and supportive meeting as opposed to what happens in many project reviews. The product management leader is responsible for maintaining an environment of positive reinforcement for Investment and technical owners. Presenters must see their management as empowering and supportive. Don't use the meeting to punish. If there are performance concerns, that's a private discussion with an individual's manager.

This may involve a significant behavior change on the part of the meeting leader to move from the left to right side of the motivation curve presented in Chapter 13. Those leaders who have attained success by getting results from negative reinforcement may find it difficult to change.

I hope the behavior model has convinced leaders that they must choose one side or the other to get organizational results. This takes strong leadership qualities. A strong leader will shield people from negative consequences. The leader should not expect to get the results described in this book if they are not ready to establish strong and frequent positive reinforcement in the daily work in their organizations. Empowering people without motivation reduces performance.

There are some methods that the meeting leader can use to help them make this transition. They can appoint a trusted individual who works for them to observe and provide feedback on the extent to which they are effectively applying consequences. It should be someone capable of providing frank corrective feedback after meetings in which they observe any resurgence of negative consequences. It could be an assistant who attends meetings to take notes.

Not everyone will be comfortable with asking for feedback from subordinates. That makes the change more challenging. Alternately, they can keep score during meetings by marking a note pad with an "x" for every time they apply threats or punishment, and a checkmark for positive reinforcement. Maintain a log with an objective of increasing positive reinforcement and reducing negative behaviors over time.

You won't have to do this forever. You will receive positive reinforcement for applying positive reinforcement when you see the results from increased engagement. As we know, positive reinforcement shapes behaviors that become habits.

Positive reinforcement needs to become the natural way of interacting with people you want to motivate. Some guidelines:

1. Be specific so people know exactly which behavior is being reinforced. The impact of positive reinforcement is increased when people know that you know what they did, instead of the often meaningless "good job."
2. Reinforce during or as soon as possible after the desired behavior or result.
3. Use metrics and charts as opportunities to reinforce. Shorter and more frequent goals provide more opportunity for positive reinforcement.
4. Be sincere – don't say it if you don't mean it. People know.
5. Apply negative reinforcement sparingly to get a behavior started and then positively reinforce the new behaviors and/or results.
6. Personalize the reinforcement. For example, public appreciation may be punishment for some individuals where a personalized e-mail can be very effective.
7. Forget rewards – only a few people can win (usually the self-motivated), while others are often disgruntled. You need to motivate the unmotivated using positive reinforcement to achieve high organizational performance.

These are all good techniques to increase the effectiveness of your positive reinforcement, but they don't replace the need for a leader to establish the environment for peer reinforcement. Consider the time spent interacting with your staff compared to the time they are working with peers. That's where positive reinforcement can be the most frequent and meaningful.

The roadmap alignment leader must be aware of how the behavior of others add to or subtract from positive reinforcement in the meeting. Punishment from an attendee can extinguish the effect of positive reinforcement. Be prepared to provide corrective feedback to attendees as needed after the meeting. It may even require removing certain people from the attendee list.

We've discussed consequences for Investment teams in the roadmap alignment meeting. What about the individual product managers and engineers working on an Investment? The good news is that if you have implemented the practices provided in this book, you will observe collaboration and teamwork. Product managers and engineers now have common goals for Investment schedule and financial results. Common goals foster collaboration, teamwork, and peer reinforcement.

Whether or not you are using Agile development, you need to create winners in your organization. You can't make a team act like winners. They must be winners to act like winners. Put an event on your calendar as the first thing you see at the start of every week with the following note.

> What opportunities have I established this week for peer recognition for achieving shared objectives?

If the answer is, "none," you are unlikely to ever see the incredible power of high-performance teams.

16.9 Summary

1. Gain organizational support for change initiatives by addressing the pain points of influencers and decision-makers.
2. Start with a low-effort analysis of stakeholders using the methods described in this book. The exercise will provide valuable customer and market insights.
3. Market research can now be focused on specific stakeholder values.
4. Generate a potential list of Investment candidates. Use the point system to prioritize Investments based on WSJF.
5. Free committed resources where possible by using Net CoD to show financial benefit of dropping low value features.
6. Let the Investment owners create weekly targets for detailed Investment planning for Investments within the one-year WIP limit. Recognize progress.
7. Establish the Agile roadmap alignment meeting with roadmap stakeholders to frequently collaborate and synchronize expectations. Financial and schedule impacts of changes are reviewed before acceptance.
8. Assign program managers at the release level to achieve release business objectives and to minimize release opportunity costs.

9. The Agile roadmap meeting leader must accept the need to move to the strong and frequent positive reinforcement side of the motivation curve.

10. The positive consequences to motivate self-directed teams are inherent in Agile development freed from the constraints of Waterfall planning. Just support Agile the way it was envisioned.

Appendix A

General Cost of Delay Formula

Cost of Delay can be calculated in the case where the cumulative income curves can be represented as functions of time.

Consider the cumulative income curves of Investments 1–3 represented by $f_1(t)$, $f_2(t), f_3(t)$ with cycle times T_1, T_2, T_3, respectively, where $f_1(t) = 15t, f_2(t) = 10t^{1.5}$, and $f_3(t) = 8t^{1.8}$. Time units are in quarters, income in \$K. Figure A.1 shows the development order $f_1(t), f_2(t), f_3(t)$.

$f_2(t)$ is delayed by T_1 while Investment 1 is developed. The deferred income from $f_2(t)$ is what would have been produced by $f_2(t)$ when the first Investment was completed, which is $f_2(T_1)$. $f_3(t)$ is delayed by $T_1 + T_2$ by the development of Investments 1 and 2. By time T_2 Investment 3 could have generated $f_3(T_1 + T_2)$. The order $f_1(t), f_2(t), f_3(t)$ produces the lowest Net Cost of Delay if $f_2(T_1) + f_3(T_1 + T_2)$ is the minimum for all permutations of $f_1(t), f_2(t), f_3(t)$.

This requires computation of Net CoD for values for the permutations as shown in Table A.1.

Net Cost of Delay for each combination is calculated in Table A.2.

The order f_1, f_3, f_2 has the lowest Net Cost of Delay in this example.

The calculations can be completed for any set of Investments. However, the number of calculations is $N!$ where N is the number of Investments. There are 120 permutations for five Investments and increases to over 3 million for 10 permutations.

There is an inherent assumption that the order of Investment development does not impact cycle time. This is true for interchangeable resources but not when development must wait for specific skills. For example, there could be limited database or backend developers to support all the Investments. This requires a more complex algorithm where cycle times are based on availability of critical path skills.

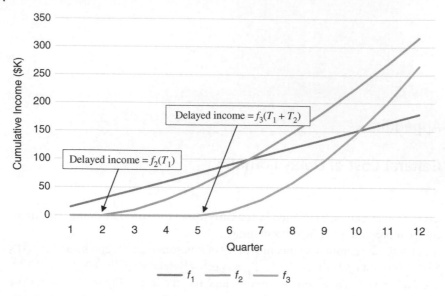

Figure A.1 Cumulative income based on project order.

Table A.1 Net Cost of Delay formulas for three Investments.

Order	Net Cost of Delay
$f_1(t), f_2(t), f_3(t)$	$f_2(T_1) + f_3(T_1 + T_2)$
$f_1(t), f_3(t), f_2(t)$	$f_3(T_1) + f_2(T_1 + T_3)$
$f_2(t), f_1(t), f_3(t)$	$f_1(T_2) + f_3(T_2 + T_1)$
$f_2(t), f_3(t), f_1(t)$	$f_3(T_2) + f_1(T_2 + T_3)$
$f_3(t), f_1(t), f_2(t)$	$f_1(T_3) + f_2(T_3 + T_1)$
$f_3(t), f_2(t), f_1(t)$	$f_2(T_3) + f_1(T_3 + T_2)$

Table A.2 Net Cost of Delay calculation example for three Investments.

Order	Net CoD ($K)
f_1, f_2, f_3	230
f_1, f_3, f_2	175
f_2, f_1, f_3	261
f_2, f_3, f_1	247
f_3, f_1, f_2	316
f_3, f_2, f_1	297

A.1   Reinertsen WSJF

The general Cost of Delay formula is another way to prove Reinertsen's Weighted Shortest Job First (WSJF) formula. Consider two Investments (or projects) with Costs of Delay C_1 and C_2. If Investment 1 is developed first, the Net Cost of Delay for Investment 2 is $f_2(T_1)$. For the opposite order, the Net Cost of Delay is $f_1(T_2)$.

$$f_2(T_1) = C_2 T_1$$
$$f_1(T_2) = C_1 T_2$$

Investment 1 should be prioritized if

$$C_1 T_2 > C_2 T_1$$

or

$$\frac{C_1}{T_1} > \frac{C_2}{T_2}$$

Unfortunately, the cross-multiplication only works for the linear case of income generated at a constant rate. Otherwise, a calculation table as shown in the example must be generated for all Investment combinations.

A.2   Income Curve Approximation

There are two options for determining the cumulative income profile function based on quarterly cumulative income projections. The first is to fit the curve to a power function of the form.

$$y = ax^b$$

This can be done with the Excel LINEST linear regression formula. Taking the logarithm of both sides of the formula gives:

$$\log(y) = \log + b \, \log(x)$$

Consider the projected cumulative income example shown in Table A.3.

The logarithms of the x and y variables are shown in Table A.4.

The Excel LINEST linear regression can be used to estimate the slope and y-intercept.

$$\text{slope} = 1.8$$
$$y\text{-intercept} = -0.086$$

Table A.3 Cumulative income example.

Quarter	Cumulative income ($K)
1	1
2	3
3	5
4	10
5	14
6	16
7	20
8	36
9	45
10	60
11	70
12	90

Table A.4 Logarithms of quarter and cumulative income.

Log (Quarter)	Log (Cumulative income)
0.0	0.0
0.3	0.5
0.5	0.7
0.6	1.0
0.7	1.1
0.8	1.2
0.8	1.3
0.9	1.6
1.0	1.7
1.0	1.8
1.0	1.8
1.1	2.0

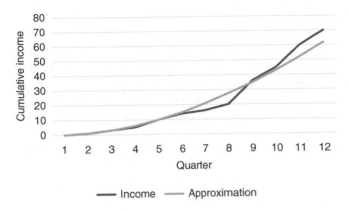

Figure A.2   Income profile nonlinear regression.

The y-intercept is $\log(a)$ so:

$$a = 10^{-0.086} = 0.82$$

The best fit for the income ramp is:

$$f(t) = 0.82t^{1.8}$$

Figure A.2 shows that this formula provides a close fit for cumulative income, certainly well within the income estimation variance.

Separate log and linear regression Excel functions were used for this example to illustrate the method. There is also an Excel LOGEST function that may be used to directly calculate the coefficient and exponent.

The "logistics curve" can also be used to estimate annual income, known as the "S-curve" given by:

$$f(t) = \frac{L}{1 + e^{-k(t-T_0)}}$$

$L =$ maximum value
$k =$ slope of the curve at the inflection point, also called "the logistics growth rate"
$T_0 =$ the time value at the inflection point

The curve is often used to describe physical phenomena like population growth where growth increases gradually at first, more rapidly in the middle growth period, leveling off as saturation occurs. It can be used to model deployment of software upgrades.

A.3   Summary

- Net Cost of Delay can be calculated for income curves that can be represented as a function of time, but complexity of the calculation increases significantly with the number of Investments. The formula has been included for completeness; but in most cases, the rate at which income is shifted out of a three-year planning period will suffice for the Cost of Delay calculation because most large companies are more concerned with near-term income predictability.
- The general formula reduces to Reinertsen's WSJF for the case of linear income ramps.
- Most cumulative income ramps can be estimated by fitting a power curve to quarterly forecasts or using the logistics formula.

Appendix B

Investment Income Profile Forecasts

Investment income profile targets can be established based on development cost, payback period, and a relative annual income profile.

Assume annual income is x_i where i is the year number. Let p_i be the relative weight for each year i *relative to Year 1*. For example, if Year 1 income is x then Year 3 income is $p_3 x$. The italics emphasize that the coefficients are relative to Year 1, and not the same as annual growth rates.

By definition, p_1 is 1. The income generated over a five-year period would be:

$$x_1 + p_2 x_2 + p_3 x_3$$

We also know the following relationships:

$$x_2 = p_2 x_1$$
$$x_3 = p_3 x_1$$

Therefore, the income S returned after three years is:

$$S = x_1 + p_2 x_1 + p_3 x_1$$

Therefore,

$$x_1 = \frac{S}{(1 + p_2 + p_3)}$$

Assume a development cost of $570K and a relative income profile projection as shown in Table B.1.

Table B.1 Annual income profile.

Year	Relative income
Year 1	100%
Year 2	105%
Year 3	110%

Unlocking Agile's Missed Potential, First Edition. Robert Webber.
© 2022 The Institute of Electrical and Electronics Engineers, Inc. Published 2022 by John Wiley & Sons, Inc.

Substituting the values for p_2 and p_3 gives

$$x_1 = \frac{\$570K}{(1 + 1.05 + 1.10)} = \$181K$$

Years 2 and 3 can be calculated as

$$x_2 = (1.05)(\$181K) = \$190K$$

$$x_3 = (1.10)(\$181K) = \$199K$$

The income for the first three years returns the development cost of $570. The forecast can be extended to any number of years by multiplying the growth rate by Year 1 income. Revenue can be estimated by dividing by the projected margins. In A margin of 80% is assumed in Table B.2, but different values could be used for each year.

This example assumes a payback period expressed in whole years. The formula can account for a partial year. For a 2.75 year payback period, the relative percent for the fractional year is multiplied by 0.75 to reflect income from the first three quarters of the third year.

$$x_1 = \frac{\$570K}{(1 + 1.05 + (0.75)(1.10))} = \$198K$$

Annual income for Years 2 and 3 can be calculated

$$x_2 = (1.05)(\$198K) = \$208K$$

$$x_3 = (1.10)(\$198K) = \$218K$$

The payback can be verified by

$$\$198K + \$208K + (0.75)(\$218K) = \$570K$$

A downloadable Investment Income Profile Calculator spreadsheet is available at www.construx.com/product-flow-optimization-calculators.

Table B.2 Revenue profile based on income and margin.

	Year 1	Year 2	Year 3
Income ($K)	181	190	199
Margin (%)	80	80	80
Revenue ($K)	226	238	249

Appendix C

Release Cycle Productivity Formula

Consider the case of releases with quarterly Cost of Delay "C" and cycle time "T." Assume the release can be split into quarterly releases with Cost of Delay $C/4$, assuming a quarter of the release value is delivered each quarter. Figure C.1 stacks the Investments within a one-year period by Cost of Delay, so the gray area represents income generated by each Investment. Within each gray area, the income generated is $\text{Time} \times \text{Cost of Delay}$.

The additional income generated within the gray area is

$$\frac{C}{4}(3+2+1) = 1.5C$$

This represents additional income pulled into this year by quarterly releases. The income generated by the prior annual release would be $4C$. Therefore, the ratio of income in the quarterly release case to that of annual release is:

$$\frac{I_2}{I_1} = \frac{4C + 1.5C}{4C} = 1.375$$

For the general case where the annual release cycle is divided by "N," the additional income in the year is:

$$\frac{C}{N}((N-1) + (N-2) + \ldots + 1)$$

The series can be replaced with:

$$\frac{N(N-1)}{2}$$

The income ratio is given by:

$$\frac{I_2}{I_1} = \frac{NC + \dfrac{C}{N}\dfrac{N(N-1)}{2}}{NC} = 1 + \frac{(N-1)}{2N}$$

Unlocking Agile's Missed Potential, First Edition. Robert Webber.
© 2022 The Institute of Electrical and Electronics Engineers, Inc. Published 2022 by John Wiley & Sons, Inc.

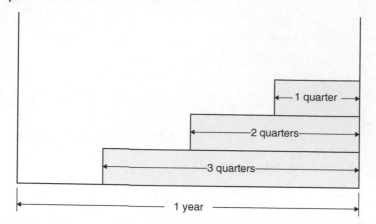

Figure C.1 Quarterly release income generation.

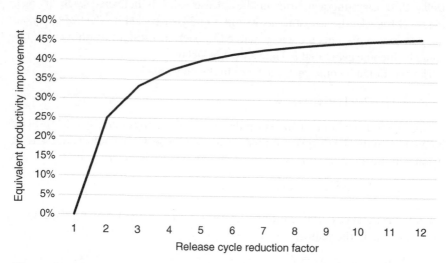

Figure C.2 Income ratio by release segments.

Figure C.2 shows the resulting calculation for a reduction factor of up to 12, which corresponds to adopting monthly releases.

We can account for release overhead costs. Assume there is a fixed overhead for each release independent of release size. This accounts for system regression testing, field testing, and deployment cost. Assume the fixed overhead R_0 can be expressed as a fraction of the development cost D of an annual release.

$$R_0 = \alpha D$$

The annual release cost is $(1 + \alpha)D$.

Assume a quarterly release cycle is adopted. Each release experiences the fixed overhead cost so the development cost increases by a factor of $(1 + 4\alpha)$. For the general case of reduction in cycle time by a factor of N, the release cost is $(1 + N\alpha)D$:

$$P_1 = \frac{I_1}{(1 + \alpha)D}$$

$$P_2 = \frac{I_2}{(1 + N\alpha)D}$$

$$\frac{P_2}{P_1} = \frac{(1 + \alpha)}{(1 + N\alpha)} \frac{I_2}{I_1}$$

From above,

$$\frac{I_2}{I_1} = 1 + \frac{(N - 1)}{2N}$$

Therefore,

$$\frac{P_2}{P_1} = \frac{(1 + \alpha)}{(1 + N\alpha)} \left(1 + \frac{(N - 1)}{2N}\right)$$

Figure C.3 shows the productivity ratio for release cycle time reduction factors of 1 to 12 with release overhead cost ratios of 10%, 20%, and 30% as shown in the legend.

The top line shows that productivity is lower for release reduction factors greater than five if the fixed overhead cost of each release is 10% of your development

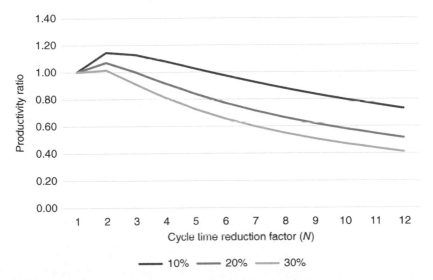

Figure C.3 Productivity ratio as a function of release overhead cost and cycle time reduction factor.

cost. Beyond that, the additional income generated by releasing more frequently is more than offset by the release overhead cost. Note how quickly the advantage of releasing more frequently decreases with increasing overhead cost, stressing the importance of reducing release overhead costs to take advantage of Agile development.

Appendix D

Rework and Productivity

The following variables represent the fractional components of the Cost of Quality model:

> A – Appraisal
>
> W – Waste
>
> P – Production

They add to 100% so:

$$P = 1 - W - A$$

We want to calculate the relative increase in production when rework is reduced:

$$\frac{P_2}{P_1} = \frac{(1 - W_2 - A_2)}{(1 - W_1 - A_1)}$$

The ratio of appraisal to production costs is assumed to be the same in both cases. This assumes that, on average, appraisal hours are proportional to development effort.

$$\frac{A_2}{P_2} = \frac{A_1}{P_1}$$

A_2 can be replaced by:

$$A_2 = \frac{A_1 P_2}{P_1}$$

Let

$$\frac{P_2}{P_1} = x$$

Therefore,

$$x = \frac{(1 - W_2 - xA_1)}{(1 - W_1 - A_1)}$$

Unlocking Agile's Missed Potential, First Edition. Robert Webber.
© 2022 The Institute of Electrical and Electronics Engineers, Inc. Published 2022 by John Wiley & Sons, Inc.

Solving for x gives:

$$\frac{P_2}{P_1} = \frac{(1 - W_2)}{(1 - W_1)}$$

Since x is the ratio of the increase in production, $x - 1$ is the productivity improvement. For example, if production rises by a factor of 1.25, the productivity improvement is 25%.

Appendix E

Innovation Behavior Survey

I posted an innovation survey on the Construx website to determine a relationship between positive reinforcement and one's perception of the level of innovation taking place within their organization. I have also used it in numerous seminars. Not a single individual has disagreed with the standing of their company predicted by the survey.

The following survey questions are rated on a six-point Likert scale:

- Strongly Disagree
- Disagree
- Somewhat Disagree
- Somewhat Agree
- Agree
- Strongly Agree

Points are assigned from 0 to 5, respectively.

Survey Questions

1. My manager feels that innovation is important.
2. My peers recognize and support new ideas.
3. My department encourages and supports new ideas.
4. Our product or solution planning people encourage and support new ideas.
5. I have the opportunity to demonstrate innovative solutions.
6. I collaborate on ideas outside my team.
7. I make time to understand what our users want.
8. I make time to keep up with technologies that could improve our product.
9. Our product/solution introduction process lets me innovate.
10. I make time to innovate.
11. Innovation is important here.
12. We are an innovative organization.

Unlocking Agile's Missed Potential, First Edition. Robert Webber.
© 2022 The Institute of Electrical and Electronics Engineers, Inc. Published 2022 by John Wiley & Sons, Inc.

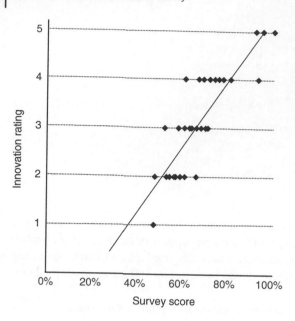

Figure E.1 Innovation survey scores.

I put the survey on the Construx website and received 35 responses. Figure E.1 plots answers to question 12 relative to the maximum score of the other 11 questions, which is $11 \times 5 = 55$.

The chart supports a relationship between scores on the first 11 questions and the respondent's perception of the level of innovation taking place in their organization.

I chose the wording of the questions carefully. For example, I did not ask if an individual was given time to innovate. The question was, "I make time to innovate." People will find the time to innovate if the organizational consequences support it.

The chart below shows the survey distribution based on the percentage of the maximum score for the 11 questions (Figure E.2).

The chart has the bell-shaped curve we would expect.

I calculated the linear regression correlation with each of the questions to determine which questions had the greatest influence on the perception of the level of innovation in their organization. It measures the proportion of the variation in the dependent variable that can be attributed to the independent variable. In this case, the percent score is the independent variable. The answer to question 12, "We are an innovative organization," is the dependent variable. The chart below shows questions with a correlation value greater than 0.5 (Figure E.3).

The strongest correlation is, "Our product planning people encourage and support new ideas," which supports early involvement of engineers in Investment

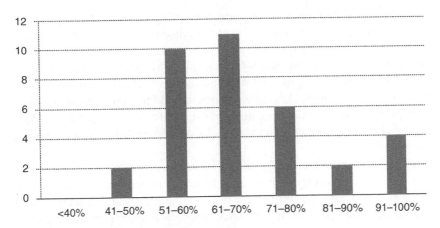

Figure E.2   Innovation survey histogram.

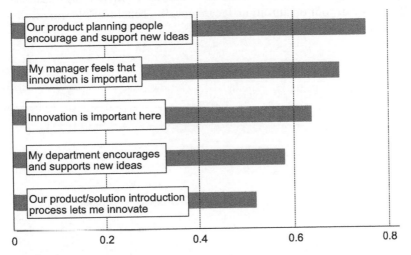

Figure E.3   Innovation survey linear regression R^2 correlation.

planning. It is the single most important factor in innovative organizations. You wouldn't expect a high score in companies "throwing features over the wall" to engineering.

The second highest correlation is the degree to which an individual perceives that innovation is important to their management. At first, I was surprised that this item was more significant than peer reinforcement, which had a correlation of 0.32. Then I realized that although the manager has fewer opportunities to reinforce the team than their peers, they control the work of their employees. Innovation leaders find a way to make innovation a priority.

It is interesting that encouraging and supporting ideas at the department level was more significant than peer. I don't think someone would view their organization as innovative unless it were widespread in a department. Support at the department level is necessary for individuals to observe innovation being implemented, which is largely controlled by budgets at the department level. It implies that it is very difficult to establish pockets of innovation in an organization. Department-level leaders in control of engineering budgets need to make a full and visible commitment to innovation. Innovation must be ingrained within the "culture."

Although this was not a comprehensive survey involving hundreds of companies, it seems to support the importance of innovation being a frequent topic in your organization, and the importance of providing positive reinforcement and support at the department level. It is also consistent with my experience in dozens of innovation seminars where attendees have completed the survey. They consistently agree that their scores reflect the level of innovation in their organizations.

Try the survey in your organization. It can provide a benchmark for innovation improvement for the leadership team.

Glossary

Agile	A software development framework where teams develop increments with short cycle times by pulling work from queues at a pace they decide.
Agile Roadmap	A database containing Investment schedules and features that can be quickly adapted to development effort changes.
Agile Technology Roadmap	A component of the Agile roadmap that identifies the dependencies and target completion dates to make new technology available for implementation in an Investment.
API	Application Programming Interface. Documented software interfaces exposing functionality that can be used by other programmers.
Appraisal	The software development cost associated with effort to detect defects in a development artifact. Used in the Cost of Quality model.
Assumption Validation	Creation of test plans to verify critical product assumptions prior to development to avoid product failures.
B – B	Business to Business. A business model where other companies are customers.
B – C	Business to Consumer. A business model where the product or services are purchased by individuals.
Balance Sheet	A business financial report that estimates the total value of a company.

Unlocking Agile's Missed Potential, First Edition. Robert Webber.
© 2022 The Institute of Electrical and Electronics Engineers, Inc. Published 2022 by John Wiley & Sons, Inc.

Behavior	Action by a person that can be observed.
Bundling	Inclusion of multiple Investments within a release.
Burndown Chart	A graph that shows the progress of an Agile team toward completion of a release.
Business Plan	A detailed plan that shows actions and responsibilities to achieve business objectives.
CoD	Cost of Delay. The income or profit lost by delaying a software project by a unit of time.
Cone of Uncertainty	A characteristic curve that shows how software estimation accuracy varies depending on the development phase in which estimates are made.
Consequences	The impact on an individual after performing a behavior.
Constrainer	Individuals or groups who can constrain product requirements that can affect the success of a product.
Continuous Delivery (CD)	Customer software is updated when value is available instead of having to wait for periodic releases.
Cost of Quality	The money that a company invests to ensure product quality.
Culture	A set of behaviors effectively reinforced throughout an organization that determines commonly observed behaviors.
Cycle Time	The time from the start of development of an Investment until it could potentially be released.
Cycle Time Reduction Factor	The ratio of current release cycle time to a reduced cycle time.
DevOps	Investments in resources and tools to reduce development and deployment durations to reduce cycle time.
Epic	A problem to be solved in software.
Feature	An increment of software functionality with benefits understood by business and technical product development participants.
Feature-Based Planning	Features defined as a first step in product or release planning.

Five Whys	A structured quality analysis method to identify root causes.
Flat File	A spreadsheet or Comma Separated Values (CSV) file that maintains relationships among elements.
FTE	Full-Time Equivalent – The hours an individual would contribute each week to a project if they were 100% dedicated to the project.
Functional Testing	Verification of software against a set of functional requirements.
Go-to-Market Plan	The tasks, responsibilities, and dependencies necessary to market and sell a product.
Headcount	The number of individuals working on a project.
Income Statement	A financial report that shows company income and profit.
Initiative	A plan to achieve a business objective.
Innovation	A nonobvious improvement provided by a product, process, or solution that results in a notable increase in product stakeholder value.
Integration Testing	Verification of interfaces among unit tested software components.
Internal Rate of Return (IRR)	The discount rate that makes Net Present Value zero in a discounted cash flow analysis.
Investment	The smallest increment of software functionality with the potential to increase income if it could be released. A capital "I" is used to distinguish it from general investments.
Investment Backlog	A set of Investments prioritized with consideration of potential near-term income based on Weighted Shortest Job First (WSJF).
Investment Team	A cross-functional team responsible for achieving the business and technical objectives of an Investment.
Kanban	A manufacturing method to limit Work in Process (WIP). Also, an Agile software development method that limits WIP.
Key Performance Indicator (KPI)	A measure that represents the state of a key business result.
Logistics Curve	A characteristic growth curve often found in business and nature. Also known as an S-curve.

Microservices	A software architectural style that structures an application as a set of services defined by an API.
Minimal Marketable Feature Set (MMFS)	A small increment of software functionality functionality that delivers value to customers.
Minimum Viable Product (MVP)	A small increment of a software product deployed to learn more about the product.
Motivation	The desire to perform a behavior.
Negative Reinforcement	A threat of punishment to increase a desired behavior.
Net Cost of Delay (Net CoD)	The money lost within a planning period by not being able to develop a set of software projects simultaneously because of resource or other constraints. Also known as the opportunity cost of prioritizing projects above others.
Net Present Value (NPV)	The value of money today that will be received in the future based on the potential value of that money considering future return rates.
Operations	Company departments responsible for providing goods and services to customers or other departments.
Payback Period	The time required by a product to pay back development cost.
Program Management Office (PMO)	A company department staffed with project. and/or program managers responsible for achieving project predictability in terms of schedule, cost, scope, and quality.
Profit and Loss Center (P&L Center)	A subset of a company with accounting to determine profit and loss.
Portfolio	The set of projects and related funding in which a company invests.
Positive Reinforcement	Applying a consequence wanted by an individual following a desired behavior.
Product Backlog	A prioritized list that determines the priority of development of software functionality.
Product Owner	A role in Scrum responsible for defining and prioritizing work for a Scrum team.
Product Stakeholder	Someone who receives benefit from your product.
Product Stakeholder Analysis	Identification of the value a product stakeholder obtains from your product.

Production	Effort and cost in the Cost of Quality model that results in perceived product value.
Productivity	There are two types of productivity measures. The first is total productivity measured by Value Out/Value In. Unit productivity counts the rate at which "units" are produced.
Program	A plan to achieve a company objective.
Proxy Business Case	An example business case prepared by an Investment team to learn how the purchase of their Investment can be justified by customers.
Punishment	Applying an unwanted consequence to stop or reduce a behavior.
Recognition	Positive acknowledgment of a desired behavior.
Regression Test	A set of software tests executed to verify that previously tested functionality works correctly.
Release	Software deployed that contains one or more Investments, features, or other functionality.
Release Opportunity Cost	The Net Cost of Delay of completed Investments awaiting release.
Release Overhead Cost	Fixed costs associated with regression testing and release deployment.
Return on Investment (ROI)	The ratio of profit returned within a specific period and the cost of the investment.
Reward	A gift with tangible value given to an individual to encourage the individual and others to repeat the desired behavior.
Rework	Effort and cost in the Cost of Quality Model for correcting defects found in design artifacts or code.
Roadmap	A multi-year plan for the output of product development.
S-Curve	A characteristic growth curve often found in business and nature. Also known as a logistics curve.
Sales	The department responsible for selling a product.
Scaled Agile Framework (SAFe)	A popular software development framework used for multi-team Agile projects.
Scrum	An Agile method where teams build short increments of usable functionality under the guidance of a product owner.

Service-Oriented Architecture (SOA)	A software architecture that provides access to data in an enterprise application.
Software Inventory	The capital cost tied up in Investments prior to release.
Sprint	A periodic software increment planned and developed by a Scrum team.
Sprint Backlog	The set of prioritized user stories to be included in the next sprint.
Sprint Retrospective	A team review after each sprint to determine ways to increase Scrum efficiency and effectiveness.
Sprint Review	A review of sprint functionality to declare it "done" or to provide corrections or improvements.
Stakeholder Value	A desired benefit of a product stakeholder.
Strategic Investment	An Investment with a payback greater than three years.
Support & Maintenance	The portion of R&D budget allocated to correct defects and maintain product viability.
System Testing	Verification of a release against system non-functional requirements.
T-Shirt Sizing	A prioritization method where business value and effort are independently rated based on T-shirt sizes.
Tactical Investment	An Investment with a payback of three or less years.
Timebox	A target cycle time of an Investment.
Top-Down Estimation	Software estimation techniques that can be used prior to software decomposition and design.
Unit Testing	A set of tests created by a developer to achieve a level of code coverage.
Use Case	A software design element used in structured requirements analysis.
User Scenario	A description of a single user interaction with the system from initial to end state.
User Story	An expression of a user need in Scrum in a specific format that can be implemented in a single sprint.
Variable Content	The ability to trade-off functionality to maintain an Investment schedule.

Waterfall	A traditional software development framework where release requirements are created in the initial planning phase.
Waterfall Planning	Retention of fixed schedule, content, and resources characteristic of Waterfall.
Weighted Shortest Job First (WSJF)	A software project prioritization method determined by Cost of Delay/Cycle Time that optimizes the income for a set of projects.
Work in Process (WIP)	The cost invested in partially completed Investments.

Index

a

AccuWiz   1–6, 55–56, 59, 64, 88, 90, 103,
       115, 117, 132, 133, 137, 195–209
Apple   135, 176, 180, 183, 185–188, 191

b

balance sheet   16–18, 63
Bringing Out the Best in People   156

c

Cone of Uncertainty   25–29, 31
consequences   6, 62, 153–171, 181–185,
       188–190, 192, 193, 209–213,
       224–226, 244
constrainers   74, 77, 79, 122, 213
Construx   5, 9, 15, 16, 20, 28, 69, 73, 115,
       140, 147, 220, 236, 243, 244
Continuous Delivery (CD)   11, 94, 96
Cost of Delay   15, 33–51, 72, 93, 95, 97,
       101, 103, 109, 119, 127, 199, 220,
       229–233, 237
Cost of Quality   139, 141–142, 145–150,
       241
cycle time   33, 35, 39–43, 46, 48, 58, 61,
       65, 67, 69, 87, 89, 93–96, 98–100,
       102, 104, 110–112, 116, 125, 127,
       139, 195, 199, 200, 218, 219, 223,
       229, 237, 239

d

Daniels, A.C. 155   158–160
dopamine   164, 165

e

earnings per share (EPS)   17

f

five whys   79–82, 146, 198
Ford   75–77, 181

i

Income Statement   16–18
Investment Rate of Return (IRR)   48
investments   1, 6, 11, 16–18, 23–24, 28,
       33–34, 42, 47–49, 51–91, 93–129,
       131–151, 167, 172–173, 175–213,
       215–224, 226, 229–231, 234–237,
       244
iPhone   70, 80, 135, 176, 183, 187

j

Jobs, Steve   70, 71, 181, 185, 187

k

Kanban 12   14–15, 23, 63, 66, 156–158,
       161, 162, 175, 176, 191, 192, 204,
       207

Unlocking Agile's Missed Potential, First Edition. Robert Webber.
© 2022 The Institute of Electrical and Electronics Engineers, Inc. Published 2022 by John Wiley & Sons, Inc.

Key Performance Indicator (KPI) 15 63,
168, 169, 197, 204, 215

l

Lean Canvas   23, 119

m

McConnell, Steve   25, 26, 58, 144, 148,
149
Minimum Marketable Feature Set
(MMFS)   1, 39, 62, 89, 113,
224
motivation   7, 18–20, 139, 140, 146, 153,
155, 158, 159, 162, 164–172, 175,
179, 181, 183, 185, 187, 189, 190,
193, 203, 224, 227

n

negative reinforcement   157–160, 162,
165–169, 181, 182, 184, 185,
187–190, 204, 206, 210, 212, 224,
225
net income   18, 36, 67
Net Present Value (NPV)   38, 40–45, 48,
62, 63, 116

o

organizational behavior   6, 153–156,
158, 169, 171, 176, 181–193, 209,
210

p

Pink, D. 170   171
positive reinforcement   157–160,
162–172, 176, 179, 181, 182,
184–186, 188–193, 197, 203,
205–207, 210, 214, 215, 224–226,
243, 246

productivity   7, 19, 22, 36, 38, 59, 63, 72,
95, 96, 99, 100, 139–150, 237–242

r

recognition   83, 135, 146, 154–163, 165,
166, 169–171, 175, 179, 181, 183,
184, 188–192, 200, 204–205, 221,
224, 226
Reinertsen, D.G. 15   24, 33, 35, 36, 38,
39, 41, 42, 47, 64, 65, 231
Research in Motion (RIM)   70, 185–188
Return on Equity (ROE)   17, 63
Return on Investment (ROI)   1, 11, 18,
33, 34, 47–50, 54, 87–91, 93, 96,
103, 112, 113, 115–117, 202, 203
rework   22, 98, 101, 112, 113, 139,
141–150, 241, 242

s

Scaled Agile Framework (SAFe)   23, 24,
42
Scrum   12–14, 18, 22, 161, 197, 204, 217
Software as a Service (SaaS)   97
software capitalization   17, 18, 38, 131
stakeholders   9, 21, 69, 71, 73–83, 85–86,
111, 120, 122, 123, 131, 132, 135,
136, 145, 155, 167, 175–179,
181–183, 189–191, 198–201, 209,
212–217, 220–223
stakeholder value   69, 71, 73–83, 86,
111, 120, 123, 136, 167, 175–179,
181–183, 189–191, 198–201, 209,
212–216
stakeholder value analysis   69, 71,
73–83, 85, 86, 179, 181, 209,
212–214
story points   58, 65, 113, 115, 125, 140,
141, 145–147, 166, 175

t

Tableau   132–134, 137
technical debt   52, 66–68, 116

u

user scenarios   69, 82–83, 167, 179, 189,
     216–218
user stories   10, 12–14, 20, 58, 63, 66, 73,
     74, 80, 82, 83, 85–87, 101, 147,
     158, 213, 217, 218

v

voice of the customer   2, 110, 111, 178,
     200

w

waterfall planning   1–6, 10, 11, 16,
     18–20, 23, 25, 26, 28, 52, 109, 131,
     140, 153, 160, 210
Weighted Shortest Job First (WSJF)
     15, 33–43, 45, 47–51, 57, 58, 62,
     64, 66, 67, 83, 87–89, 93, 103,
     104, 110–112, 119, 124, 125,
     127, 139, 199–201, 218–221,
     231
Work in Process (WIP)   15, 52,
     63–67, 83, 93, 104–106, 111, 119,
     124, 125, 127, 200–202, 219,
     221

Printed and bound by CPI Group (UK) Ltd, Croydon, CR0 4YY
16/08/2022
03141873-0001